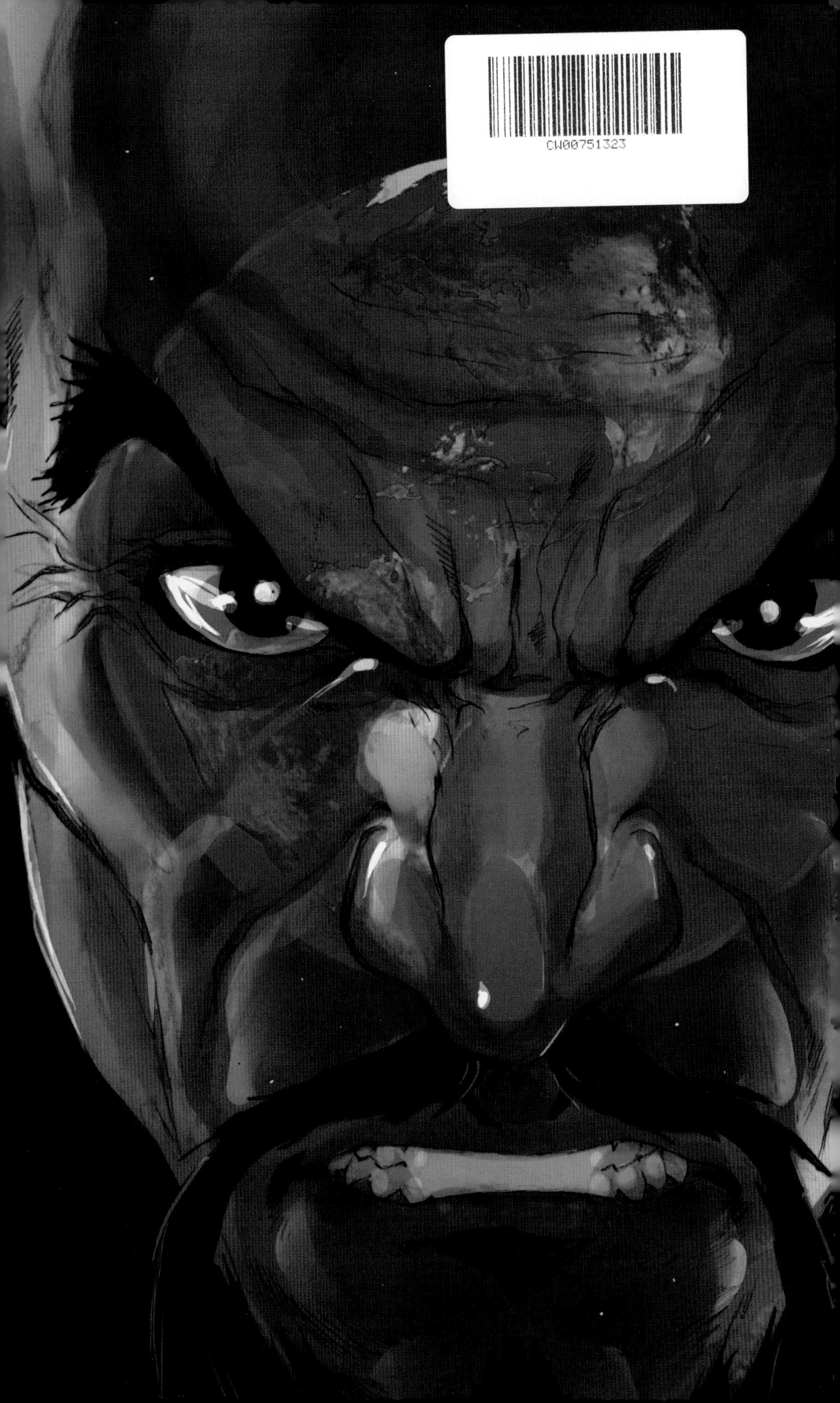

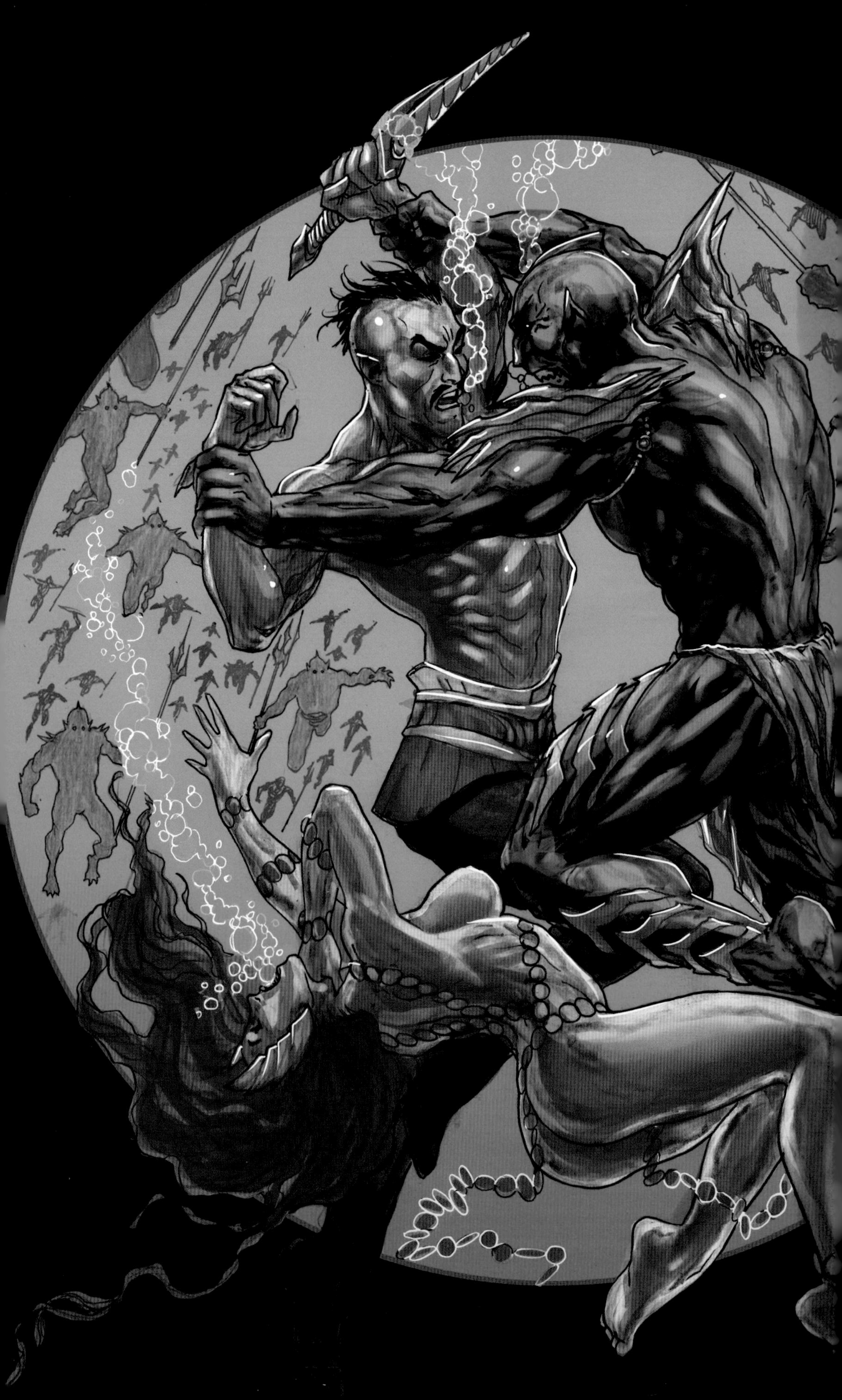

MERCILESS

THE RISE OF MING

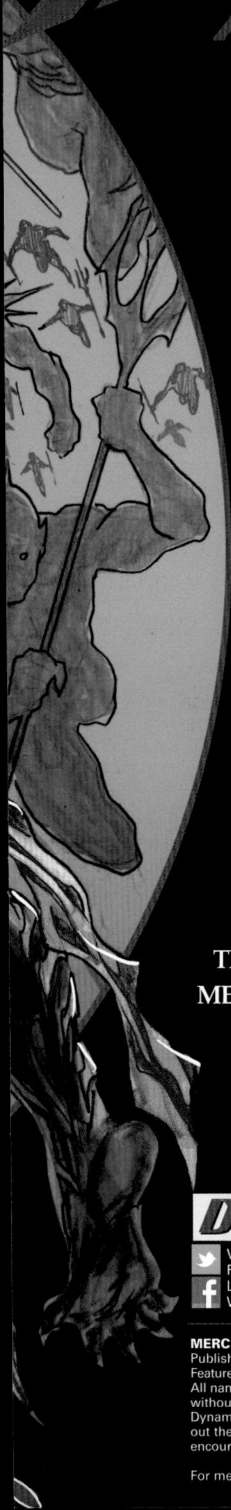

WRITTEN BY
SCOTT BEATTY

ART BY
RON ADRIAN

COLORS BY
RONI SETIAWAN

LETTERS BY
SIMON BOWLAND

COLLECTION COVER BY
ALEX ROSS

THIS VOLUME COLLECTS THE 4-ISSUE MINI SERIES
MERCILESS: THE RISE OF MING BY DYNAMITE ENTERTAINMENT

DYNAMITE®

Visit us online at **www.DYNAMITE.com**
Follow us on Twitter **@dynamitecomics**
Like us on Facebook **/Dynamitecomics**
Watch us on YouTube **/Dynamitecomics**

Nick Barrucci, CEO / Publisher
Juan Collado, President / COO
Joe Rybandt, Senior Editor
Josh Johnson, Art Director
Rich Young, Director Business Development
Jason Ullmeyer, Senior Graphic Designer
Josh Green, Traffic Coordinator
Chris Caniano, Production Assistant

First Printing
ISBN-10: 1-60690-379-9
ISBN-13: 978-1-60690-379-7
10 9 8 7 6 5 4 3 2 1

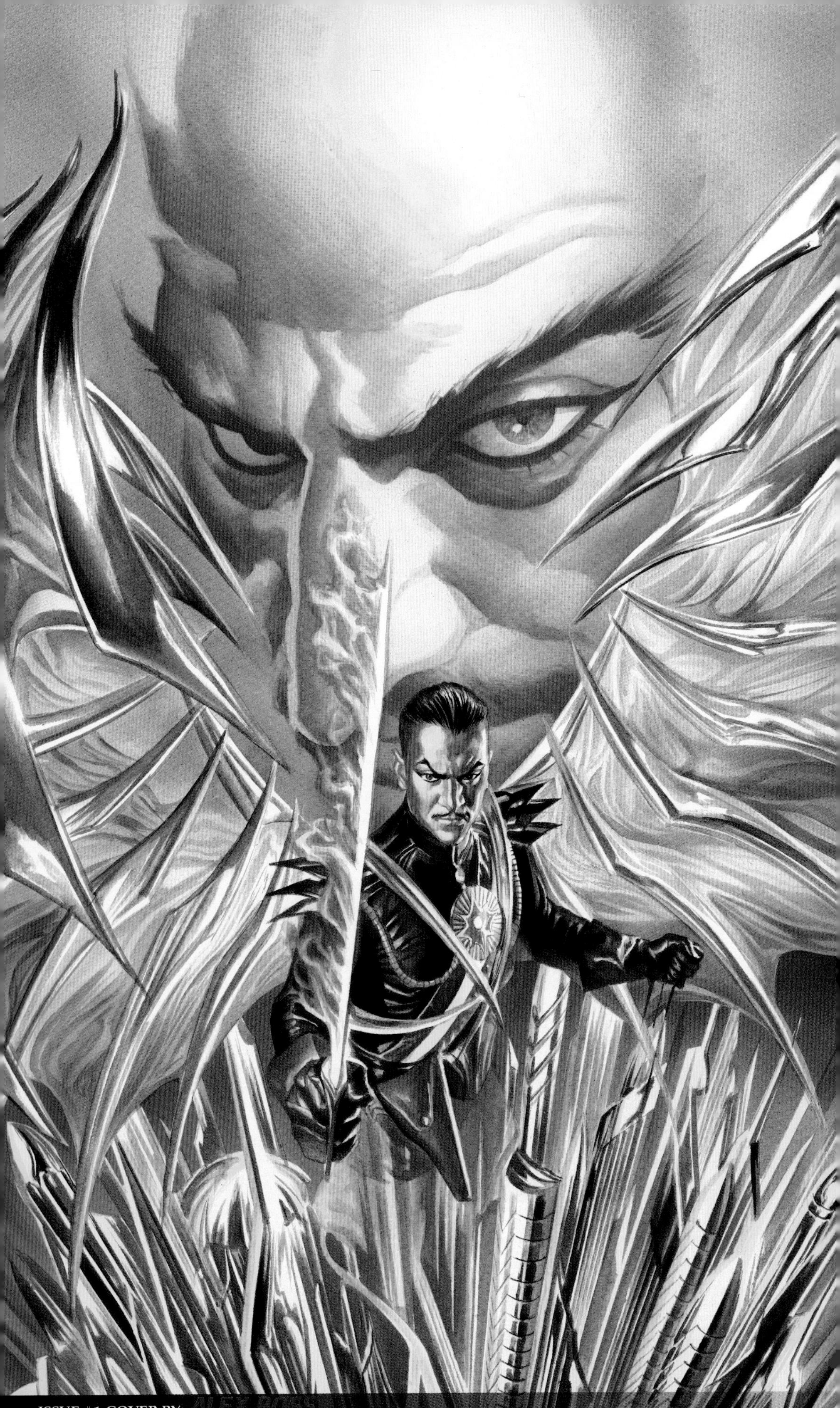

ISSUE #1 COVER BY ALEX ROSS

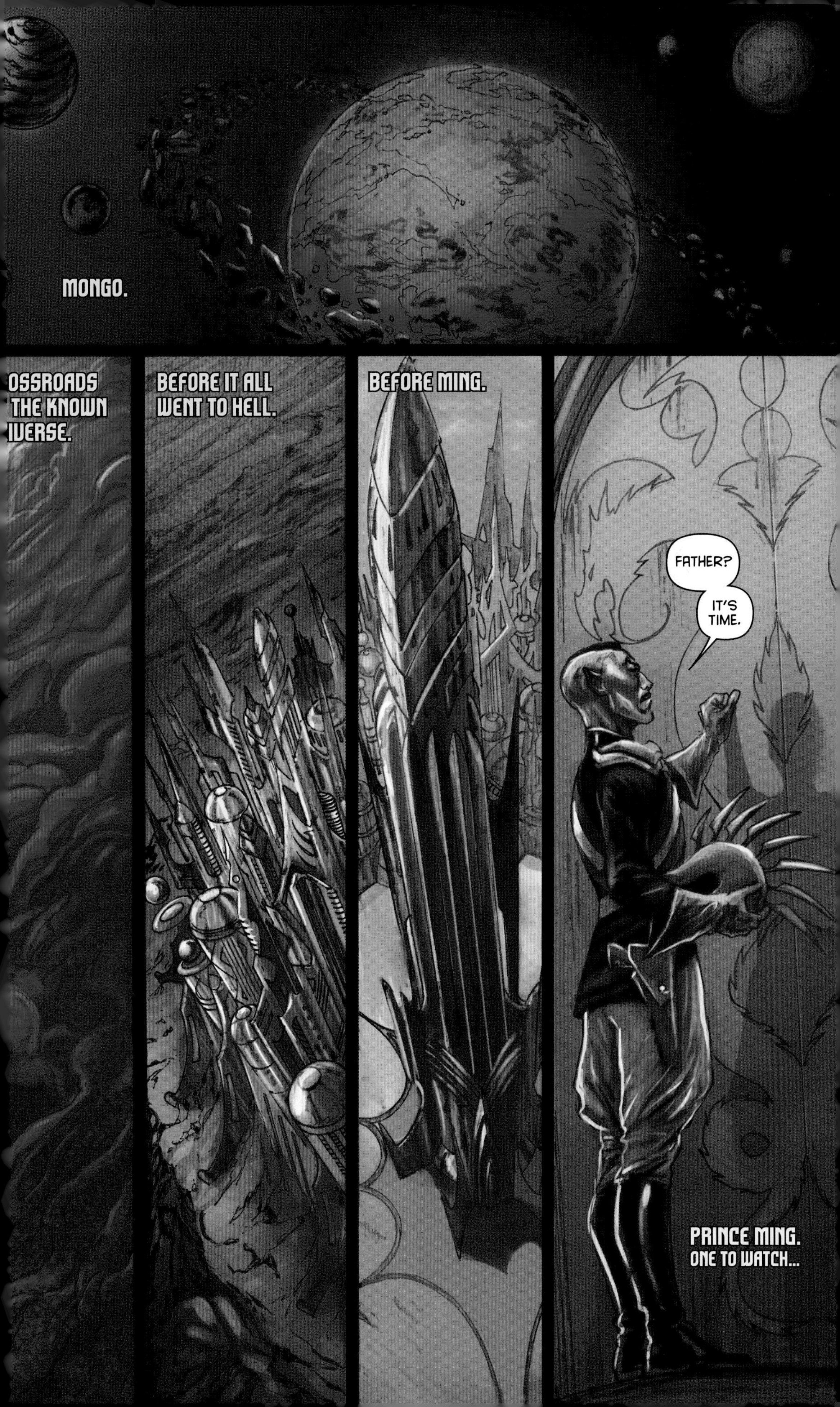
MONGO.
OSSROADS
THE KNOWN
IVERSE.
BEFORE IT ALL
WENT TO HELL.
BEFORE MING.
FATHER?
IT'S
TIME.
PRINCE MING.
ONE TO WATCH...

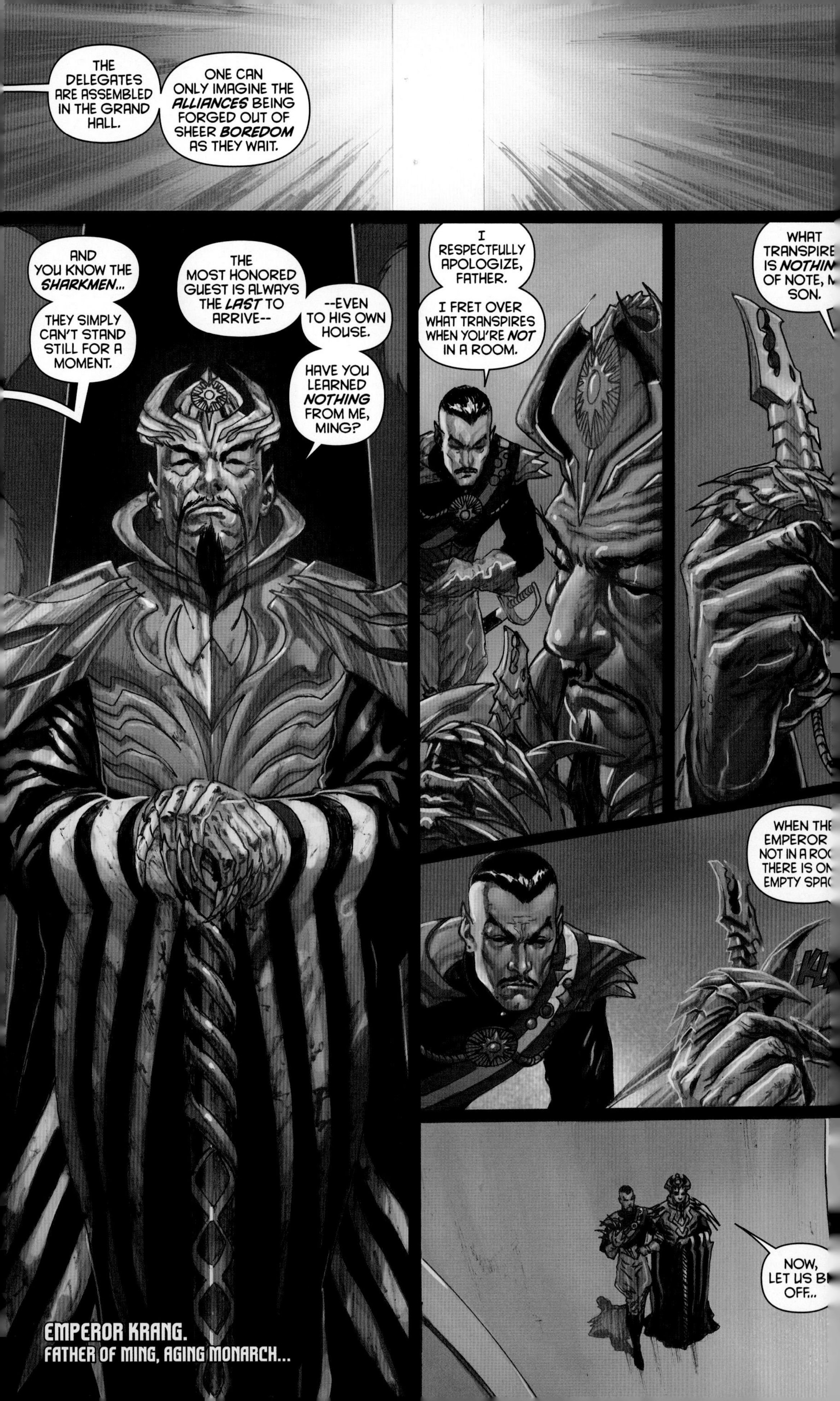
THE DELEGATES ARE ASSEMBLED IN THE GRAND HALL.
ONE CAN ONLY IMAGINE THE ALLIANCES BEING FORGED OUT OF SHEER BOREDOM AS THEY WAIT.
AND YOU KNOW THE SHARKMEN...
THEY SIMPLY CAN'T STAND STILL FOR A MOMENT.
THE MOST HONORED GUEST IS ALWAYS THE LAST TO ARRIVE--
--EVEN TO HIS OWN HOUSE.
HAVE YOU LEARNED NOTHING FROM ME, MING?
EMPEROR KRANG.
FATHER OF MING, AGING MONARCH...
I RESPECTFULLY APOLOGIZE, FATHER.
I FRET OVER WHAT TRANSPIRES WHEN YOU'RE NOT IN A ROOM.
WHAT TRANSPIRE IS NOTHIN OF NOTE, M SON.
WHEN THE EMPEROR NOT IN A ROO THERE IS ON EMPTY SPAC
NOW, LET US B OFF...

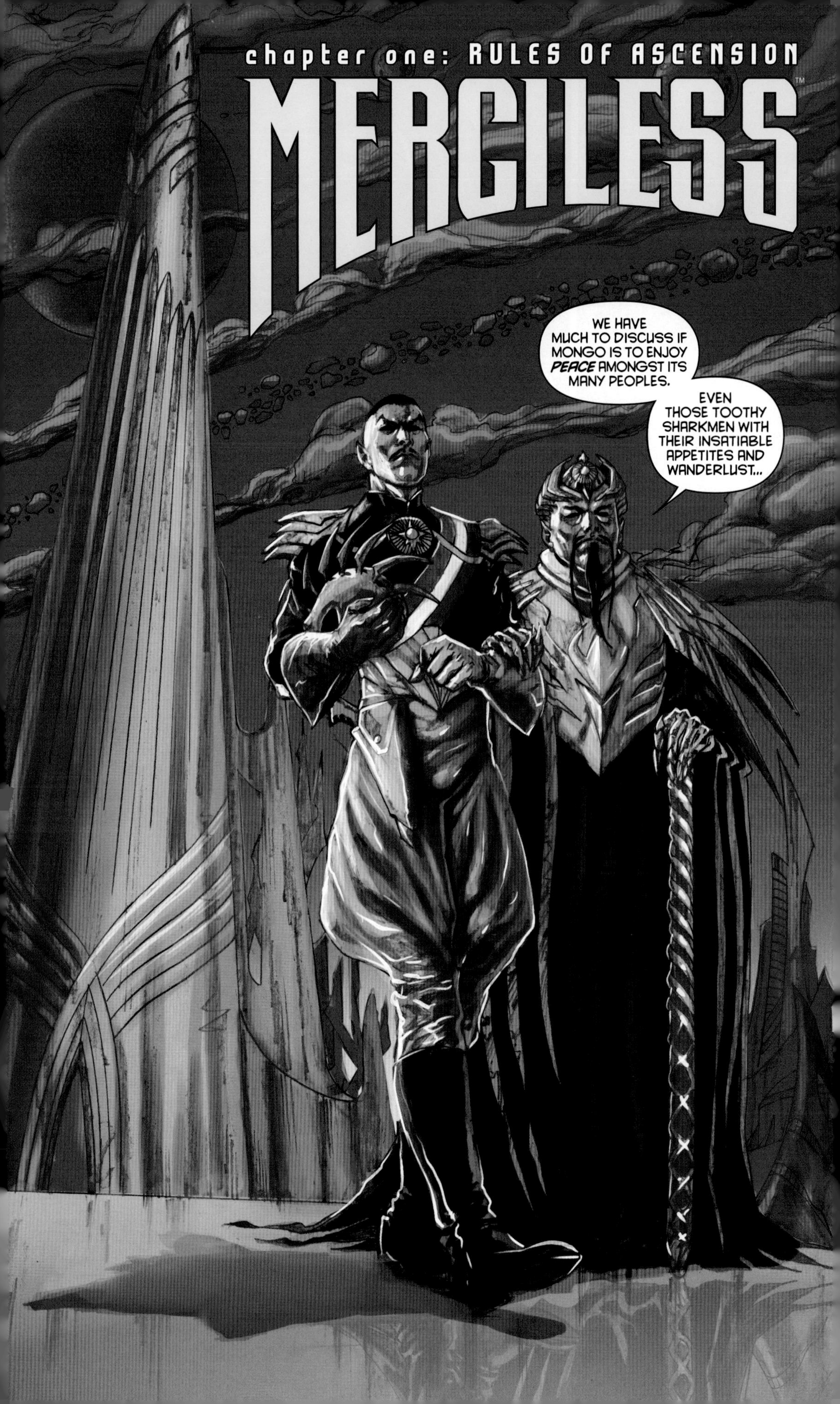
chapter one: RULES OF ASCENSION
MERCILESS™
WE HAVE MUCH TO DISCUSS IF MONGO IS TO ENJOY PEACE AMONGST ITS MANY PEOPLES.
EVEN THOSE TOOTHY SHARKMEN WITH THEIR INSATIABLE APPETITES AND WANDERLUST...

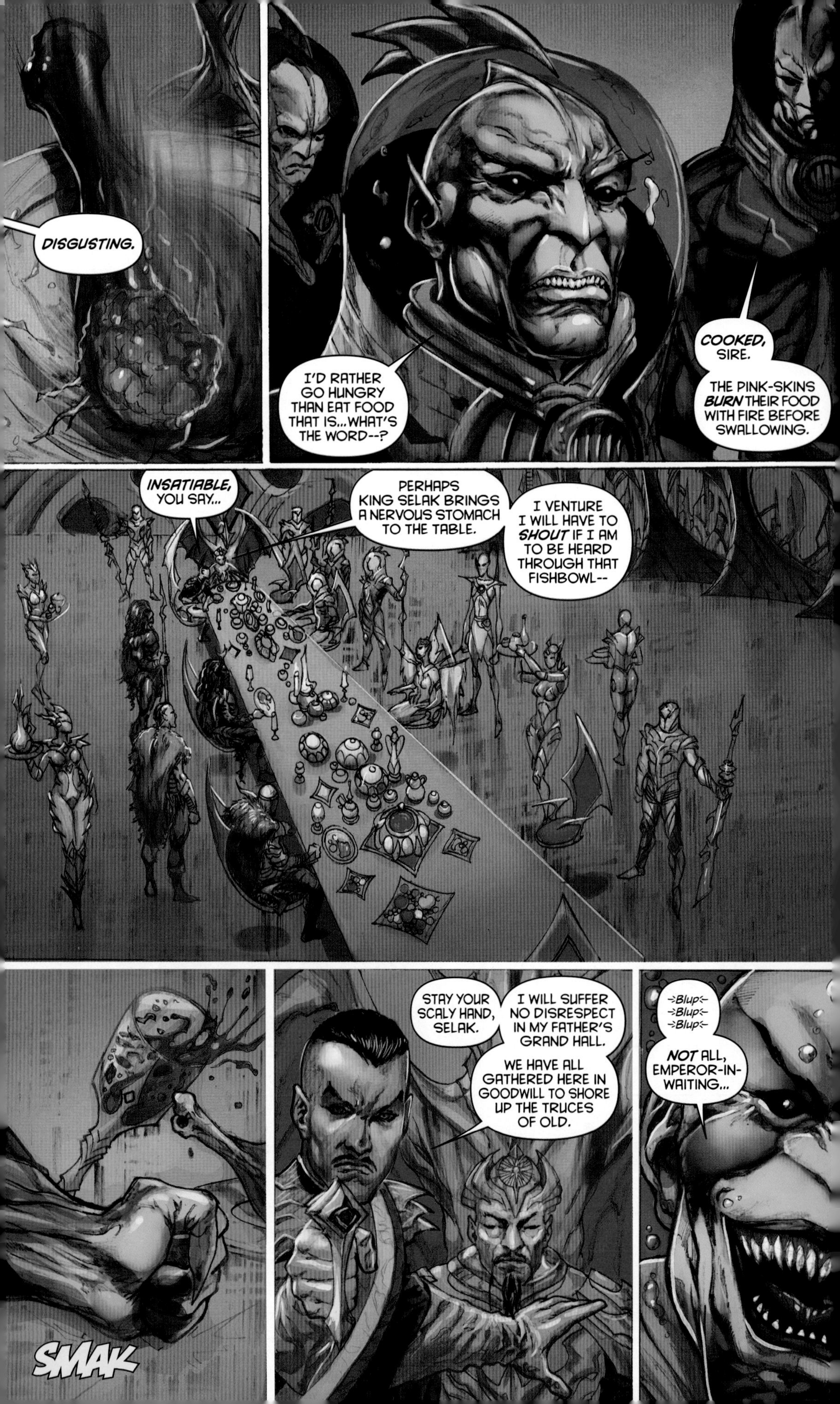

DISGUSTING.
I'D RATHER GO HUNGRY THAN EAT FOOD THAT IS...WHAT'S THE WORD--?
COOKED, SIRE.
THE PINK-SKINS BURN THEIR FOOD WITH FIRE BEFORE SWALLOWING.
INSATIABLE, YOU SAY...
PERHAPS KING SELAK BRINGS A NERVOUS STOMACH TO THE TABLE.
I VENTURE I WILL HAVE TO SHOUT IF I AM TO BE HEARD THROUGH THAT FISHBOWL--
SMAK
STAY YOUR SCALY HAND, SELAK.
I WILL SUFFER NO DISRESPECT IN MY FATHER'S GRAND HALL.
WE HAVE ALL GATHERED HERE IN GOODWILL TO SHORE UP THE TRUCES OF OLD.
Blup
Blup
Blup
NOT ALL, EMPEROR-IN-WAITING...

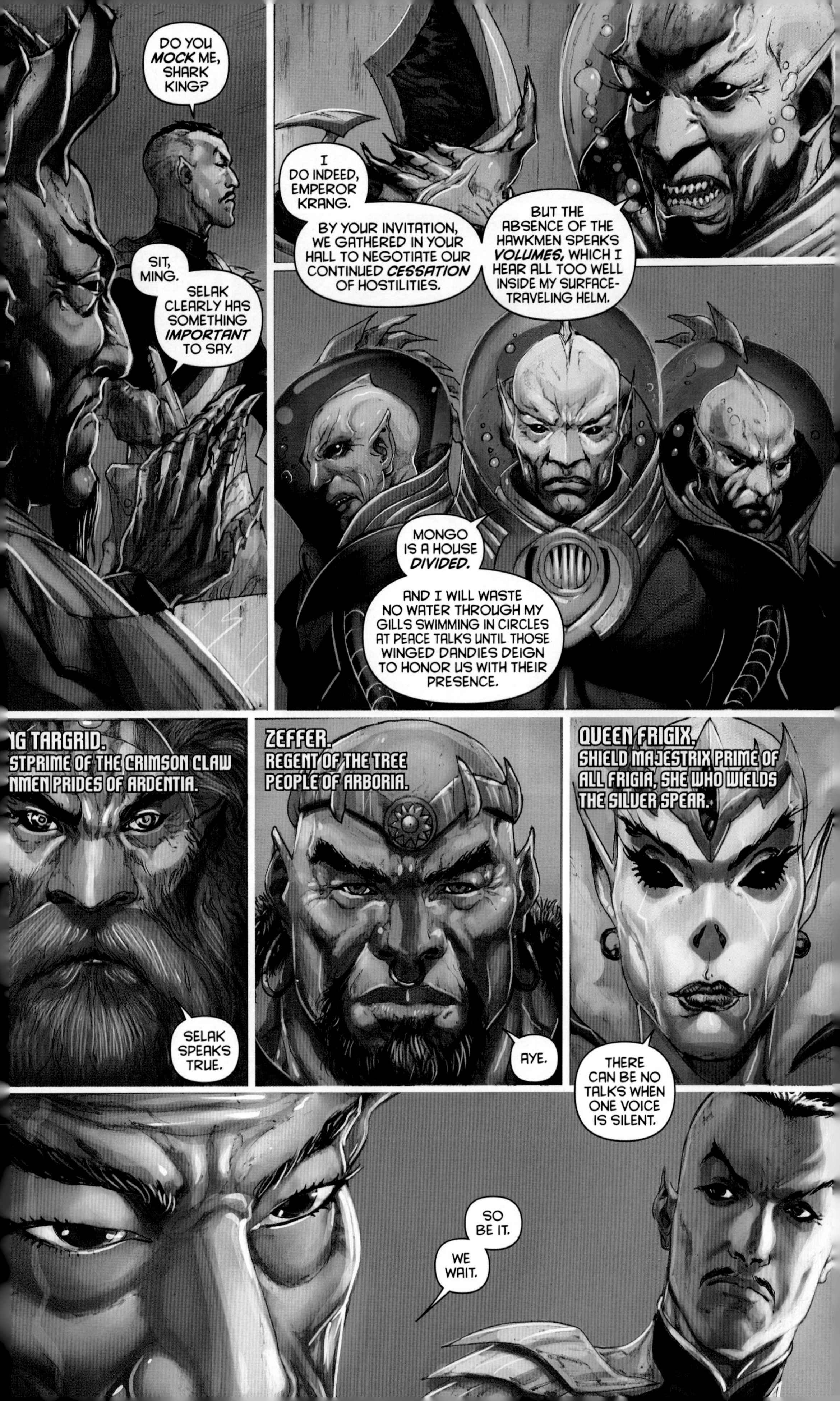
DO YOU MOCK ME, SHARK KING?
SIT, MING.
SELAK CLEARLY HAS SOMETHING IMPORTANT TO SAY.
I DO INDEED, EMPEROR KRANG.
BY YOUR INVITATION, WE GATHERED IN YOUR HALL TO NEGOTIATE OUR CONTINUED CESSATION OF HOSTILITIES.
BUT THE ABSENCE OF THE HAWKMEN SPEAKS VOLUMES, WHICH I HEAR ALL TOO WELL INSIDE MY SURFACE-TRAVELING HELM.
MONGO IS A HOUSE DIVIDED.
AND I WILL WASTE NO WATER THROUGH MY GILLS SWIMMING IN CIRCLES AT PEACE TALKS UNTIL THOSE WINGED DANDIES DEIGN TO HONOR US WITH THEIR PRESENCE.
NG TARGRID. STPRIME OF THE CRIMSON CLAW NMEN PRIDES OF ARDENTIA.
SELAK SPEAKS TRUE.
ZEFFER. REGENT OF THE TREE PEOPLE OF ARBORIA.
AYE.
QUEEN FRIGIX. SHIELD MAJESTRIX PRIME OF ALL FRIGIA, SHE WHO WIELDS THE SILVER SPEAR.
THERE CAN BE NO TALKS WHEN ONE VOICE IS SILENT.
SO BE IT.
WE WAIT.

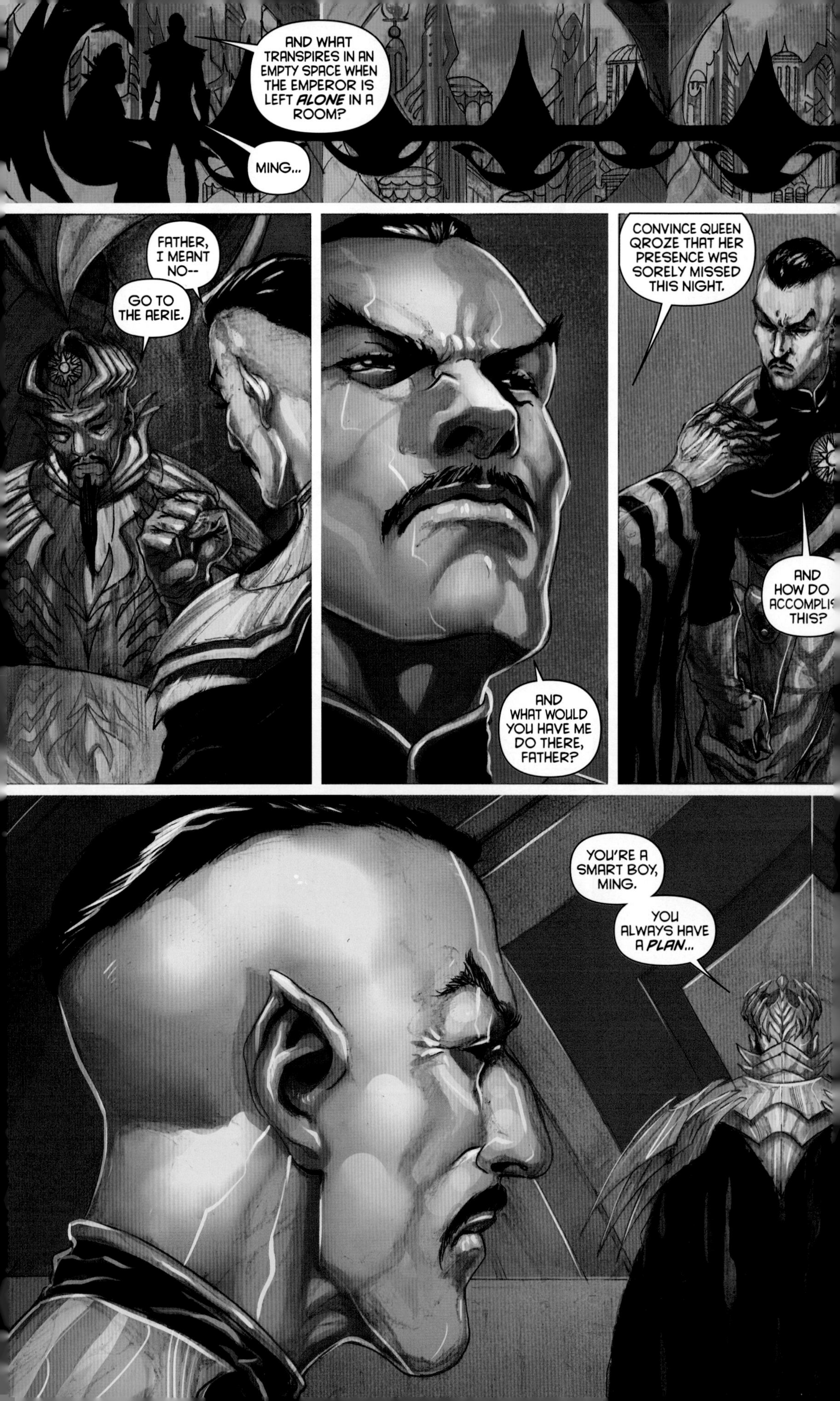
AND WHAT TRANSPIRES IN AN EMPTY SPACE WHEN THE EMPEROR IS LEFT ALONE IN A ROOM?
MING...
FATHER, I MEANT NO--
GO TO THE AERIE.
AND WHAT WOULD YOU HAVE ME DO THERE, FATHER?
CONVINCE QUEEN QROZE THAT HER PRESENCE WAS SORELY MISSED THIS NIGHT.
AND HOW DO ACCOMPLIS THIS?
YOU'RE A SMART BOY, MING.
YOU ALWAYS HAVE A PLAN...

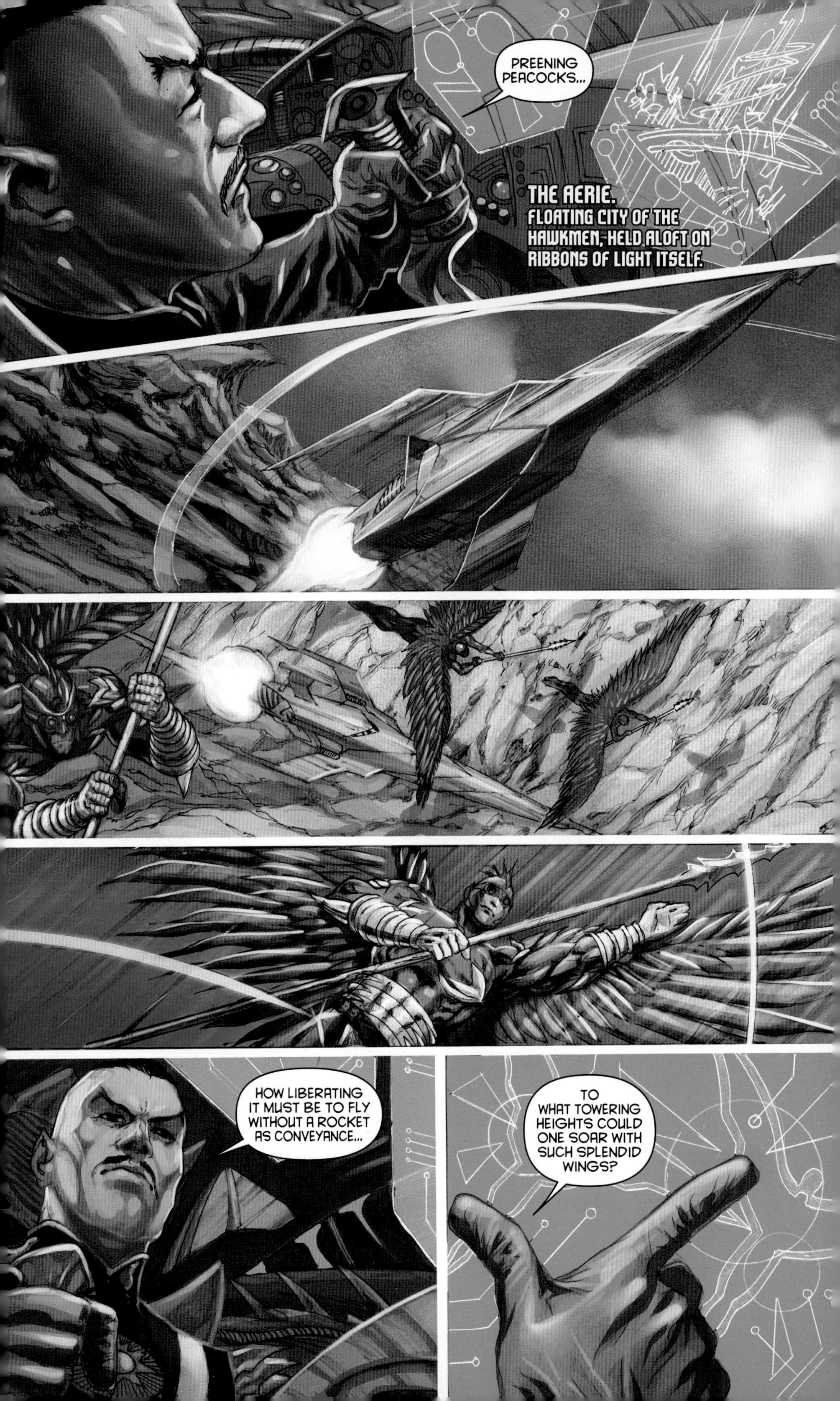
PREENING PEACOCKS...
THE AERIE.
FLOATING CITY OF THE HAWKMEN, HELD ALOFT ON RIBBONS OF LIGHT ITSELF.
HOW LIBERATING IT MUST BE TO FLY WITHOUT A ROCKET AS CONVEYANCE...
TO WHAT TOWERING HEIGHTS COULD ONE SOAR WITH SUCH SPLENDID WINGS?

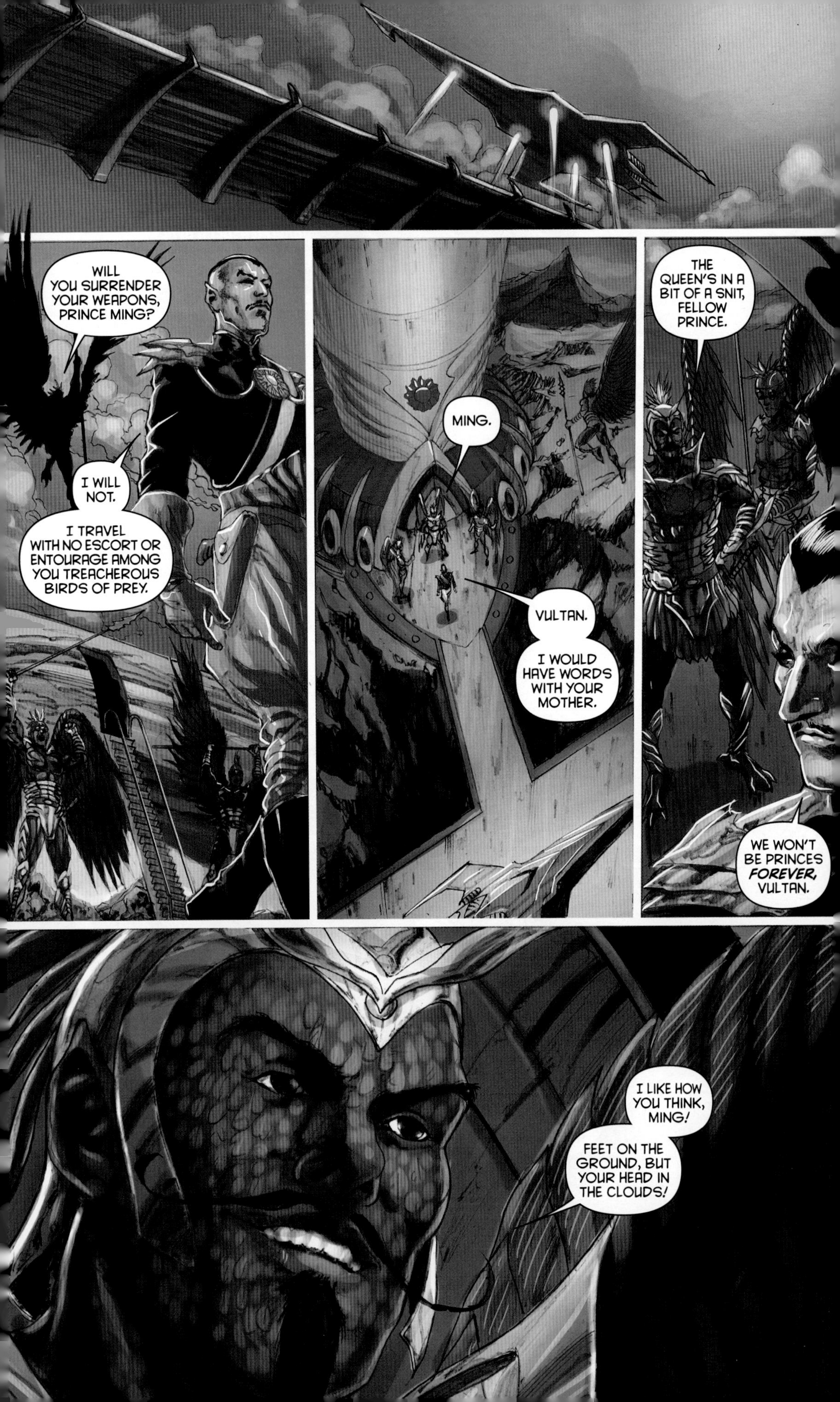

WILL YOU SURRENDER YOUR WEAPONS, PRINCE MING?
I WILL NOT.
I TRAVEL WITH NO ESCORT OR ENTOURAGE AMONG YOU TREACHEROUS BIRDS OF PREY.
MING.
VULTAN.
I WOULD HAVE WORDS WITH YOUR MOTHER.
THE QUEEN'S IN A BIT OF A SNIT, FELLOW PRINCE.
WE WON'T BE PRINCES *FOREVER,* VULTAN.
I LIKE HOW YOU THINK, MING!
FEET ON THE GROUND, BUT YOUR HEAD IN THE CLOUDS!

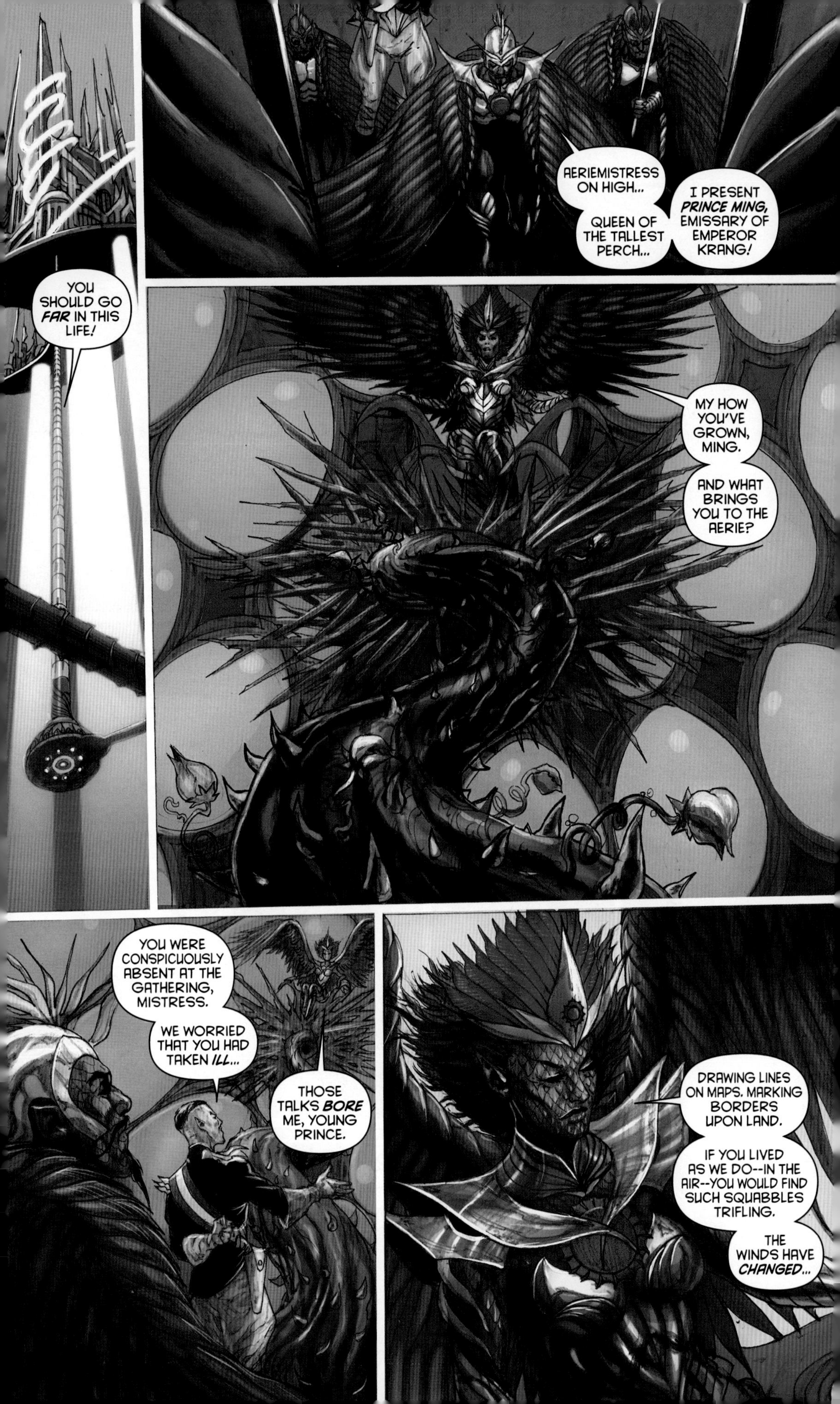
AERIEMISTRESS ON HIGH...
QUEEN OF THE TALLEST PERCH...
I PRESENT PRINCE MING, EMISSARY OF EMPEROR KRANG!
YOU SHOULD GO FAR IN THIS LIFE!
MY HOW YOU'VE GROWN, MING.
AND WHAT BRINGS YOU TO THE AERIE?
YOU WERE CONSPICUOUSLY ABSENT AT THE GATHERING, MISTRESS.
WE WORRIED THAT YOU HAD TAKEN ILL...
THOSE TALKS BORE ME, YOUNG PRINCE.
DRAWING LINES ON MAPS. MARKING BORDERS UPON LAND.
IF YOU LIVED AS WE DO--IN THE AIR--YOU WOULD FIND SUCH SQUABBLES TRIFLING.
THE WINDS HAVE CHANGED...

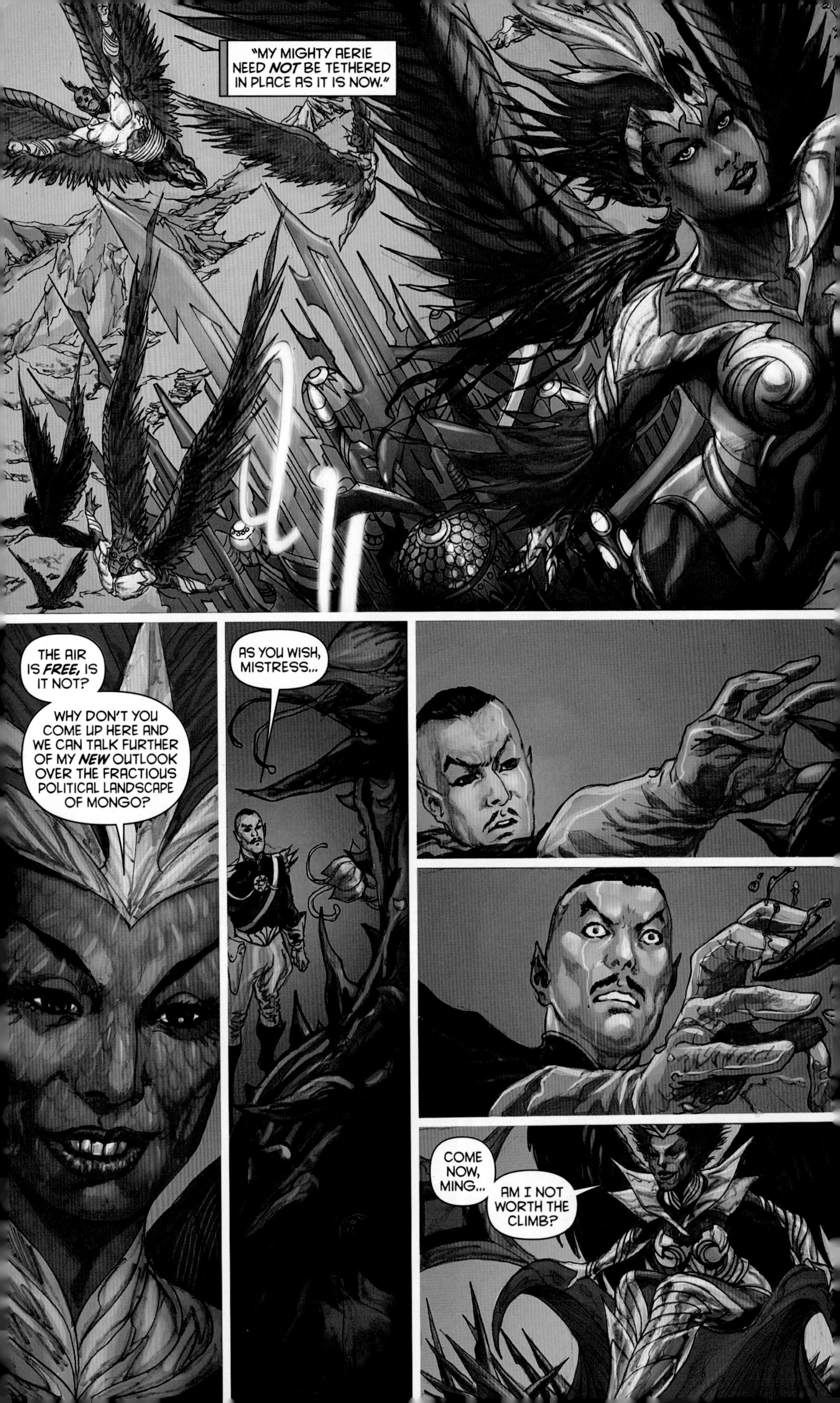
"MY MIGHTY AERIE NEED *NOT* BE TETHERED IN PLACE AS IT IS NOW."
THE AIR IS *FREE,* IS IT NOT?
WHY DON'T YOU COME UP HERE AND WE CAN TALK FURTHER OF MY *NEW* OUTLOOK OVER THE FRACTIOUS POLITICAL LANDSCAPE OF MONGO?
AS YOU WISH, MISTRESS...
COME NOW, MING...
AM I NOT WORTH THE CLIMB?

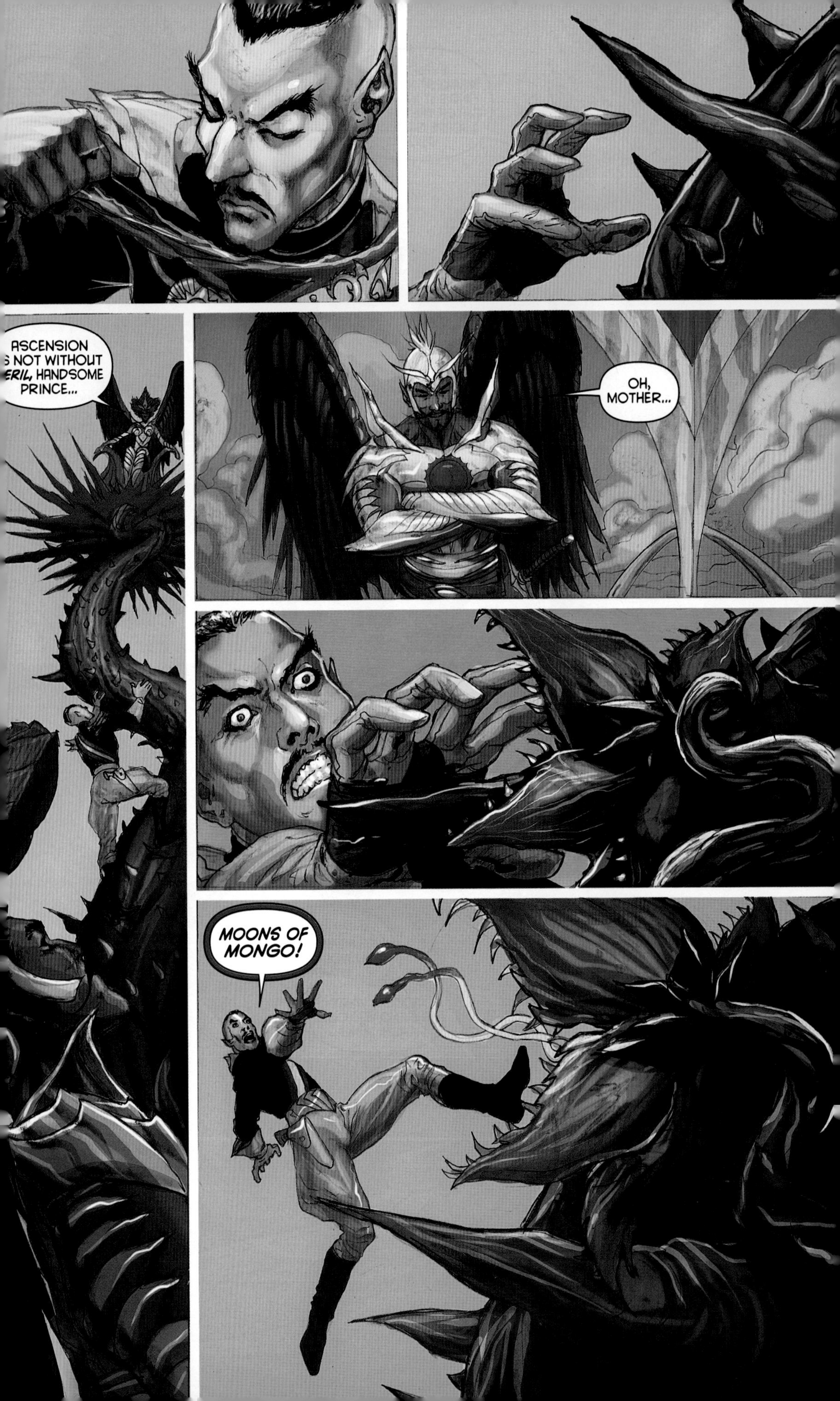
ASCENSION
S NOT WITHOUT
ERIL, HANDSOME
PRINCE...
OH,
MOTHER...
MOONS OF
MONGO!

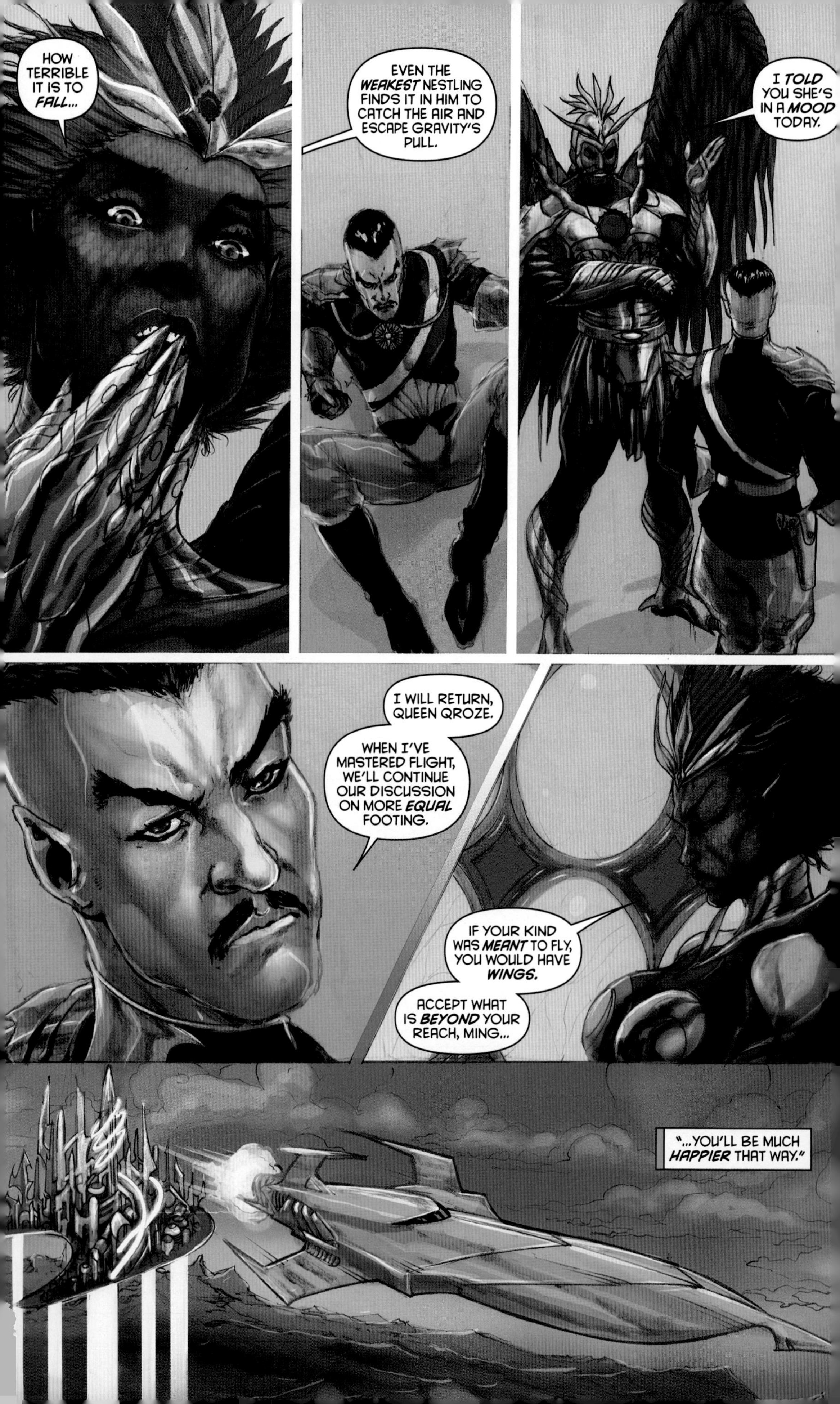
HOW TERRIBLE IT IS TO FALL...
EVEN THE WEAKEST NESTLING FINDS IT IN HIM TO CATCH THE AIR AND ESCAPE GRAVITY'S PULL.
I TOLD YOU SHE'S IN A MOOD TODAY.
I WILL RETURN, QUEEN QROZE.
WHEN I'VE MASTERED FLIGHT, WE'LL CONTINUE OUR DISCUSSION ON MORE EQUAL FOOTING.
IF YOUR KIND WAS MEANT TO FLY, YOU WOULD HAVE WINGS.
ACCEPT WHAT IS BEYOND YOUR REACH, MING...
"...YOU'LL BE MUCH HAPPIER THAT WAY."

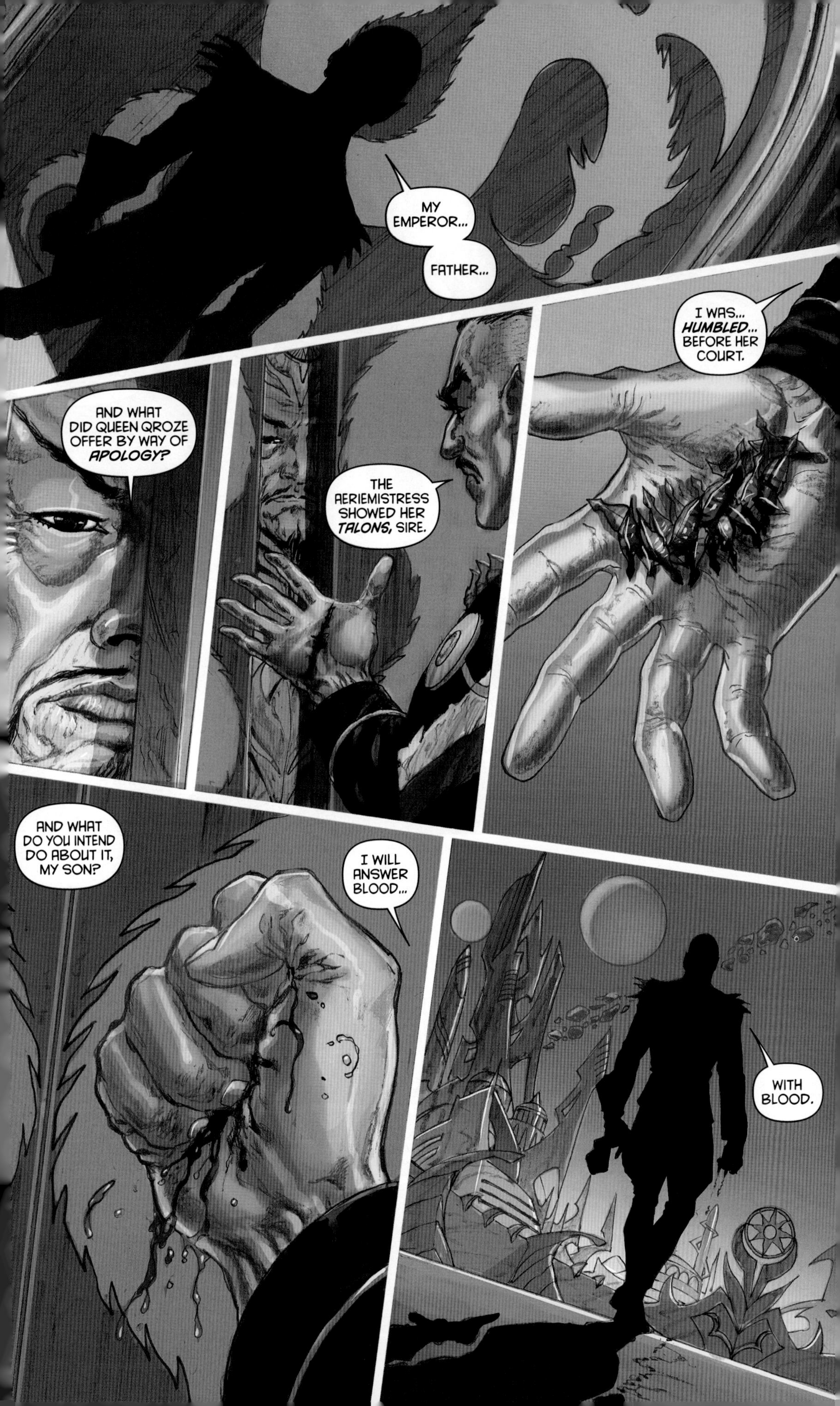
MY EMPEROR...
FATHER...
AND WHAT DID QUEEN QROZE OFFER BY WAY OF *APOLOGY?*
THE AERIEMISTRESS SHOWED HER *TALONS,* SIRE.
I WAS... *HUMBLED*... BEFORE HER COURT.
AND WHAT DO YOU INTEND DO ABOUT IT, MY SON?
I WILL ANSWER BLOOD...
WITH BLOOD.

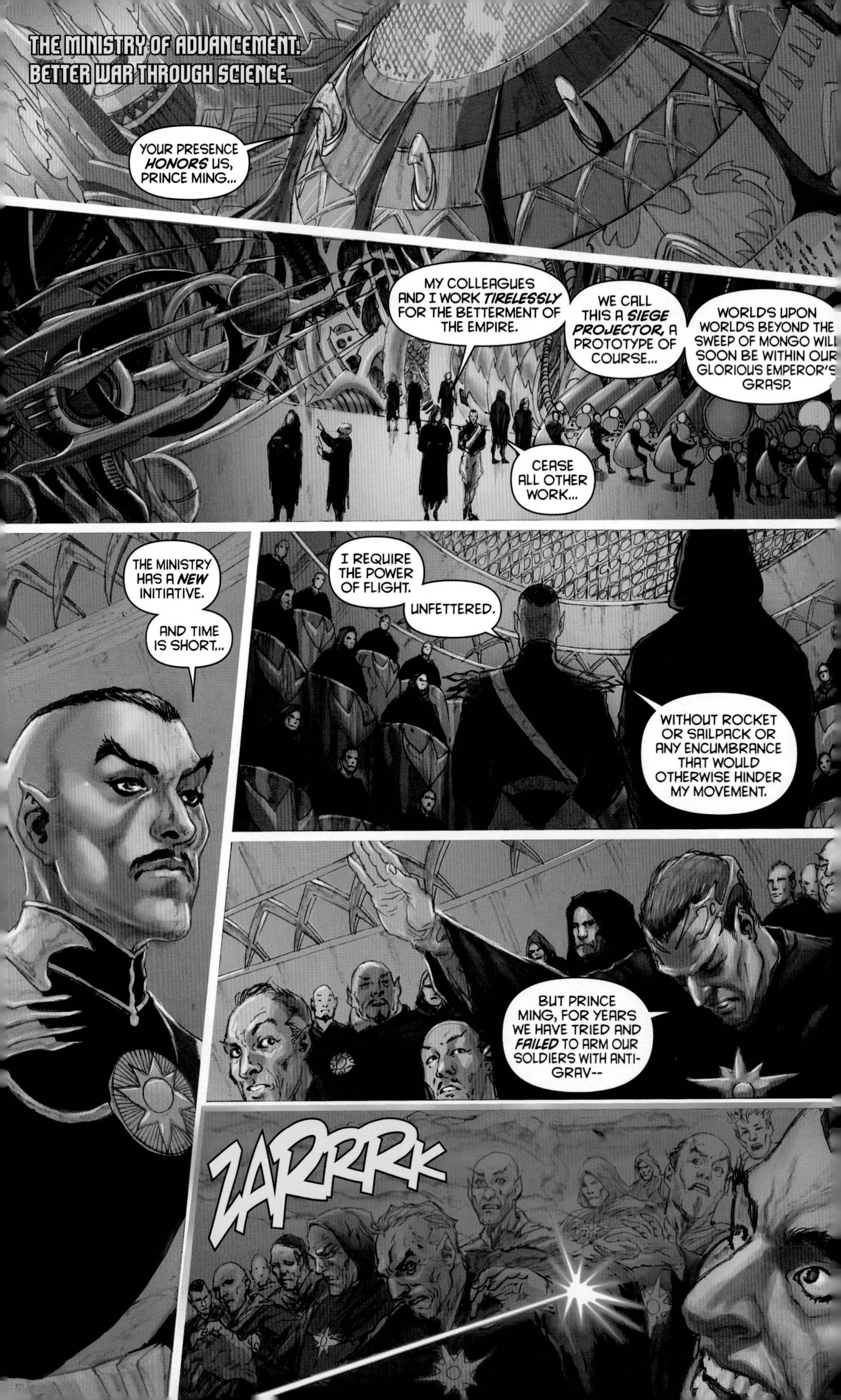

THE MINISTRY OF ADVANCEMENT.
BETTER WAR THROUGH SCIENCE.
YOUR PRESENCE HONORS US, PRINCE MING...
MY COLLEAGUES AND I WORK TIRELESSLY FOR THE BETTERMENT OF THE EMPIRE.
WE CALL THIS A SIEGE PROJECTOR, A PROTOTYPE OF COURSE...
WORLDS UPON WORLDS BEYOND THE SWEEP OF MONGO WILL SOON BE WITHIN OUR GLORIOUS EMPEROR'S GRASP.
CEASE ALL OTHER WORK...
THE MINISTRY HAS A NEW INITIATIVE.
AND TIME IS SHORT...
I REQUIRE THE POWER OF FLIGHT.
UNFETTERED.
WITHOUT ROCKET OR SAILPACK OR ANY ENCUMBRANCE THAT WOULD OTHERWISE HINDER MY MOVEMENT.
BUT PRINCE MING, FOR YEARS WE HAVE TRIED AND FAILED TO ARM OUR SOLDIERS WITH ANTI-GRAV--
ZARRRK

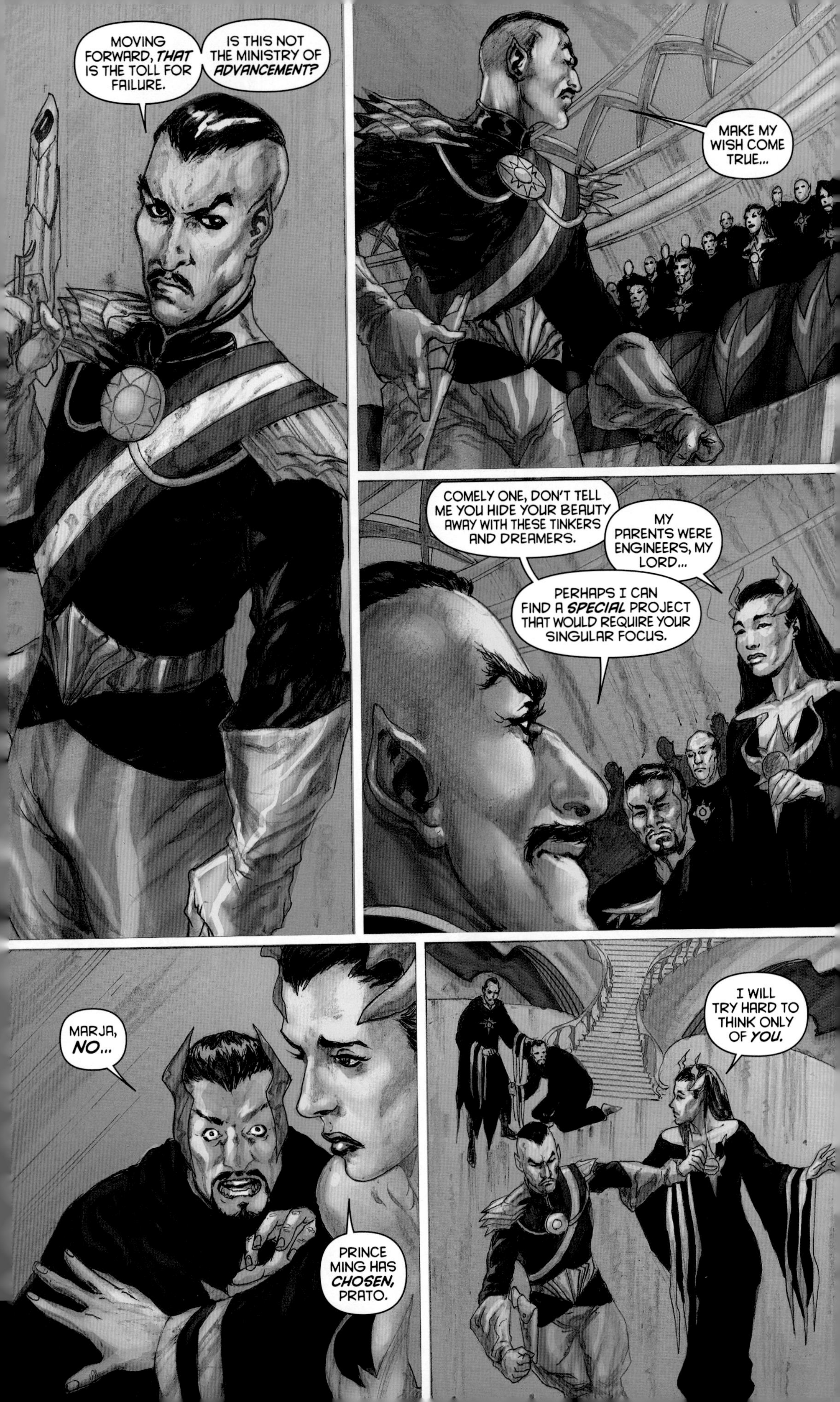
MOVING FORWARD, *THAT* IS THE TOLL FOR FAILURE.
IS THIS NOT THE MINISTRY OF *ADVANCEMENT?*
MAKE MY WISH COME TRUE...
COMELY ONE, DON'T TELL ME YOU HIDE YOUR BEAUTY AWAY WITH THESE TINKERS AND DREAMERS.
MY PARENTS WERE ENGINEERS, MY LORD...
PERHAPS I CAN FIND A *SPECIAL* PROJECT THAT WOULD REQUIRE YOUR SINGULAR FOCUS.
MARJA, *NO*...
PRINCE MING HAS *CHOSEN,* PRATO.
I WILL TRY HARD TO THINK ONLY OF *YOU.*

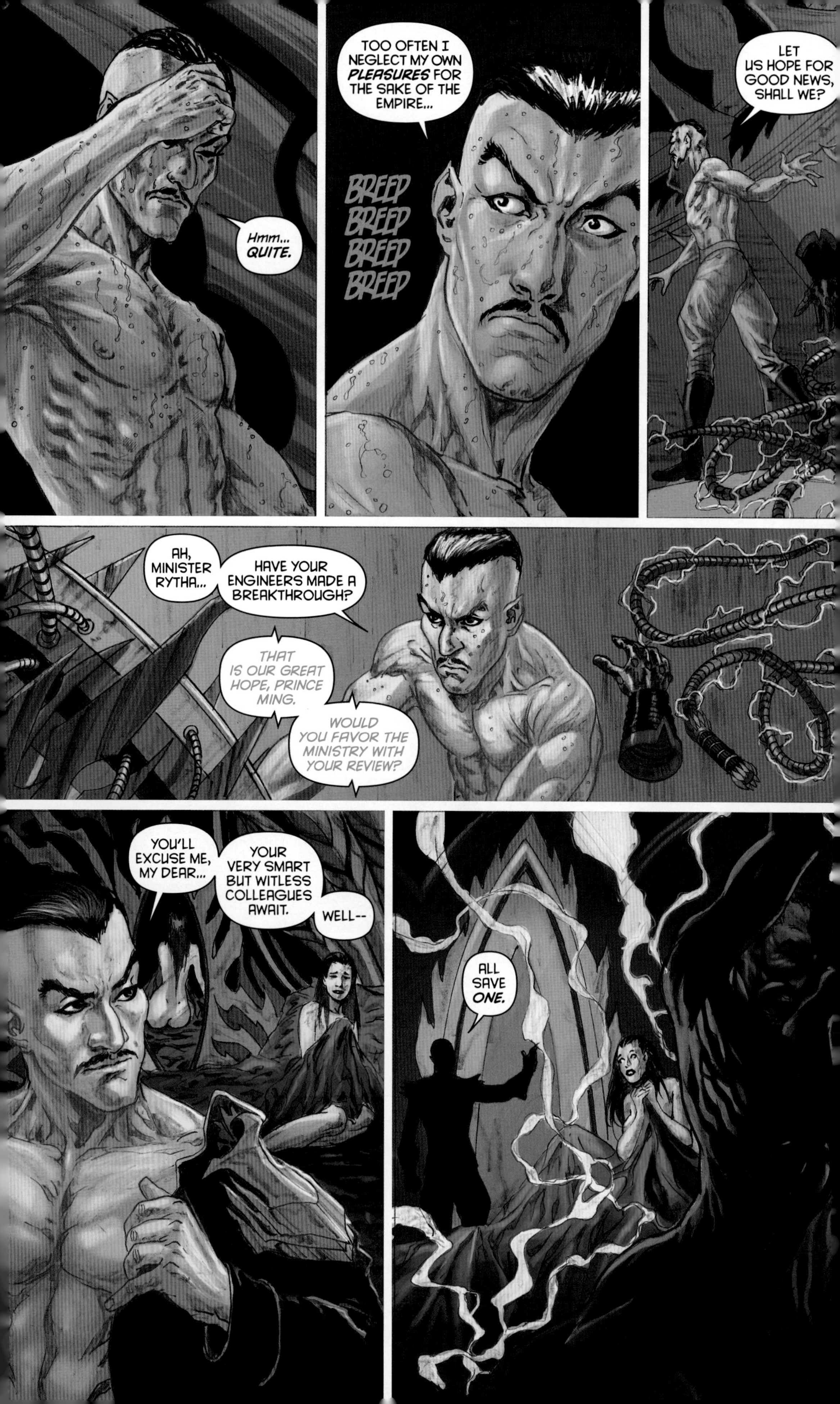
Hmm... QUITE.
TOO OFTEN I NEGLECT MY OWN PLEASURES FOR THE SAKE OF THE EMPIRE...
BREEP BREEP BREEP BREEP
LET US HOPE FOR GOOD NEWS, SHALL WE?
AH, MINISTER RYTHA...
HAVE YOUR ENGINEERS MADE A BREAKTHROUGH?
THAT IS OUR GREAT HOPE, PRINCE MING.
WOULD YOU FAVOR THE MINISTRY WITH YOUR REVIEW?
YOU'LL EXCUSE ME, MY DEAR...
YOUR VERY SMART BUT WITLESS COLLEAGUES AWAIT.
WELL--
ALL SAVE ONE.

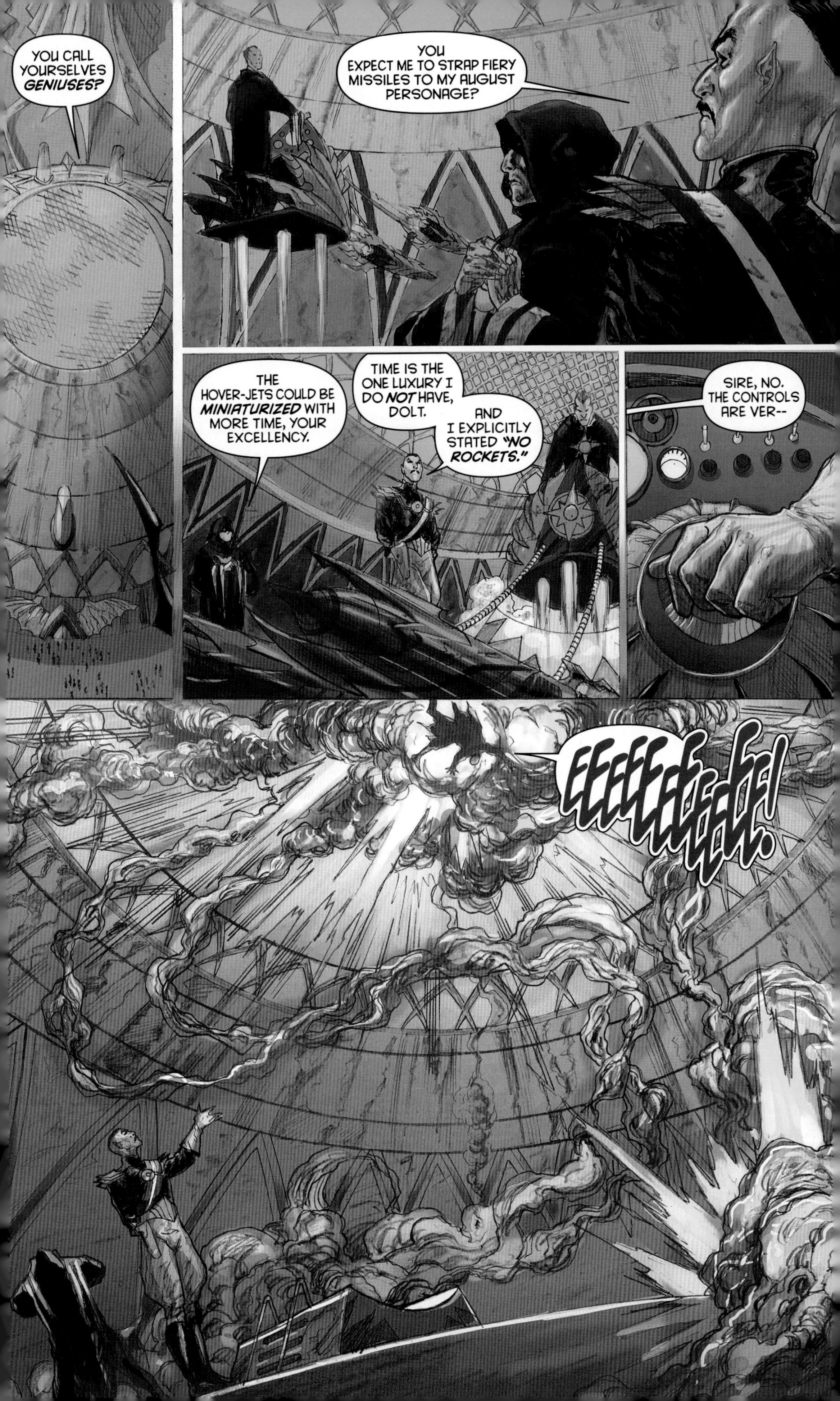

YOU CALL YOURSELVES ***GENIUSES?***
YOU EXPECT ME TO STRAP FIERY MISSILES TO MY AUGUST PERSONAGE?
THE HOVER-JETS COULD BE ***MINIATURIZED*** WITH MORE TIME, YOUR EXCELLENCY.
TIME IS THE ONE LUXURY I DO ***NOT*** HAVE, DOLT.
AND I EXPLICITLY STATED ***"NO ROCKETS."***
SIRE, NO. THE CONTROLS ARE VER--
EEEEEEEEEE!

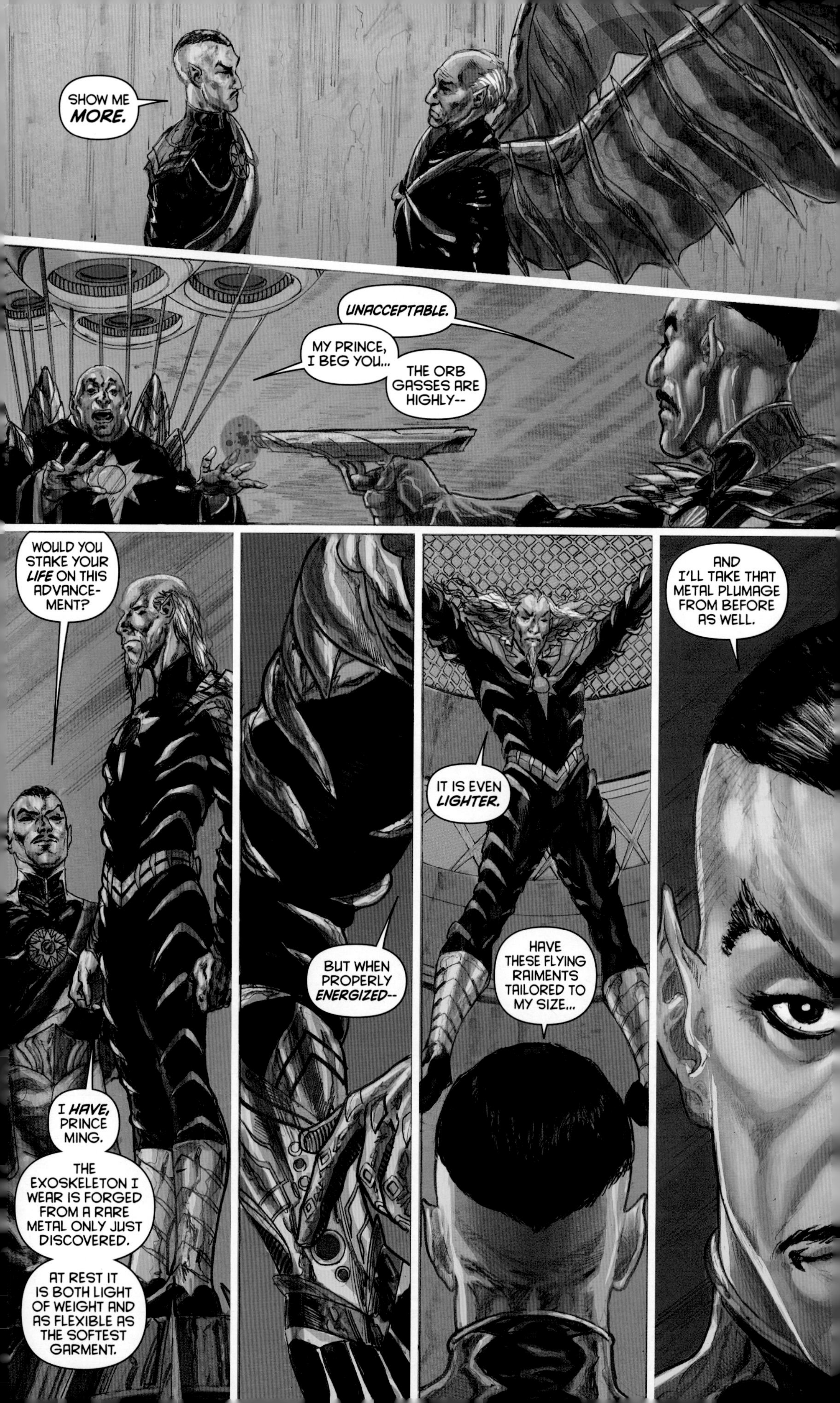
SHOW ME MORE.
UNACCEPTABLE.
MY PRINCE, I BEG YOU...
THE ORB GASSES ARE HIGHLY--
WOULD YOU STAKE YOUR LIFE ON THIS ADVANCE-MENT?
I HAVE, PRINCE MING.
THE EXOSKELETON I WEAR IS FORGED FROM A RARE METAL ONLY JUST DISCOVERED.
AT REST IT IS BOTH LIGHT OF WEIGHT AND AS FLEXIBLE AS THE SOFTEST GARMENT.
BUT WHEN PROPERLY ENERGIZED--
IT IS EVEN LIGHTER.
HAVE THESE FLYING RAIMENTS TAILORED TO MY SIZE...
AND I'LL TAKE THAT METAL PLUMAGE FROM BEFORE AS WELL.

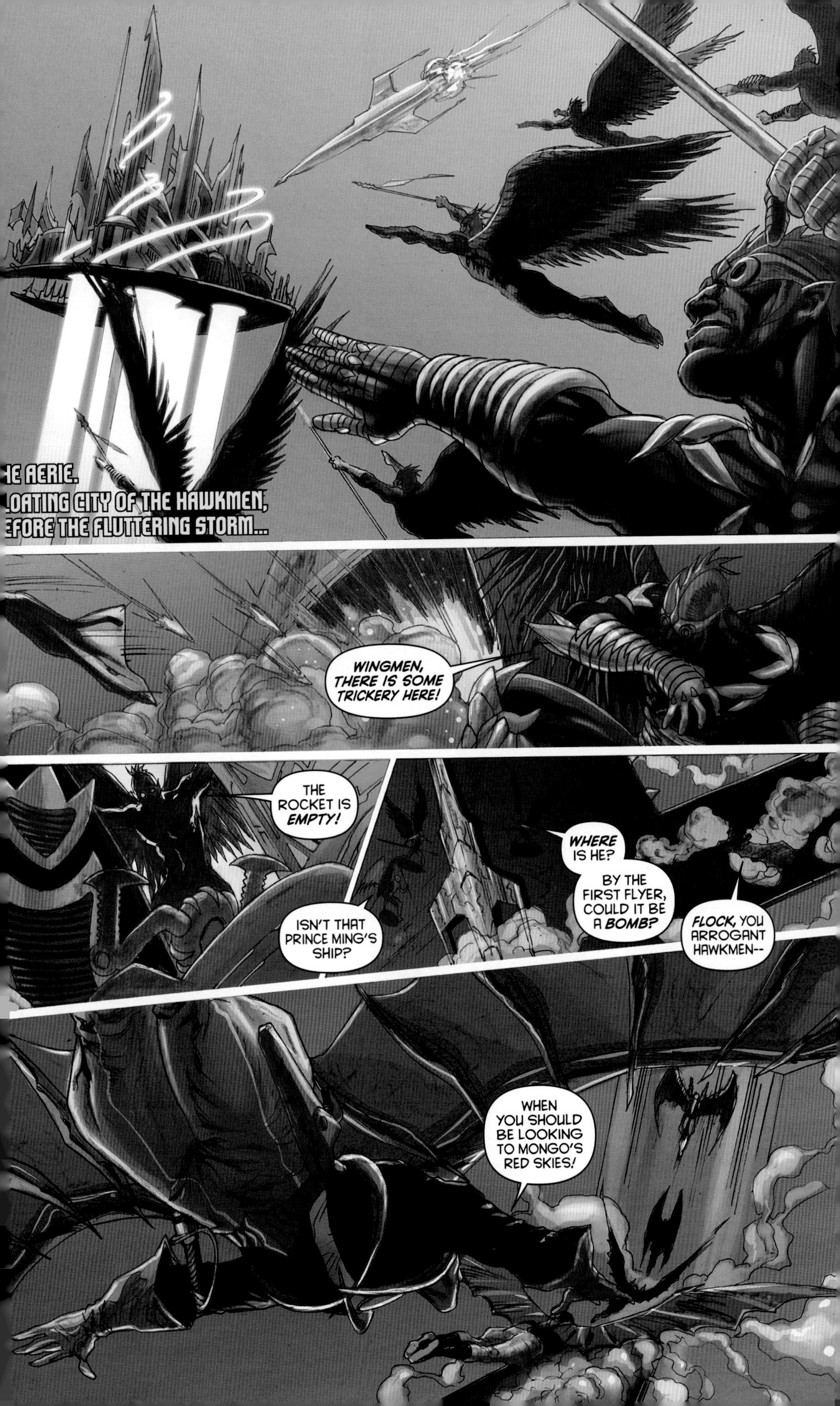

IE AERIE.
LOATING CITY OF THE HAWKMEN,
EFORE THE FLUTTERING STORM...
WINGMEN, THERE IS SOME TRICKERY HERE!
THE ROCKET IS EMPTY!
ISN'T THAT PRINCE MING'S SHIP?
WHERE IS HE?
BY THE FIRST FLYER, COULD IT BE A BOMB?
FLOCK, YOU ARROGANT HAWKMEN--
WHEN YOU SHOULD BE LOOKING TO MONGO'S RED SKIES!

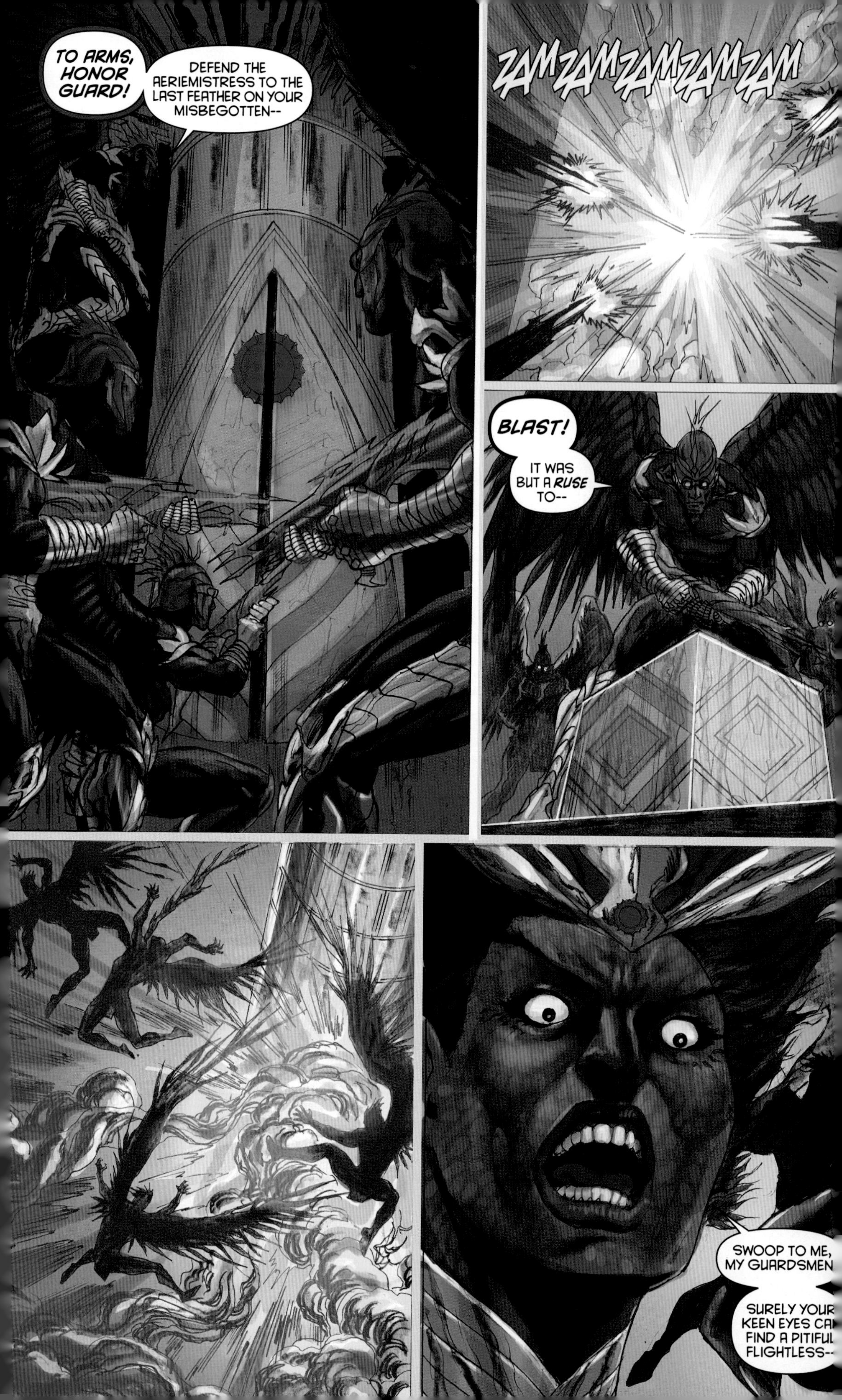
TO ARMS, HONOR GUARD!
DEFEND THE AERIEMISTRESS TO THE LAST FEATHER ON YOUR MISBEGOTTEN--
ZAMZAMZAMZAMZAM
BLAST!
IT WAS BUT A RUSE TO--
SWOOP TO ME, MY GUARDSMEN
SURELY YOUR KEEN EYES CA FIND A PITIFUL FLIGHTLESS--

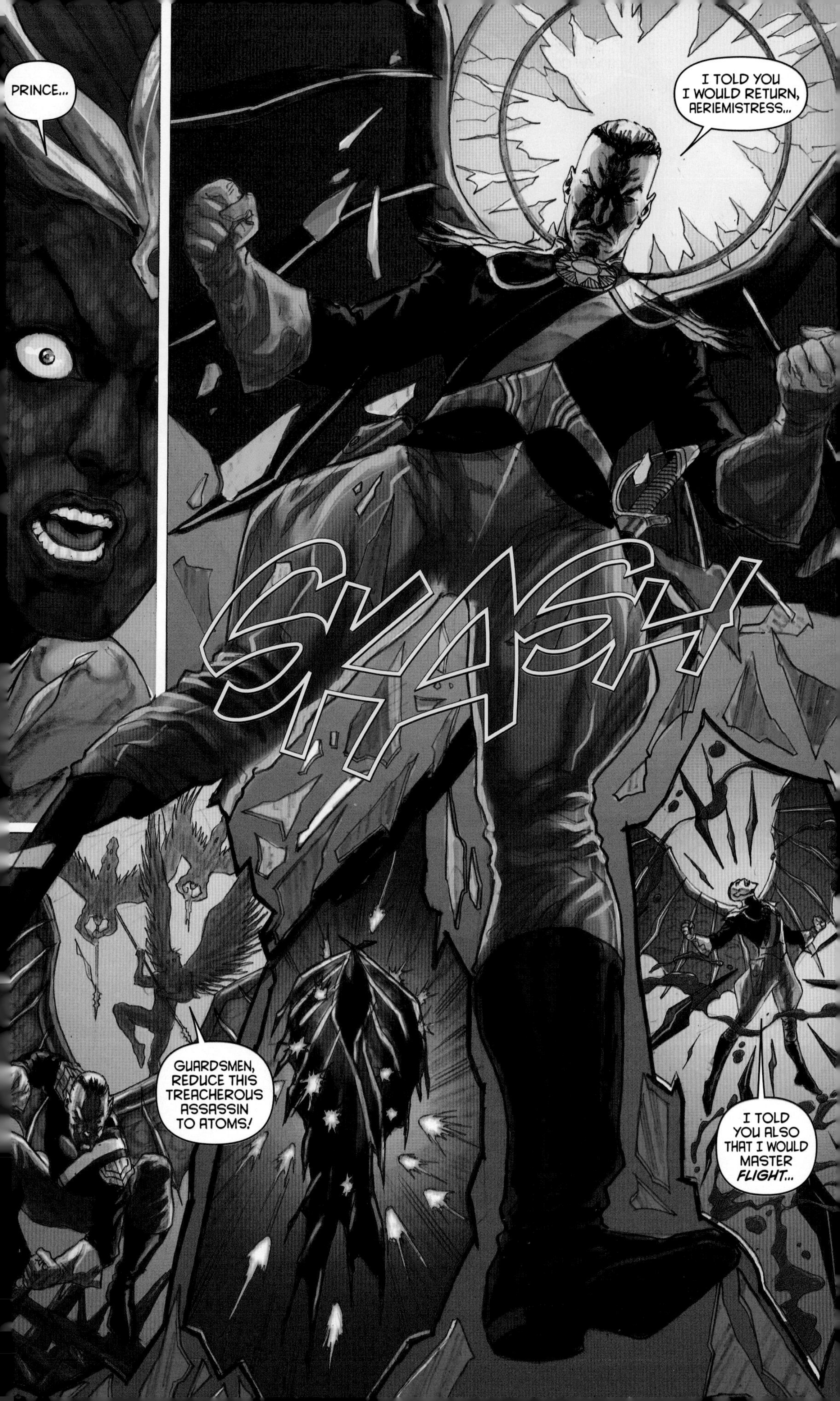
PRINCE...
I TOLD YOU I WOULD RETURN, AERIEMISTRESS...
SKASH
GUARDSMEN, REDUCE THIS TREACHEROUS ASSASSIN TO ATOMS!
I TOLD YOU ALSO THAT I WOULD MASTER *FLIGHT*...

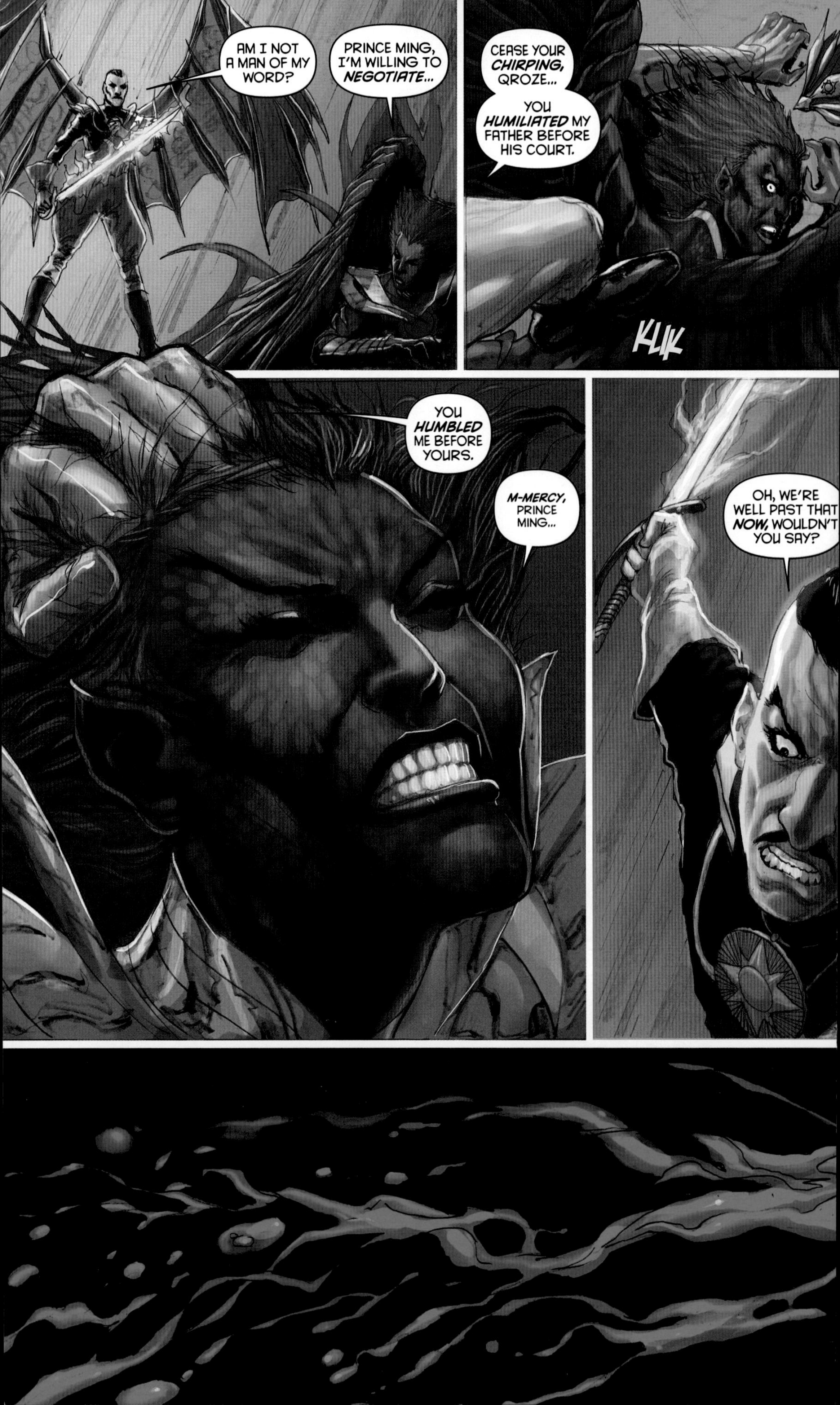
AM I NOT A MAN OF MY WORD?
PRINCE MING, I'M WILLING TO NEGOTIATE...
CEASE YOUR CHIRPING, QROZE...
YOU HUMILIATED MY FATHER BEFORE HIS COURT.
KLIK
YOU HUMBLED ME BEFORE YOURS.
M-MERCY, PRINCE MING...
OH, WE'RE WELL PAST THAT NOW, WOULDN'T YOU SAY?

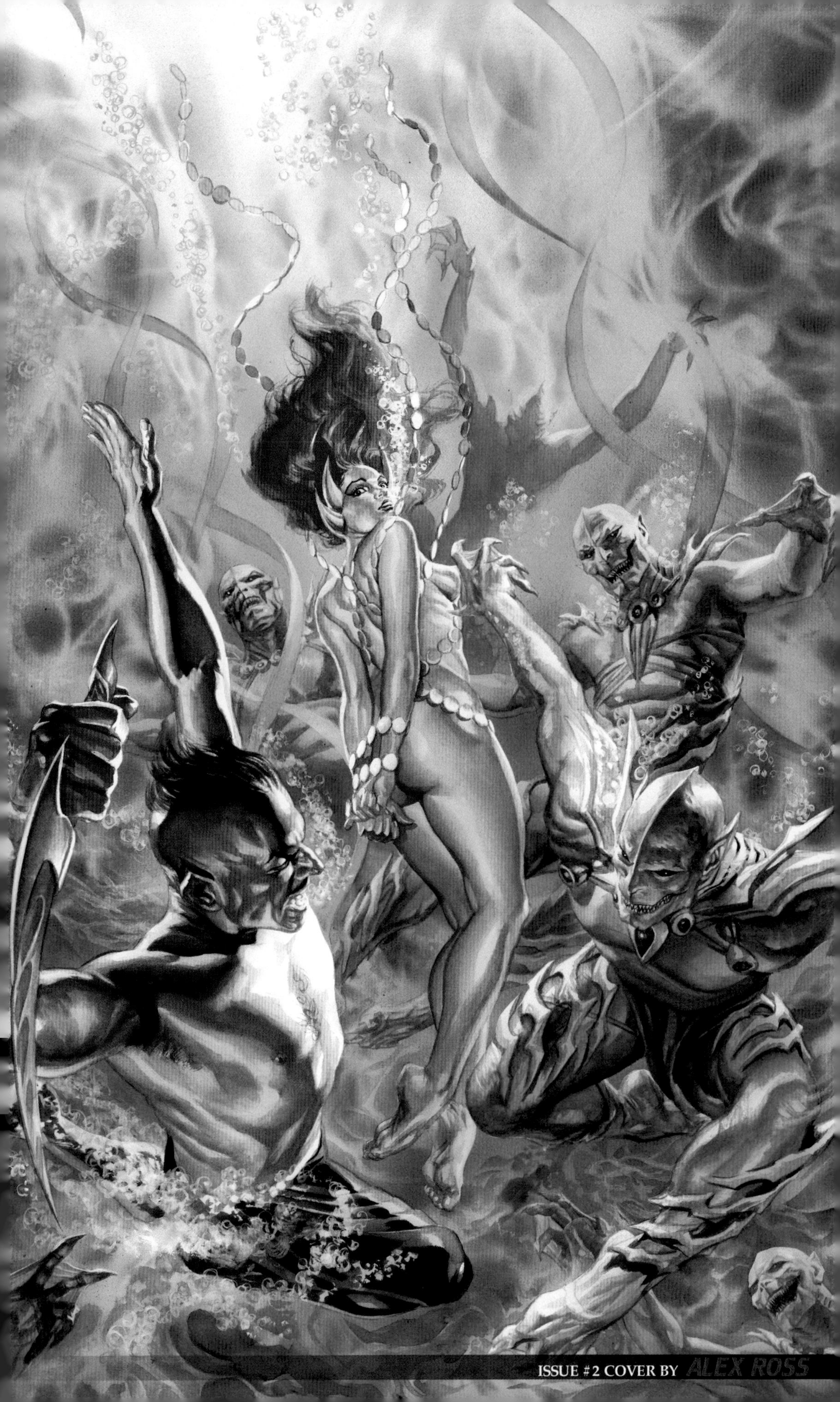

ISSUE #2 COVER BY ALEX ROSS

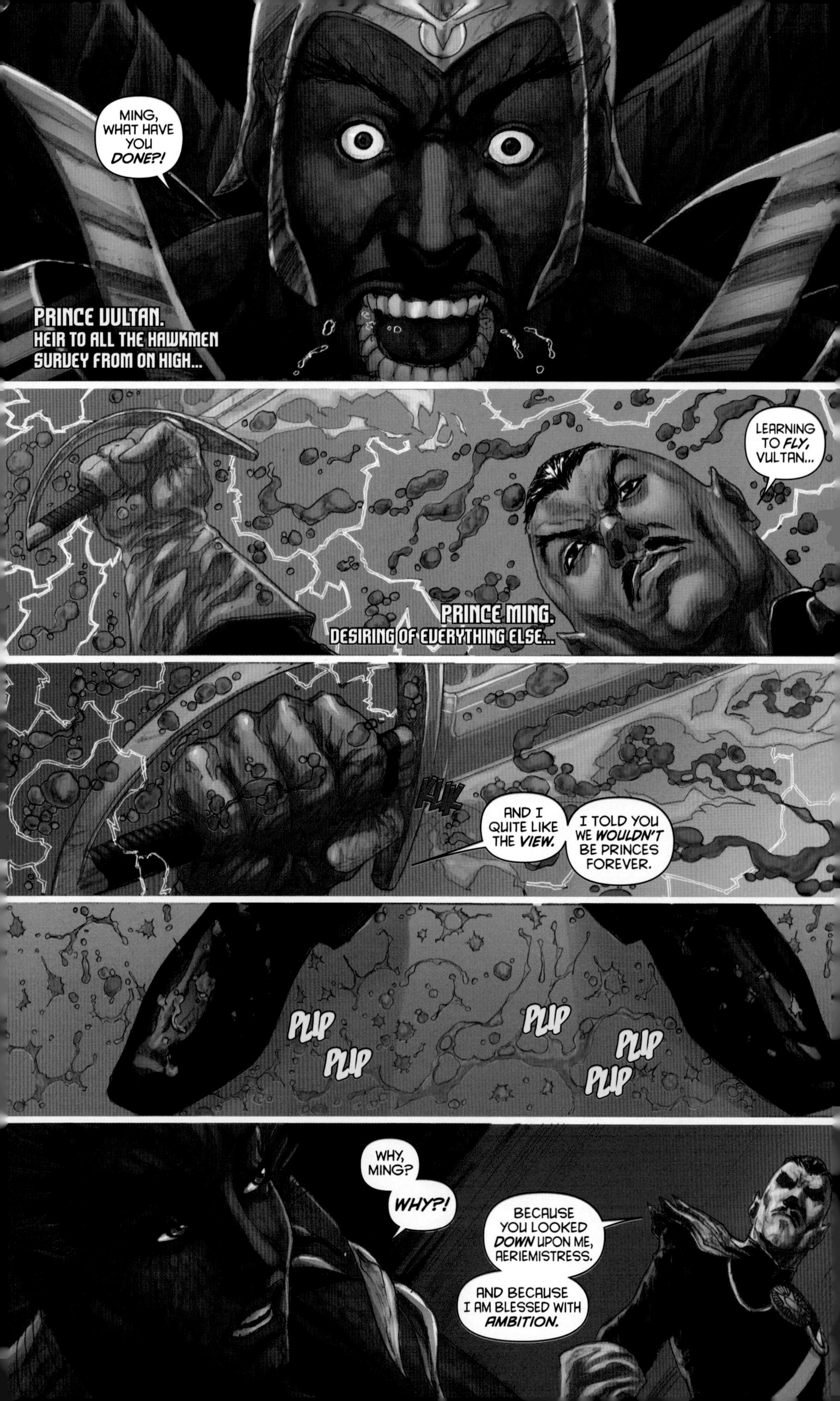
MING, WHAT HAVE YOU DONE?!
PRINCE VULTAN.
HEIR TO ALL THE HAWKMEN SURVEY FROM ON HIGH...
LEARNING TO FLY, VULTAN...
PRINCE MING.
DESIRING OF EVERYTHING ELSE...
KLIK
AND I QUITE LIKE THE VIEW.
I TOLD YOU WE WOULDN'T BE PRINCES FOREVER.
PLIP
PLIP
PLIP
PLIP
PLIP
WHY, MING?
WHY?!
BECAUSE YOU LOOKED DOWN UPON ME, AERIEMISTRESS.
AND BECAUSE I AM BLESSED WITH AMBITION.

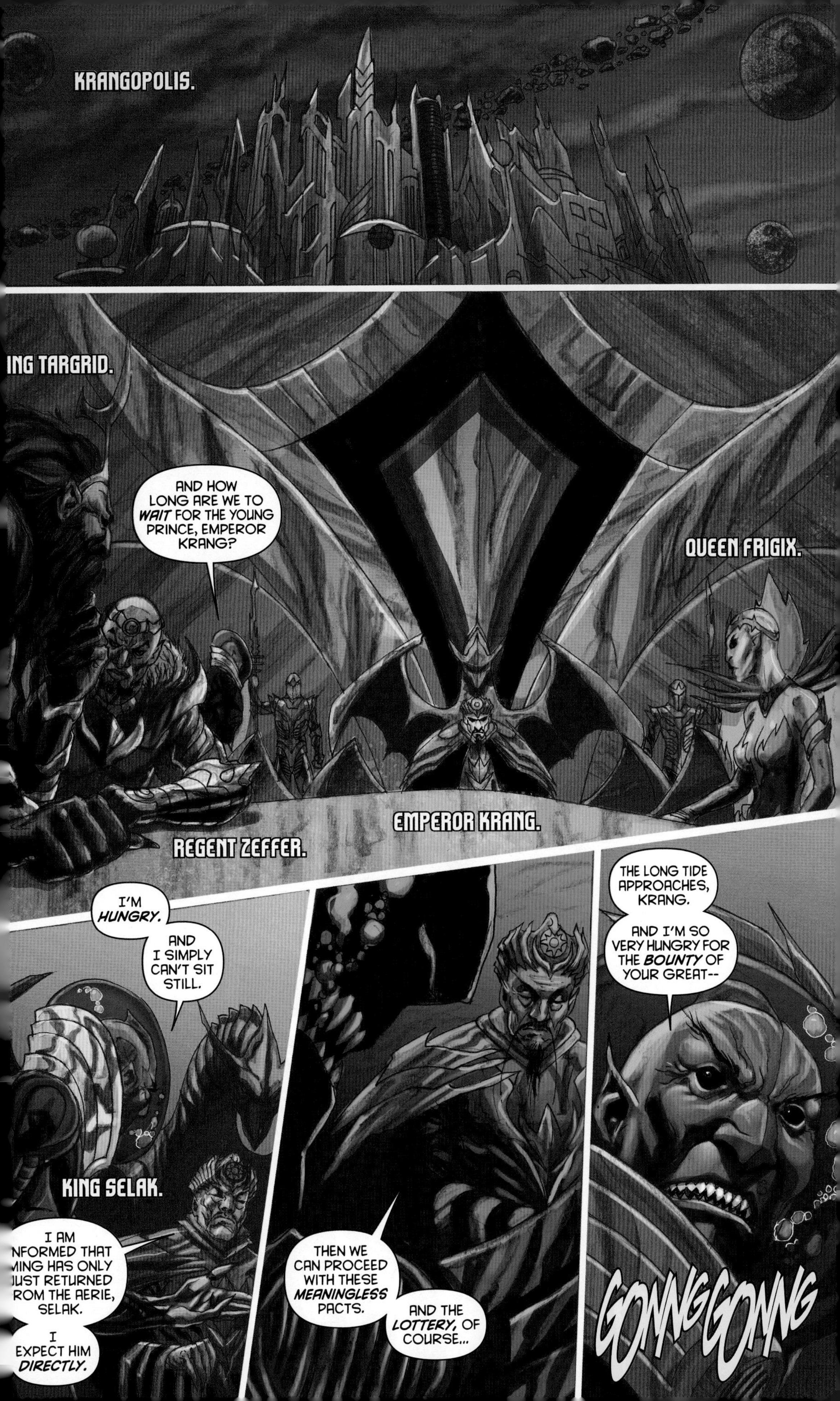
KRANGOPOLIS.
ING TARGRID.
AND HOW LONG ARE WE TO *WAIT* FOR THE YOUNG PRINCE, EMPEROR KRANG?
QUEEN FRIGIX.
EMPEROR KRANG.
REGENT ZEFFER.
I'M *HUNGRY.*
AND I SIMPLY CAN'T SIT STILL.
KING SELAK.
I AM NFORMED THAT MING HAS ONLY UST RETURNED ROM THE AERIE, SELAK.
I EXPECT HIM *DIRECTLY.*
THEN WE CAN PROCEED WITH THESE *MEANINGLESS* PACTS.
AND THE *LOTTERY,* OF COURSE...
THE LONG TIDE APPROACHES, KRANG.
AND I'M SO VERY HUNGRY FOR THE *BOUNTY* OF YOUR GREAT--
GONNG GONNG

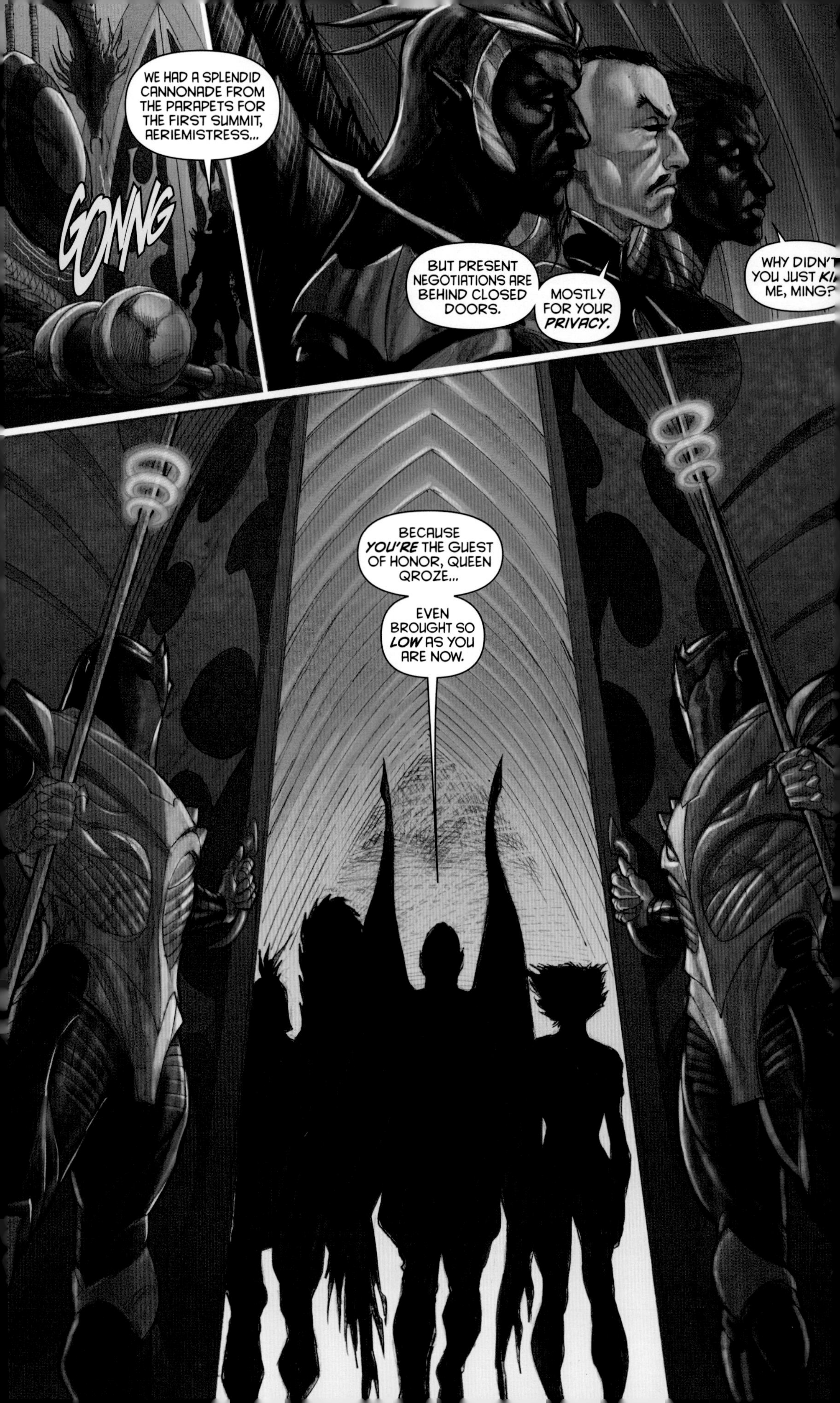
WE HAD A SPLENDID CANNONADE FROM THE PARAPETS FOR THE FIRST SUMMIT, AERIEMISTRESS...
GONNG
BUT PRESENT NEGOTIATIONS ARE BEHIND CLOSED DOORS.
MOSTLY FOR YOUR *PRIVACY.*
WHY DIDN'T YOU JUST *KI* ME, MING?
BECAUSE *YOU'RE* THE GUEST OF HONOR, QUEEN QROZE...
EVEN BROUGHT SO *LOW* AS YOU ARE NOW.

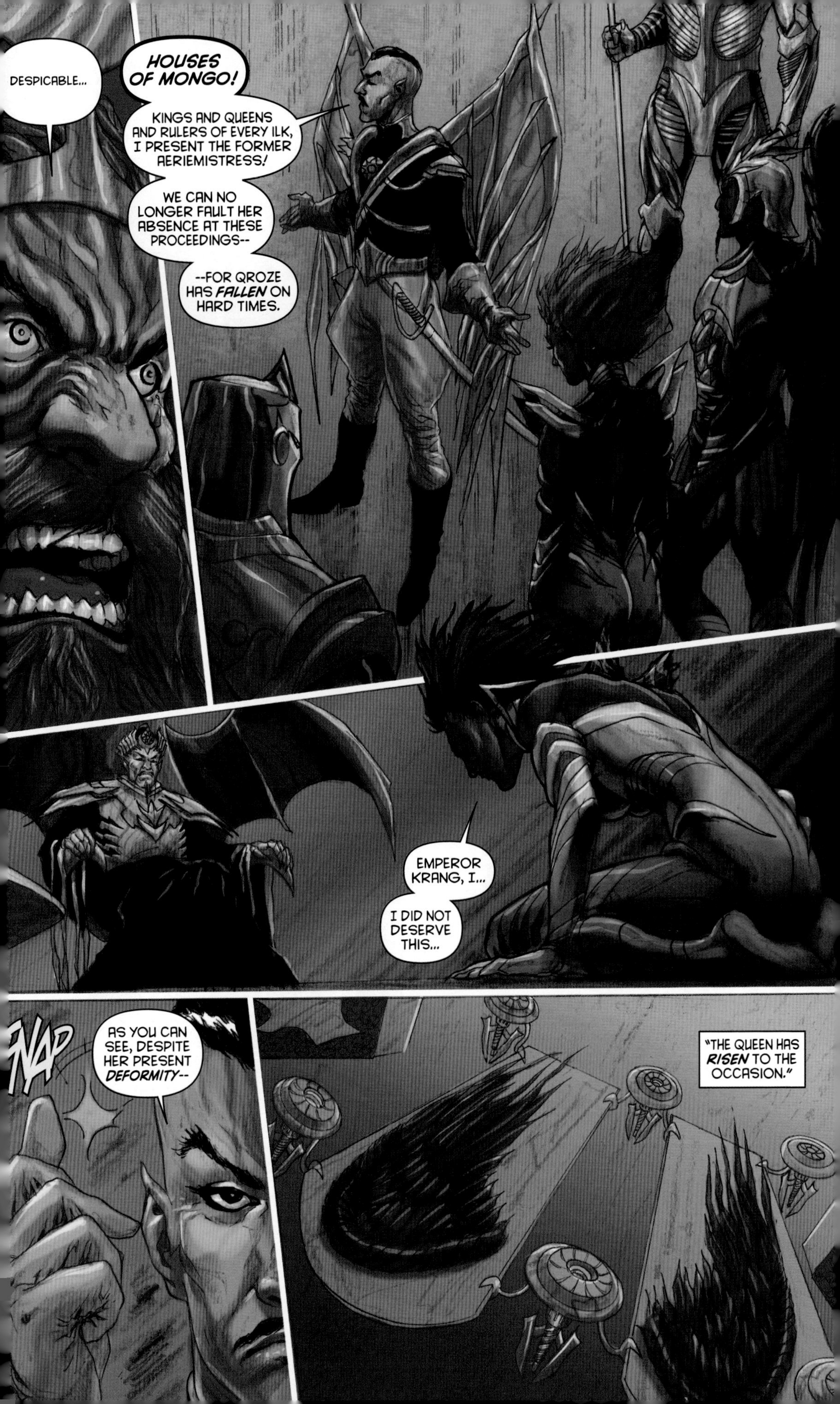

DESPICABLE...
HOUSES OF MONGO!
KINGS AND QUEENS AND RULERS OF EVERY ILK, I PRESENT THE FORMER AERIEMISTRESS!
WE CAN NO LONGER FAULT HER ABSENCE AT THESE PROCEEDINGS--
--FOR QROZE HAS FALLEN ON HARD TIMES.
EMPEROR KRANG, I...
I DID NOT DESERVE THIS...
SNAP
AS YOU CAN SEE, DESPITE HER PRESENT DEFORMITY--
"THE QUEEN HAS RISEN TO THE OCCASION."

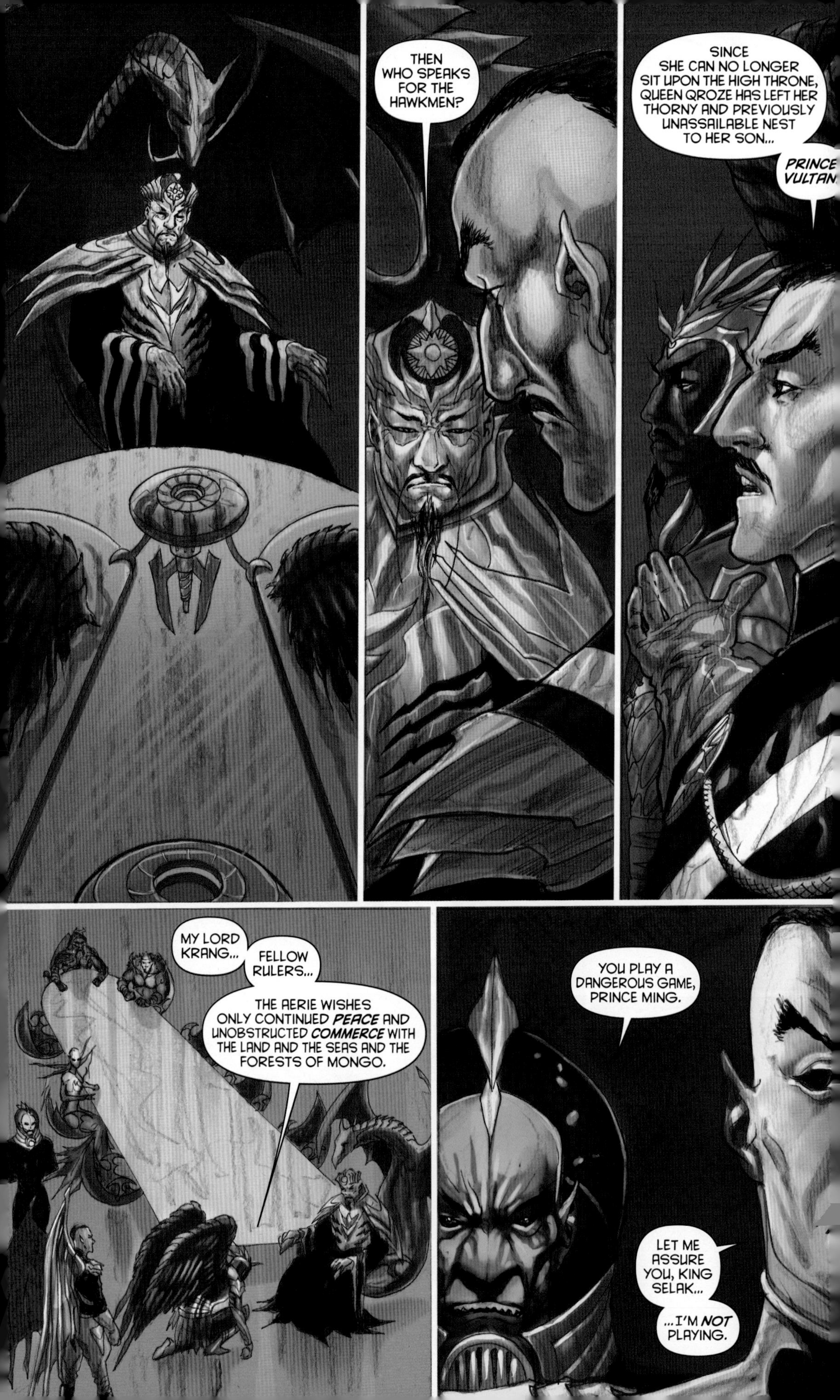
THEN WHO SPEAKS FOR THE HAWKMEN?
SINCE SHE CAN NO LONGER SIT UPON THE HIGH THRONE, QUEEN QROZE HAS LEFT HER THORNY AND PREVIOUSLY UNASSAILABLE NEST TO HER SON...
PRINCE VULTAN.
MY LORD KRANG...
FELLOW RULERS...
THE AERIE WISHES ONLY CONTINUED PEACE AND UNOBSTRUCTED COMMERCE WITH THE LAND AND THE SEAS AND THE FORESTS OF MONGO.
YOU PLAY A DANGEROUS GAME, PRINCE MING.
LET ME ASSURE YOU, KING SELAK...
...I'M NOT PLAYING.

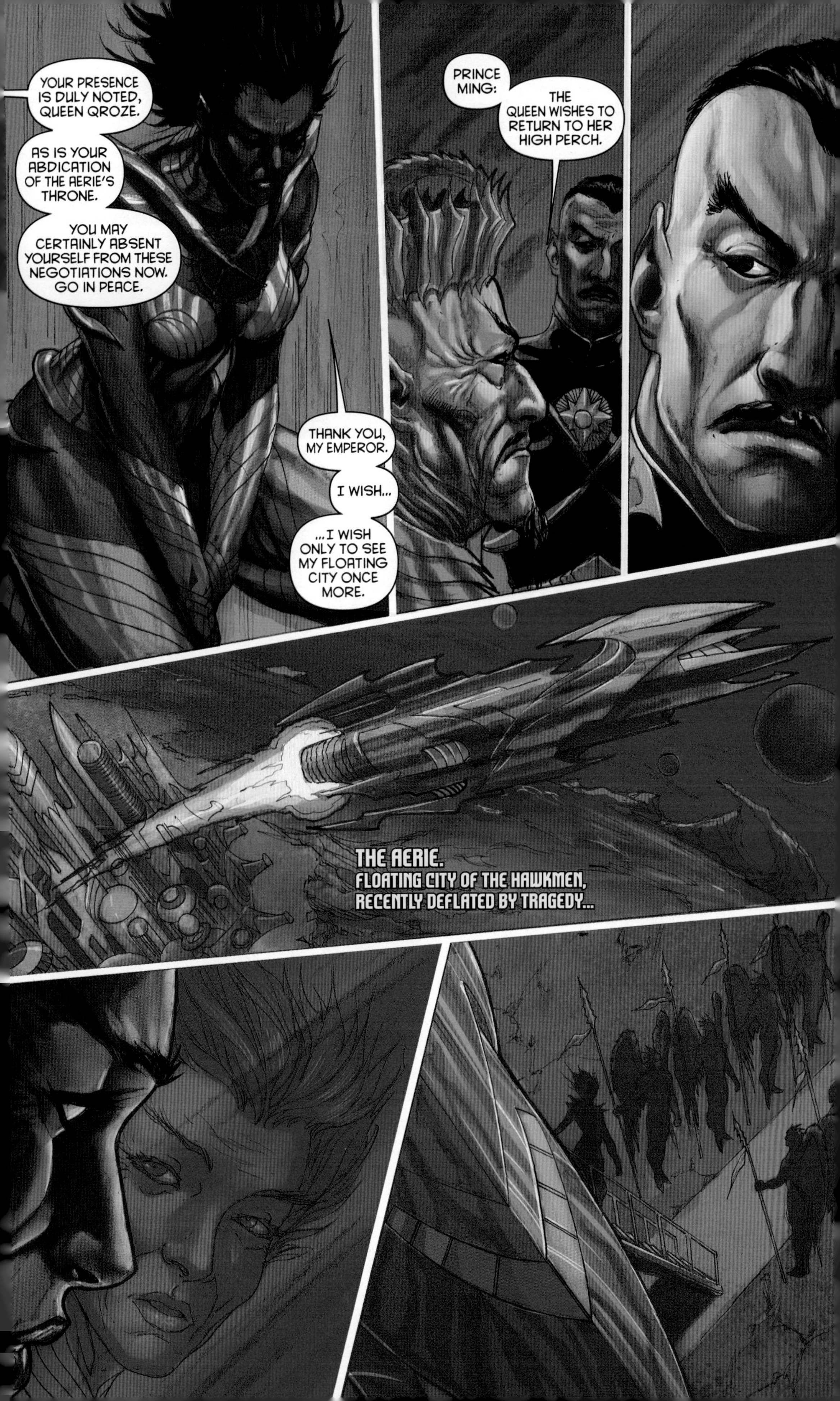
YOUR PRESENCE IS DULY NOTED, QUEEN QROZE.
AS IS YOUR ABDICATION OF THE AERIE'S THRONE.
YOU MAY CERTAINLY ABSENT YOURSELF FROM THESE NEGOTIATIONS NOW. GO IN PEACE.
THANK YOU, MY EMPEROR.
I WISH...
...I WISH ONLY TO SEE MY FLOATING CITY ONCE MORE.
PRINCE MING:
THE QUEEN WISHES TO RETURN TO HER HIGH PERCH.
THE AERIE.
FLOATING CITY OF THE HAWKMEN, RECENTLY DEFLATED BY TRAGEDY...

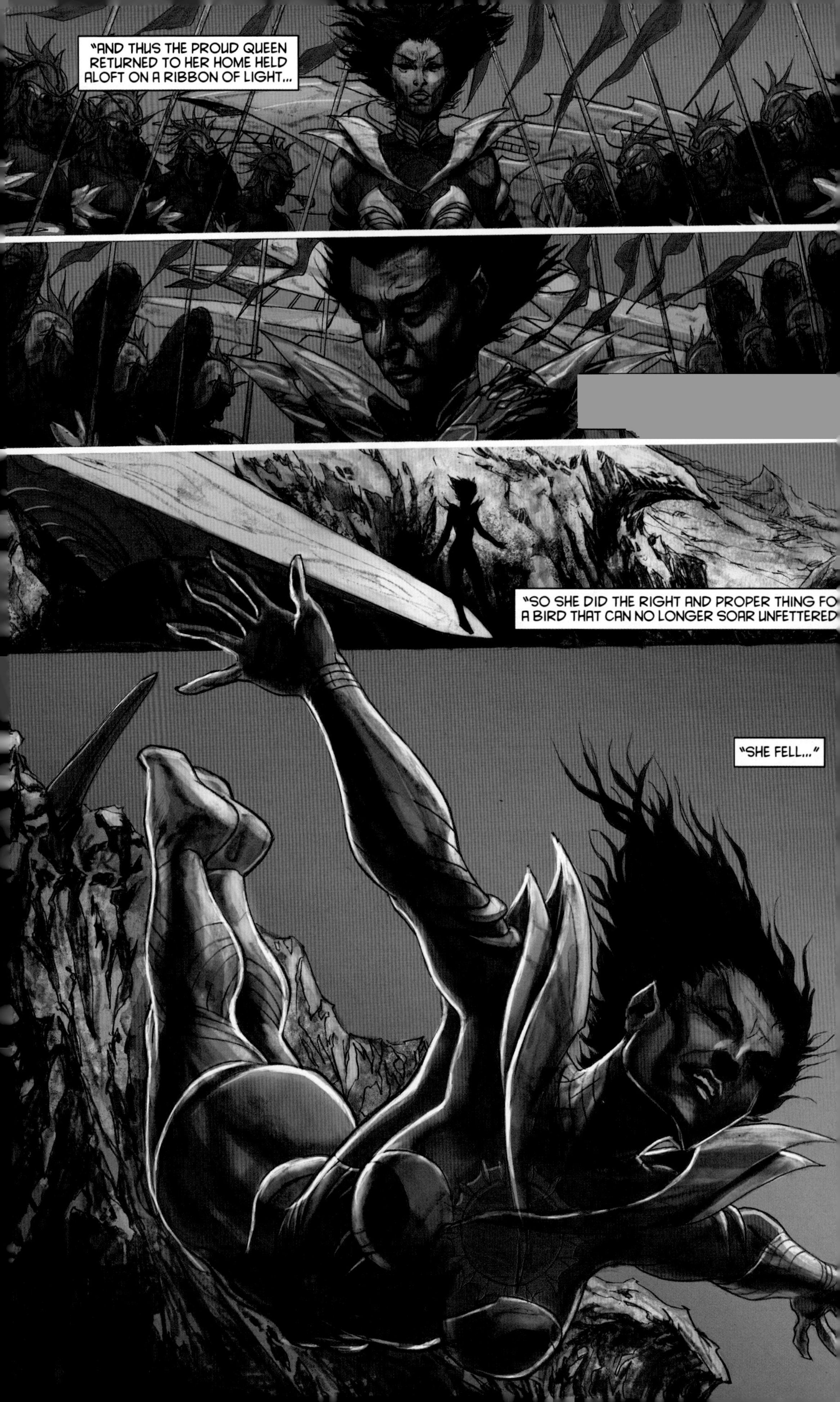
"AND THUS THE PROUD QUEEN RETURNED TO HER HOME HELD ALOFT ON A RIBBON OF LIGHT...
"SO SHE DID THE RIGHT AND PROPER THING FO
A BIRD THAT CAN NO LONGER SOAR UNFETTERED
"SHE FELL..."

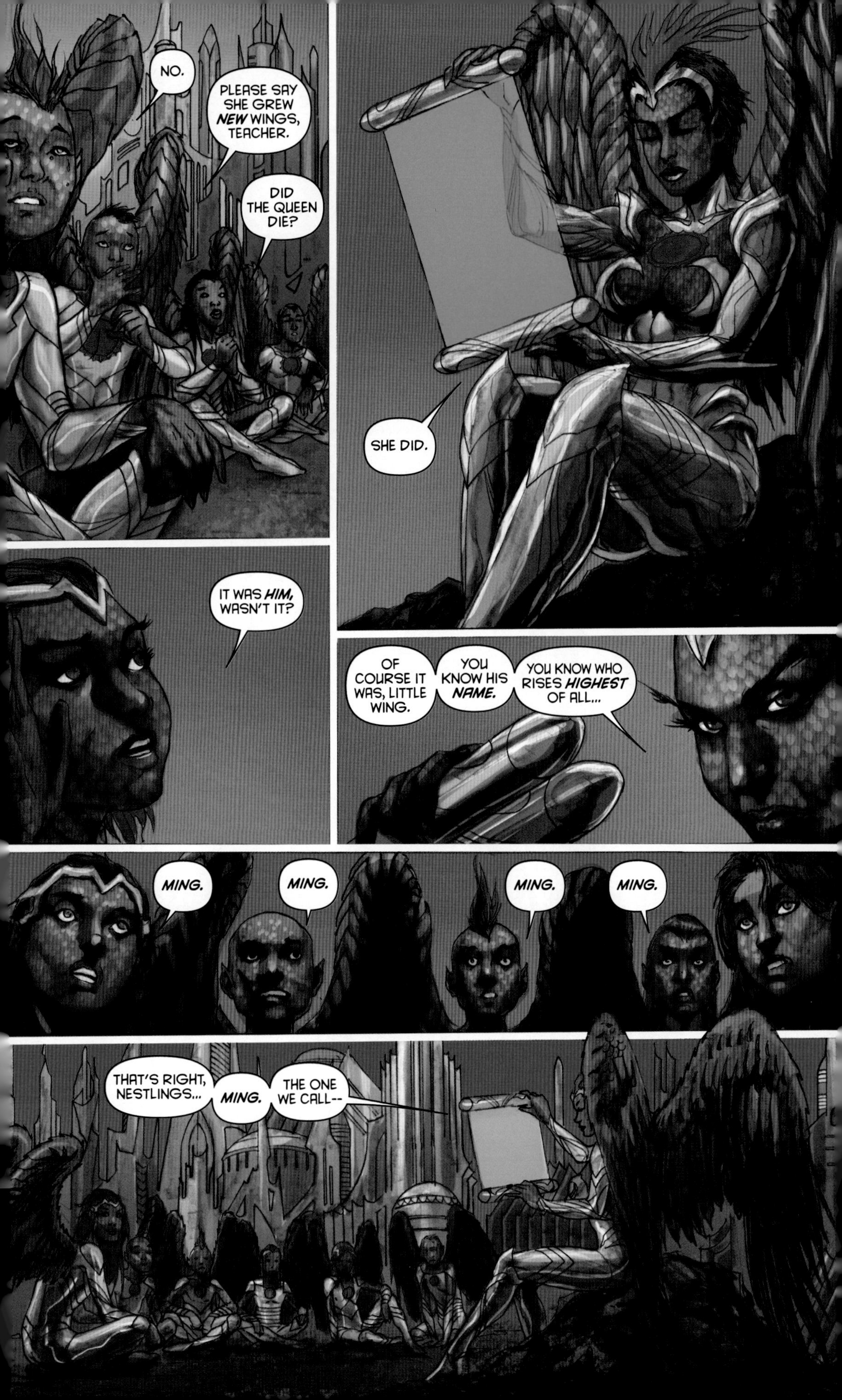

NO.
PLEASE SAY SHE GREW *NEW* WINGS, TEACHER.
DID THE QUEEN DIE?
SHE DID.
IT WAS *HIM,* WASN'T IT?
OF COURSE IT WAS, LITTLE WING.
YOU KNOW HIS *NAME.*
YOU KNOW WHO RISES *HIGHEST* OF ALL...
MING.
MING.
MING.
MING.
THAT'S RIGHT, NESTLINGS...
MING.
THE ONE WE CALL--

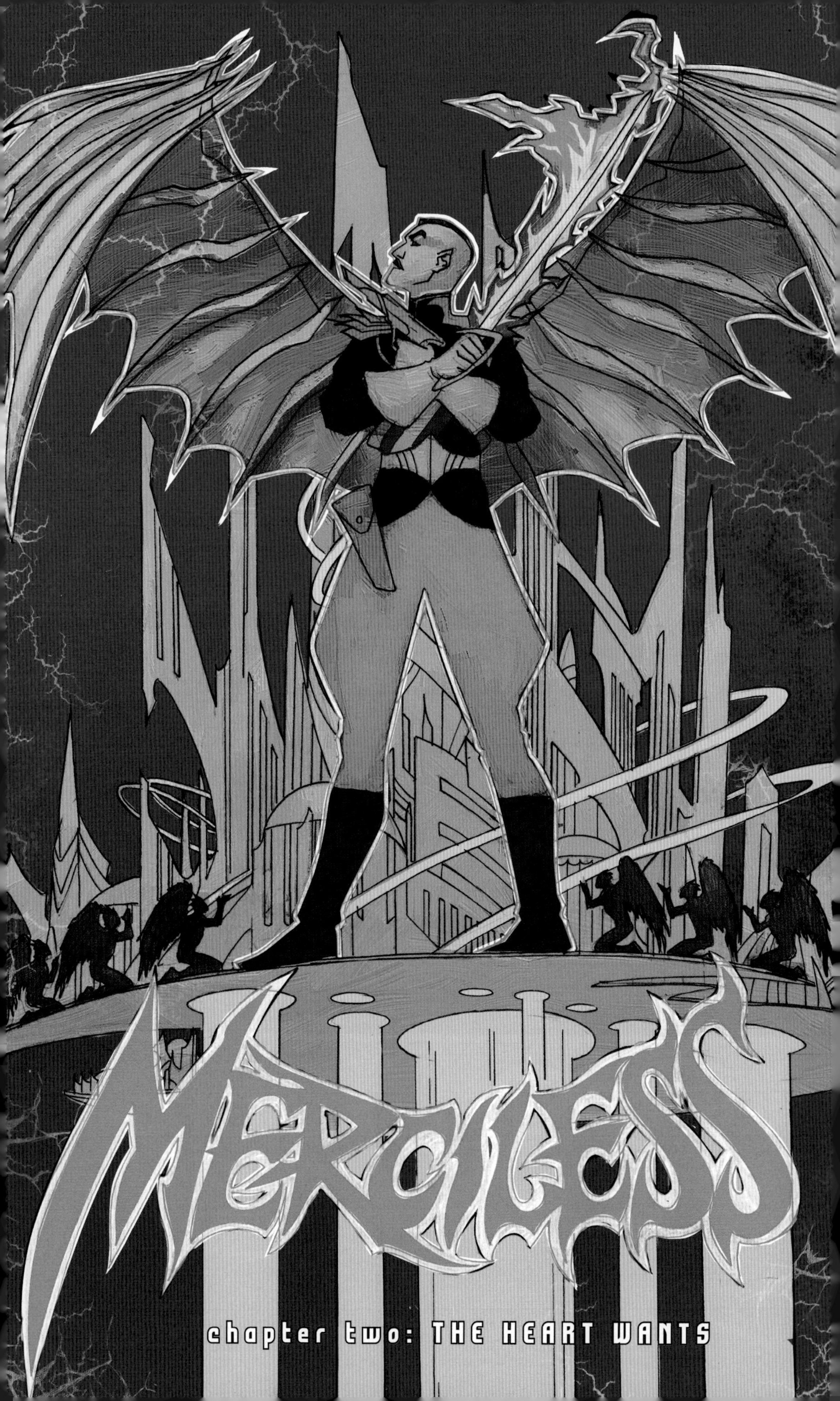
MERCILESS
chapter two: THE HEART WANTS

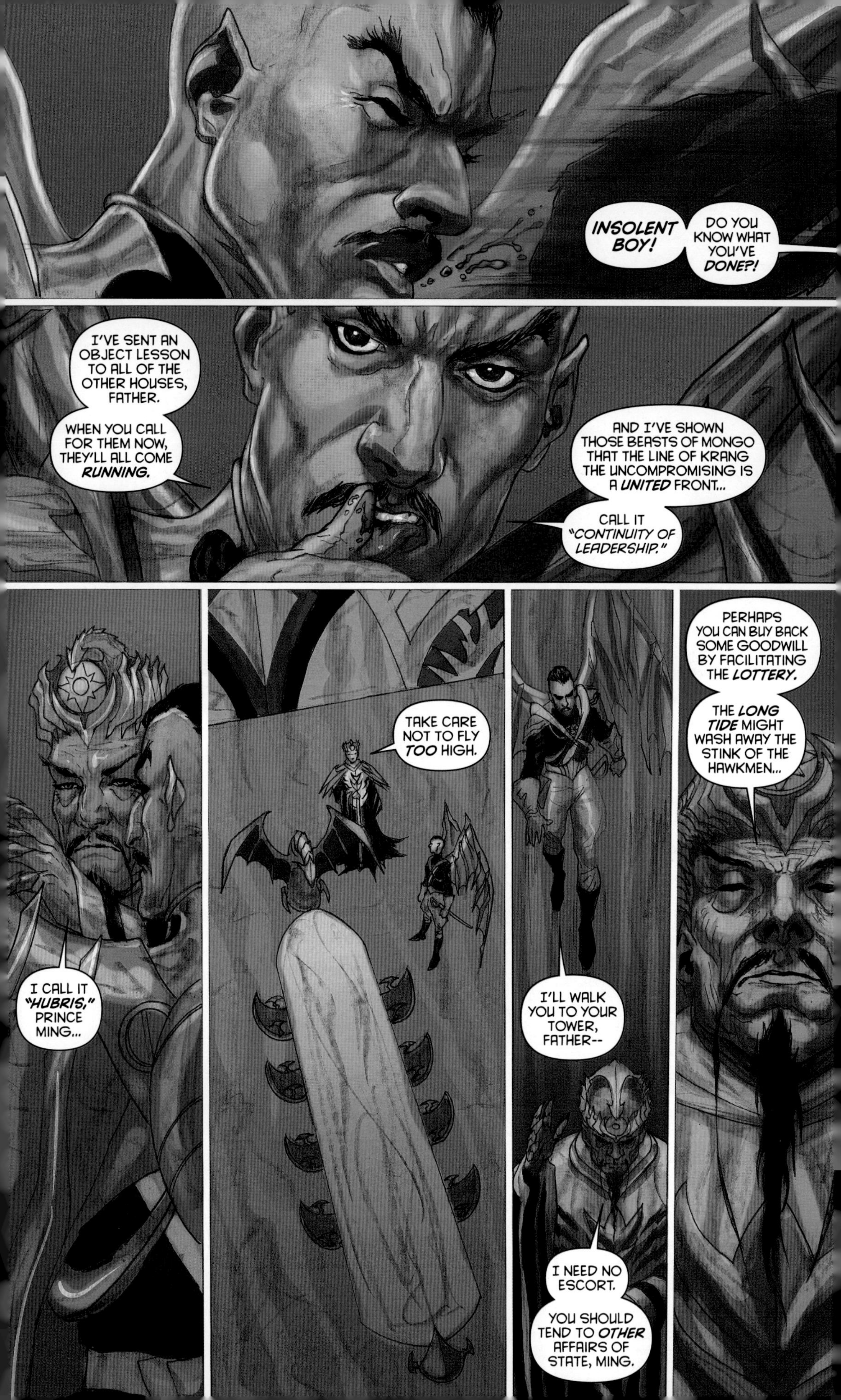
INSOLENT BOY!
DO YOU KNOW WHAT YOU'VE DONE?!
I'VE SENT AN OBJECT LESSON TO ALL OF THE OTHER HOUSES, FATHER.
WHEN YOU CALL FOR THEM NOW, THEY'LL ALL COME RUNNING.
AND I'VE SHOWN THOSE BEASTS OF MONGO THAT THE LINE OF KRANG THE UNCOMPROMISING IS A UNITED FRONT...
CALL IT "CONTINUITY OF LEADERSHIP."
I CALL IT "HUBRIS," PRINCE MING...
TAKE CARE NOT TO FLY TOO HIGH.
I'LL WALK YOU TO YOUR TOWER, FATHER--
I NEED NO ESCORT.
YOU SHOULD TEND TO OTHER AFFAIRS OF STATE, MING.
PERHAPS YOU CAN BUY BACK SOME GOODWILL BY FACILITATING THE LOTTERY.
THE LONG TIDE MIGHT WASH AWAY THE STINK OF THE HAWKMEN...

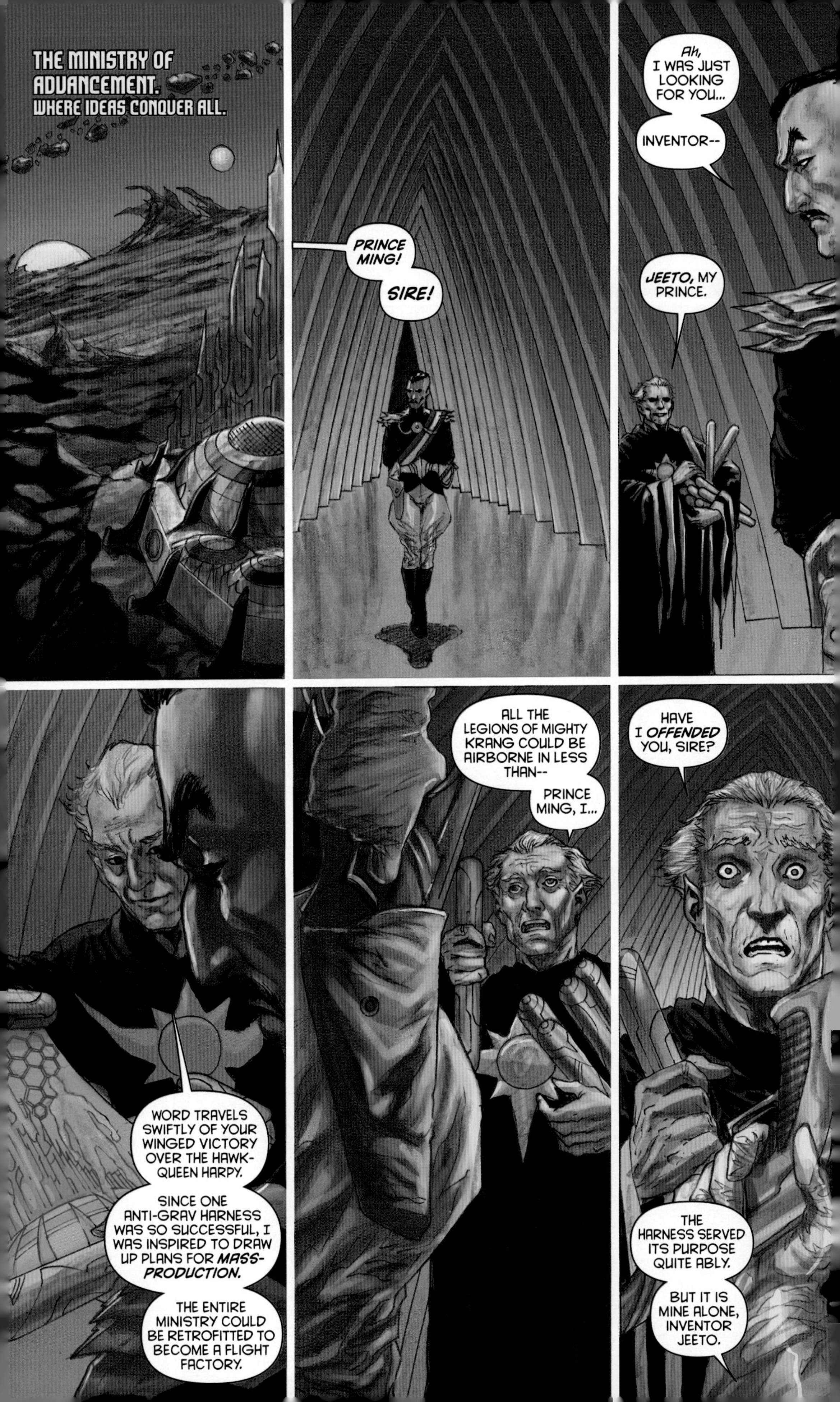

THE MINISTRY OF ADVANCEMENT.
WHERE IDEAS CONQUER ALL.
PRINCE MING!
SIRE!
AH, I WAS JUST LOOKING FOR YOU...
INVENTOR--
JEETO, MY PRINCE.
WORD TRAVELS SWIFTLY OF YOUR WINGED VICTORY OVER THE HAWK-QUEEN HARPY.
SINCE ONE ANTI-GRAV HARNESS WAS SO SUCCESSFUL, I WAS INSPIRED TO DRAW UP PLANS FOR MASS-PRODUCTION.
THE ENTIRE MINISTRY COULD BE RETROFITTED TO BECOME A FLIGHT FACTORY.
ALL THE LEGIONS OF MIGHTY KRANG COULD BE AIRBORNE IN LESS THAN--
PRINCE MING, I...
HAVE I OFFENDED YOU, SIRE?
THE HARNESS SERVED ITS PURPOSE QUITE ABLY.
BUT IT IS MINE ALONE, INVENTOR JEETO.

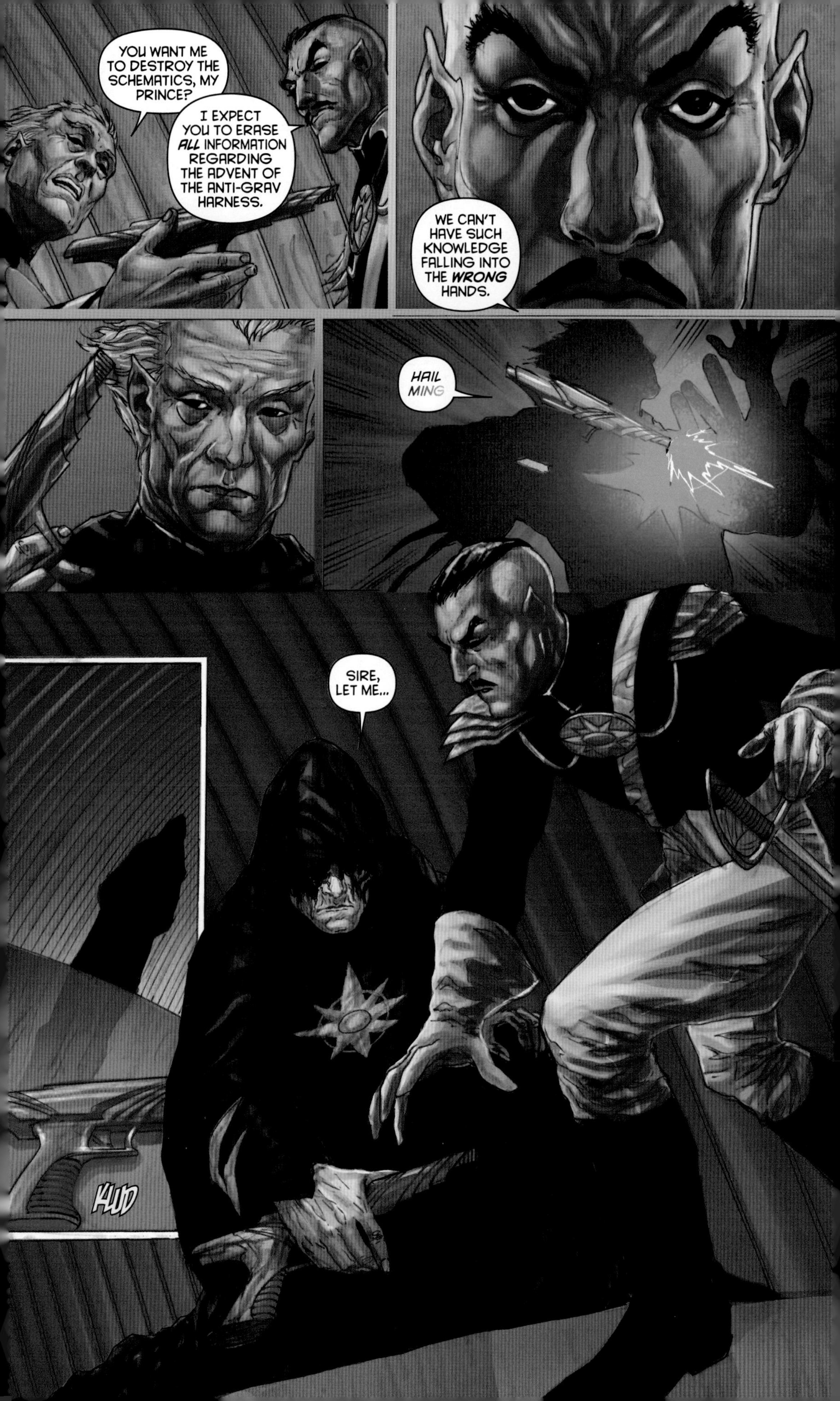
YOU WANT ME TO DESTROY THE SCHEMATICS, MY PRINCE?
I EXPECT YOU TO ERASE ALL INFORMATION REGARDING THE ADVENT OF THE ANTI-GRAV HARNESS.
WE CAN'T HAVE SUCH KNOWLEDGE FALLING INTO THE WRONG HANDS.
HAIL MING
SIRE, LET ME...
KLUD

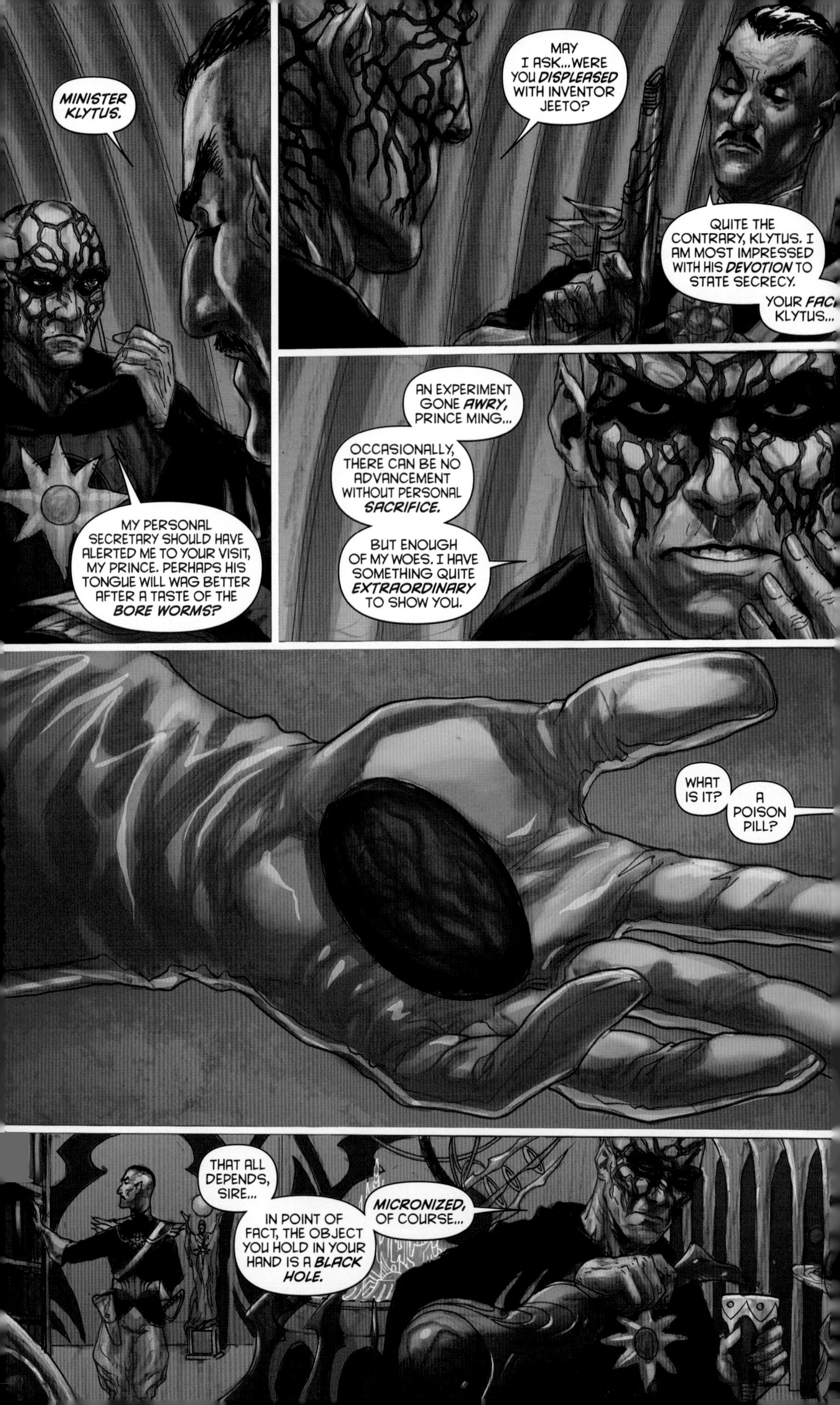

MINISTER KLYTUS.
MY PERSONAL SECRETARY SHOULD HAVE ALERTED ME TO YOUR VISIT, MY PRINCE. PERHAPS HIS TONGUE WILL WAG BETTER AFTER A TASTE OF THE BORE WORMS?
MAY I ASK...WERE YOU DISPLEASED WITH INVENTOR JEETO?
QUITE THE CONTRARY, KLYTUS. I AM MOST IMPRESSED WITH HIS DEVOTION TO STATE SECRECY.
YOUR FAC KLYTUS...
AN EXPERIMENT GONE AWRY, PRINCE MING...
OCCASIONALLY, THERE CAN BE NO ADVANCEMENT WITHOUT PERSONAL SACRIFICE.
BUT ENOUGH OF MY WOES. I HAVE SOMETHING QUITE EXTRAORDINARY TO SHOW YOU.
WHAT IS IT?
A POISON PILL?
THAT ALL DEPENDS, SIRE...
IN POINT OF FACT, THE OBJECT YOU HOLD IN YOUR HAND IS A BLACK HOLE.
MICRONIZED, OF COURSE...

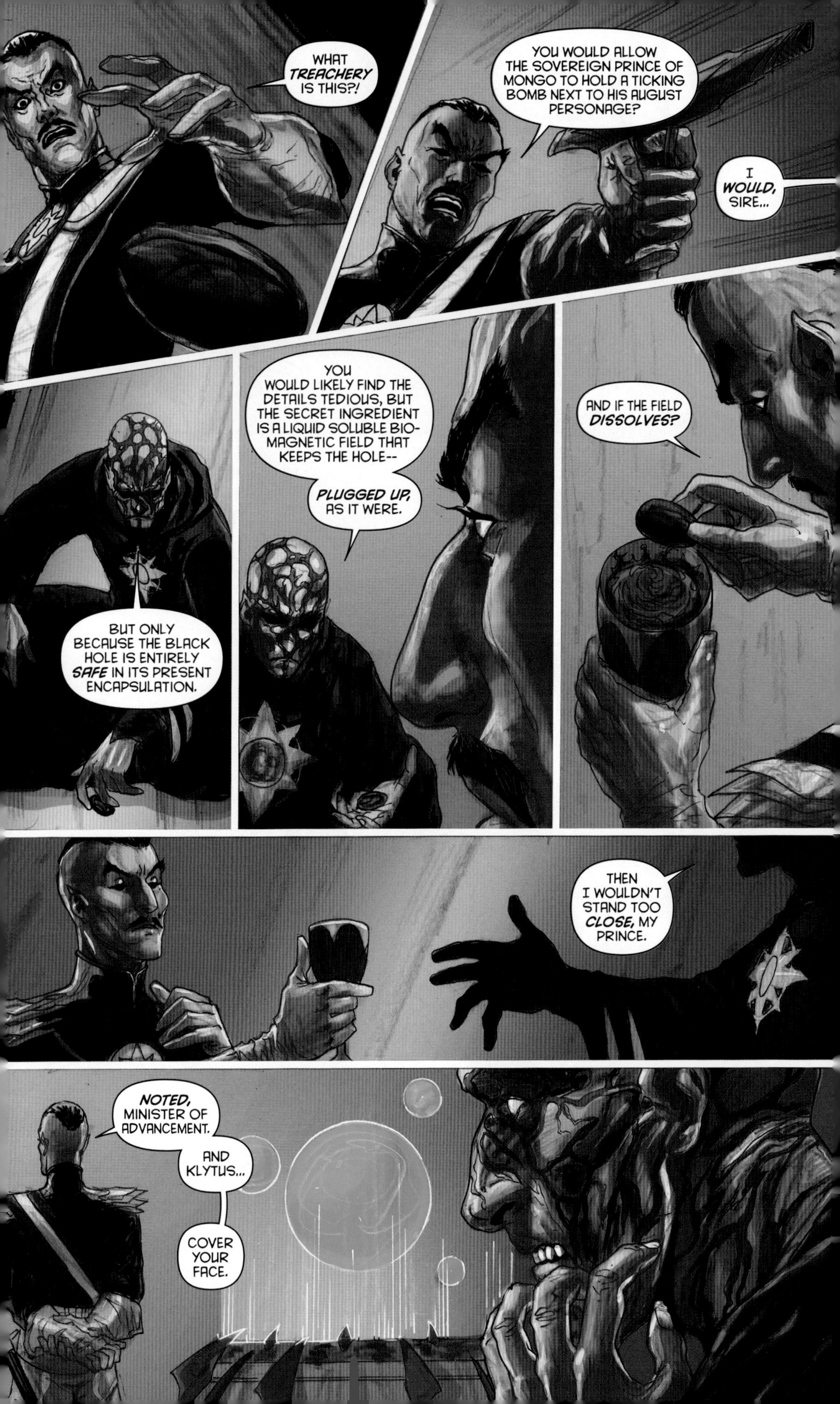
WHAT TREACHERY IS THIS?!
YOU WOULD ALLOW THE SOVEREIGN PRINCE OF MONGO TO HOLD A TICKING BOMB NEXT TO HIS AUGUST PERSONAGE?
I WOULD, SIRE...
BUT ONLY BECAUSE THE BLACK HOLE IS ENTIRELY SAFE IN ITS PRESENT ENCAPSULATION.
YOU WOULD LIKELY FIND THE DETAILS TEDIOUS, BUT THE SECRET INGREDIENT IS A LIQUID SOLUBLE BIO-MAGNETIC FIELD THAT KEEPS THE HOLE--
PLUGGED UP, AS IT WERE.
AND IF THE FIELD DISSOLVES?
THEN I WOULDN'T STAND TOO CLOSE, MY PRINCE.
NOTED, MINISTER OF ADVANCEMENT.
AND KLYTUS...
COVER YOUR FACE.

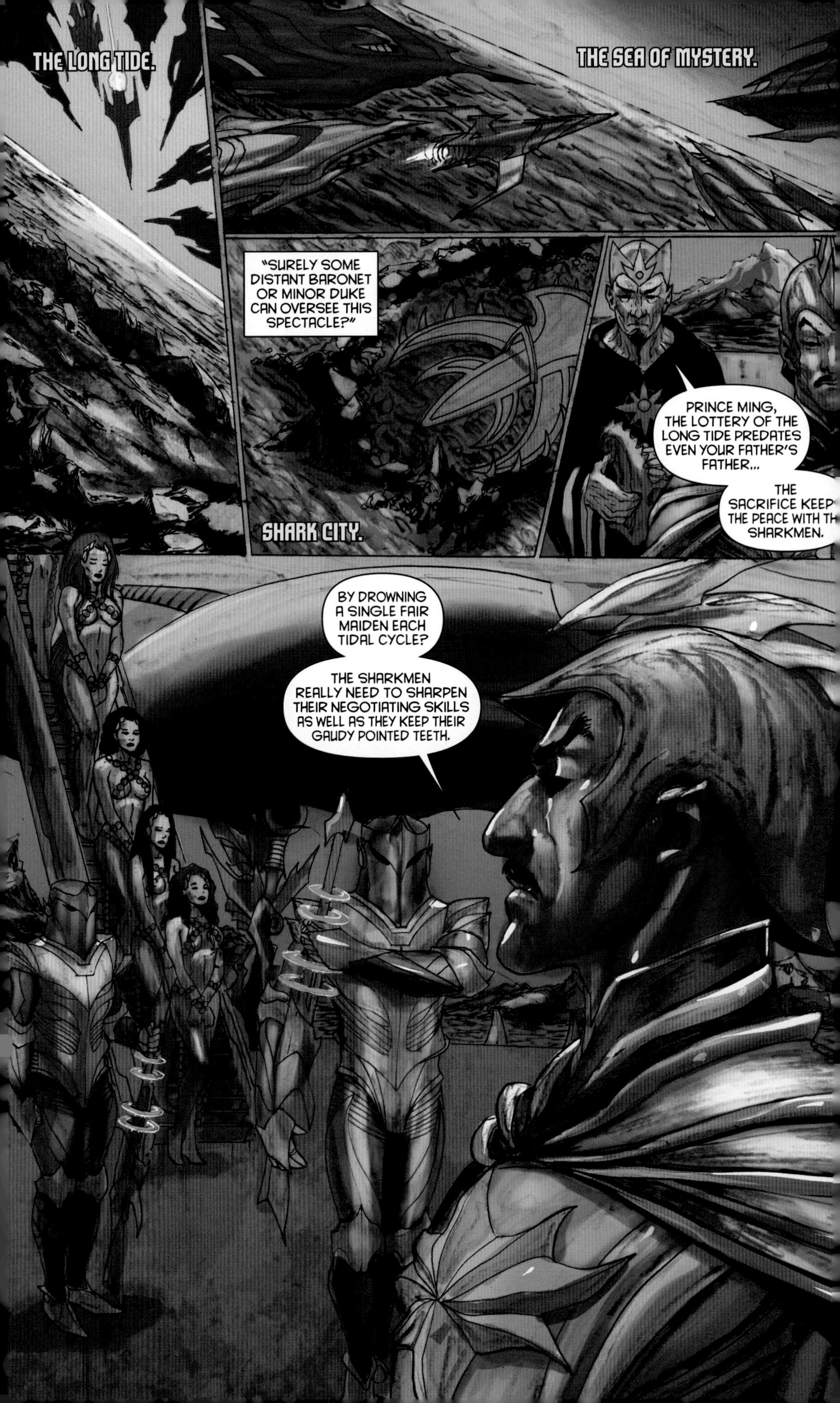

THE LONG TIDE.
THE SEA OF MYSTERY.
"SURELY SOME DISTANT BARONET OR MINOR DUKE CAN OVERSEE THIS SPECTACLE?"
SHARK CITY.
PRINCE MING, THE LOTTERY OF THE LONG TIDE PREDATES EVEN YOUR FATHER'S FATHER...
THE SACRIFICE KEEP THE PEACE WITH TH SHARKMEN.
BY DROWNING A SINGLE FAIR MAIDEN EACH TIDAL CYCLE?
THE SHARKMEN REALLY NEED TO SHARPEN THEIR NEGOTIATING SKILLS AS WELL AS THEY KEEP THEIR GAUDY POINTED TEETH.

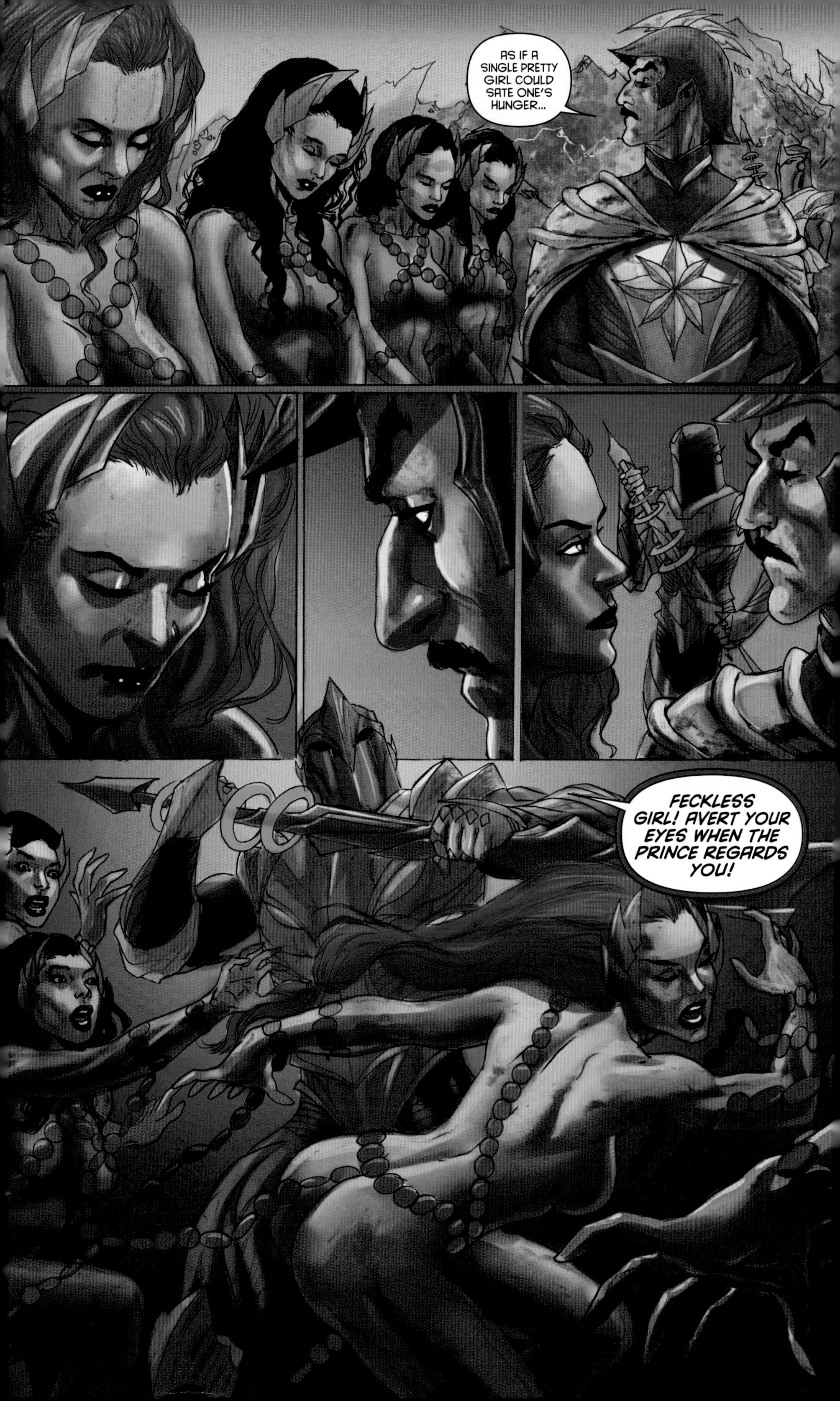
AS IF A SINGLE PRETTY GIRL COULD SATE ONE'S HUNGER...
FECKLESS GIRL! AVERT YOUR EYES WHEN THE PRINCE REGARDS YOU!

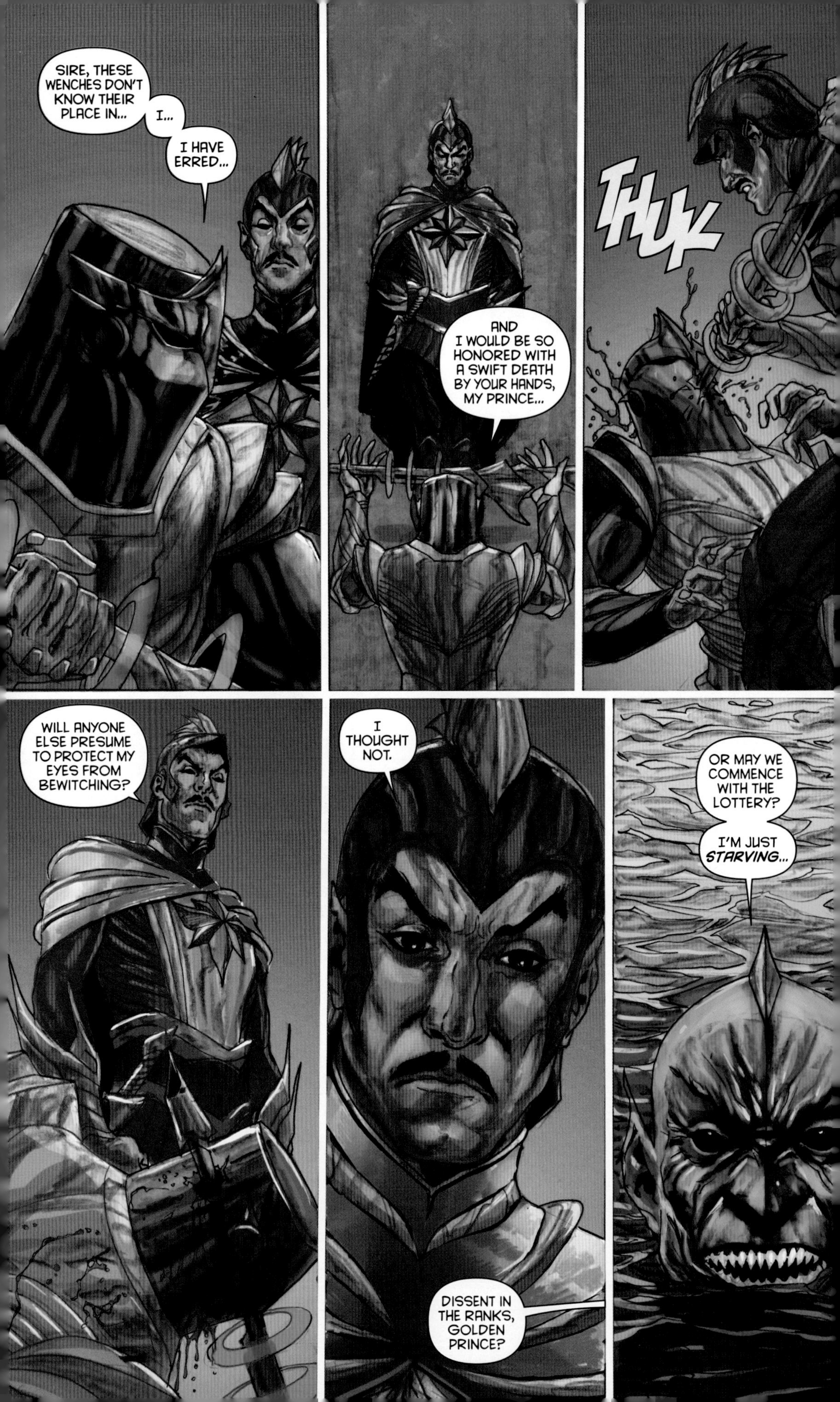
SIRE, THESE WENCHES DON'T KNOW THEIR PLACE IN...
I...
I HAVE ERRED...
AND I WOULD BE SO HONORED WITH A SWIFT DEATH BY YOUR HANDS, MY PRINCE...
THUK
WILL ANYONE ELSE PRESUME TO PROTECT MY EYES FROM BEWITCHING?
I THOUGHT NOT.
DISSENT IN THE RANKS, GOLDEN PRINCE?
OR MAY WE COMMENCE WITH THE LOTTERY?
I'M JUST *STARVING*...

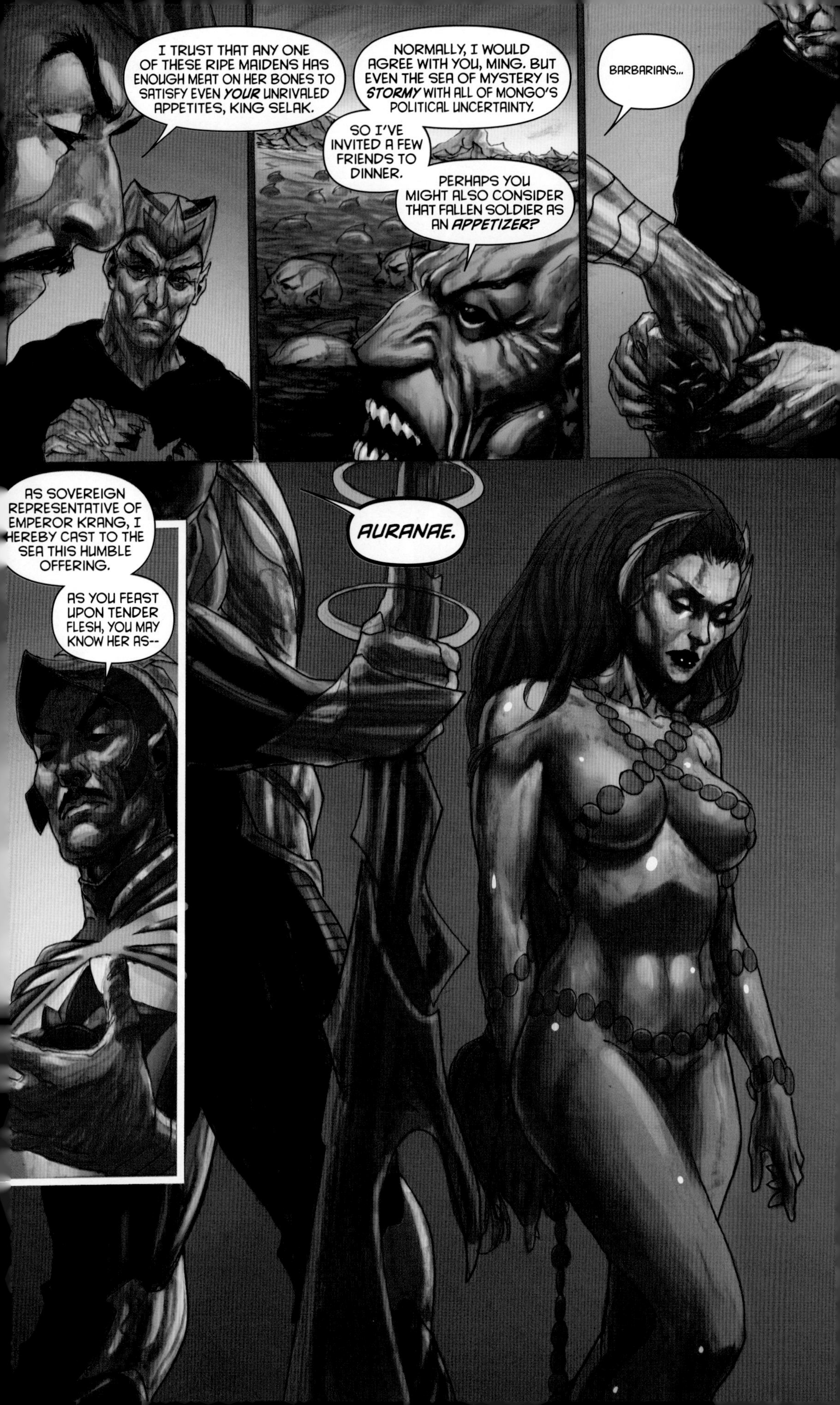
I TRUST THAT ANY ONE OF THESE RIPE MAIDENS HAS ENOUGH MEAT ON HER BONES TO SATISFY EVEN *YOUR* UNRIVALED APPETITES, KING SELAK.
NORMALLY, I WOULD AGREE WITH YOU, MING. BUT EVEN THE SEA OF MYSTERY IS *STORMY* WITH ALL OF MONGO'S POLITICAL UNCERTAINTY.
SO I'VE INVITED A FEW FRIENDS TO DINNER.
PERHAPS YOU MIGHT ALSO CONSIDER THAT FALLEN SOLDIER AS AN *APPETIZER?*
BARBARIANS...
AS SOVEREIGN REPRESENTATIVE OF EMPEROR KRANG, I HEREBY CAST TO THE SEA THIS HUMBLE OFFERING.
AS YOU FEAST UPON TENDER FLESH, YOU MAY KNOW HER AS--
AURANAE.

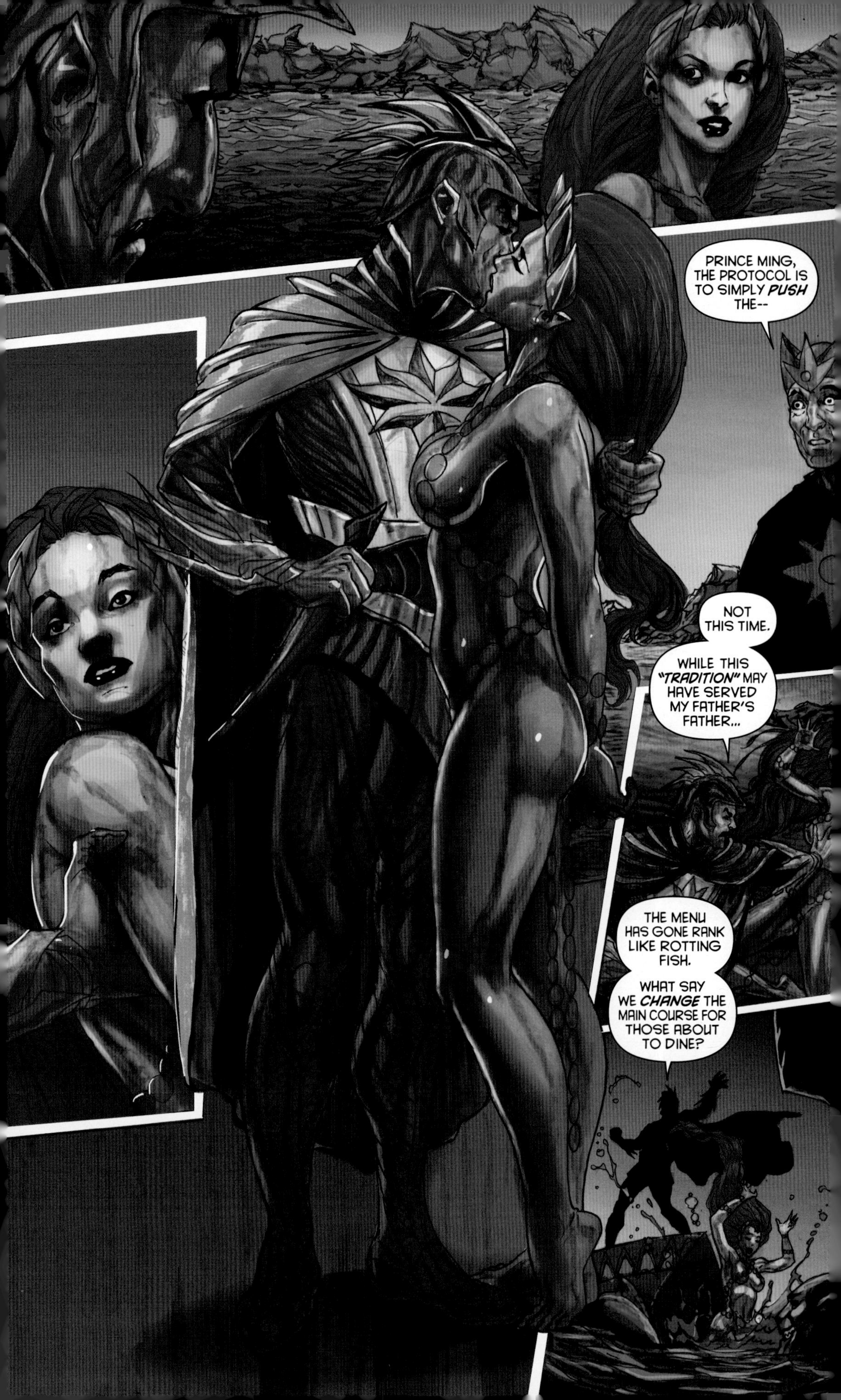
PRINCE MING, THE PROTOCOL IS TO SIMPLY *PUSH* THE--
NOT THIS TIME.
WHILE THIS *"TRADITION"* MAY HAVE SERVED MY FATHER'S FATHER...
THE MENU HAS GONE RANK LIKE ROTTING FISH.
WHAT SAY WE *CHANGE* THE MAIN COURSE FOR THOSE ABOUT TO DINE?

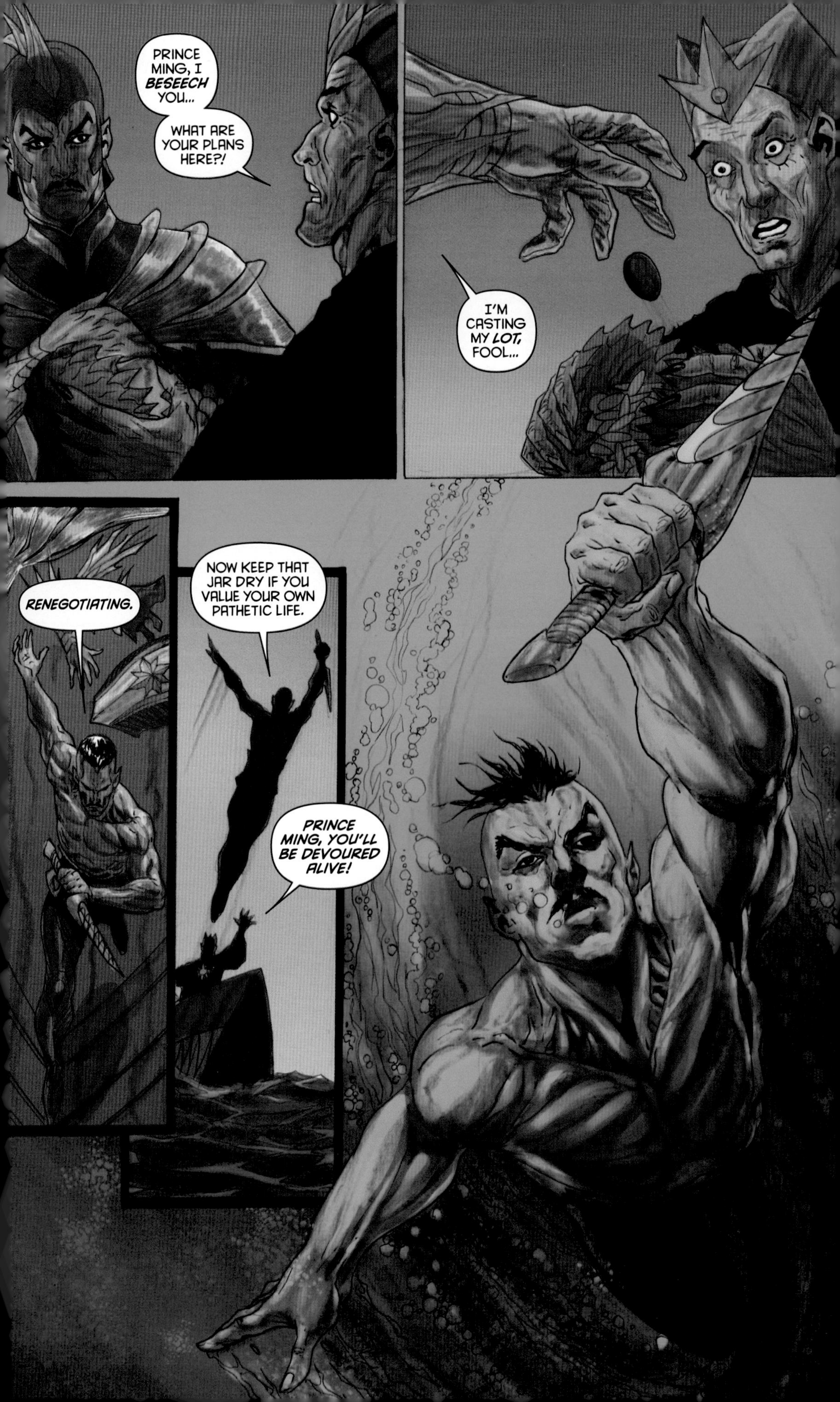
PRINCE MING, I *BESEECH* YOU...
WHAT ARE YOUR PLANS HERE?!
I'M CASTING MY *LOT,* FOOL...
RENEGOTIATING.
NOW KEEP THAT JAR DRY IF YOU VALUE YOUR OWN PATHETIC LIFE.
PRINCE MING, YOU'LL BE DEVOURED ALIVE!

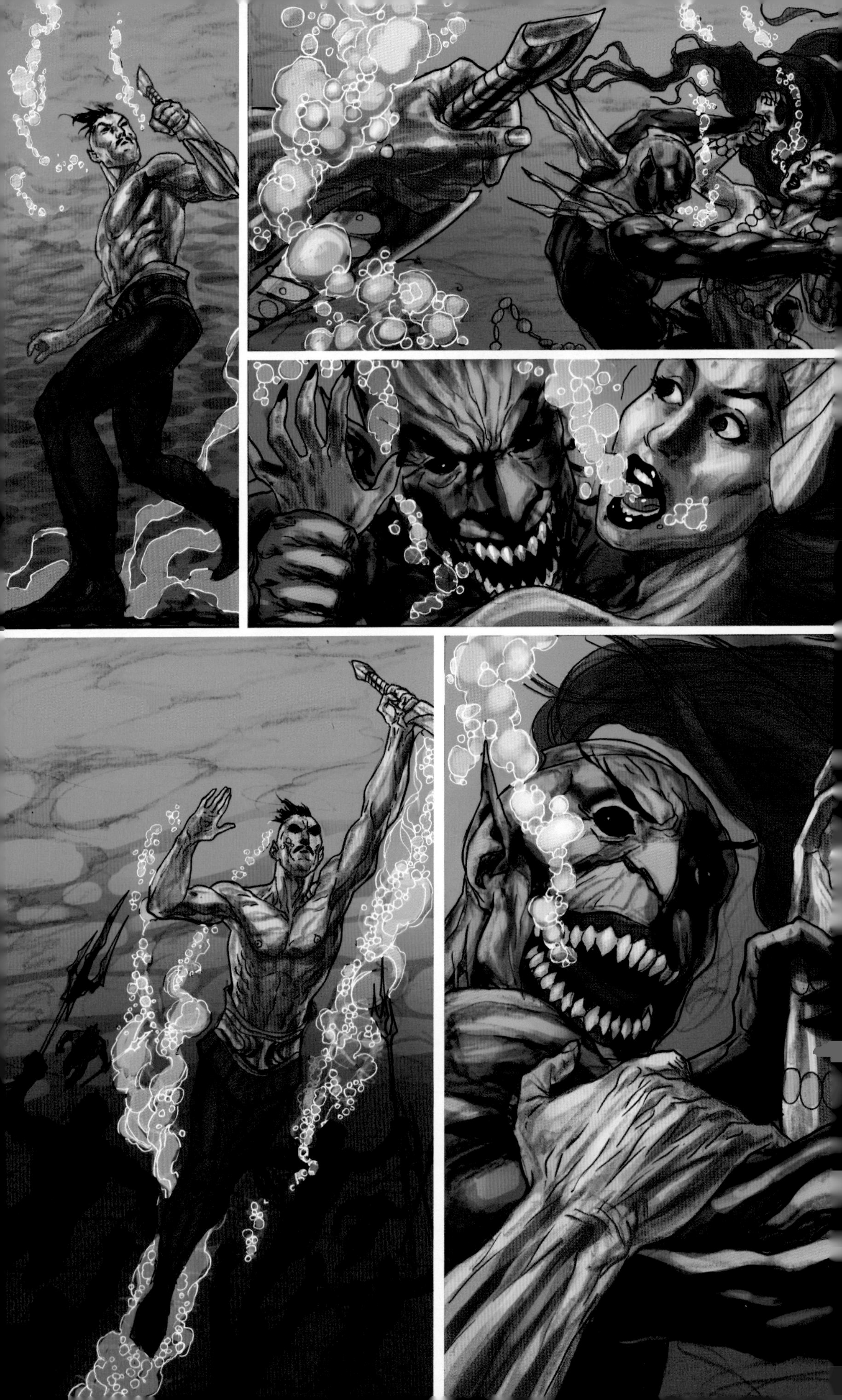

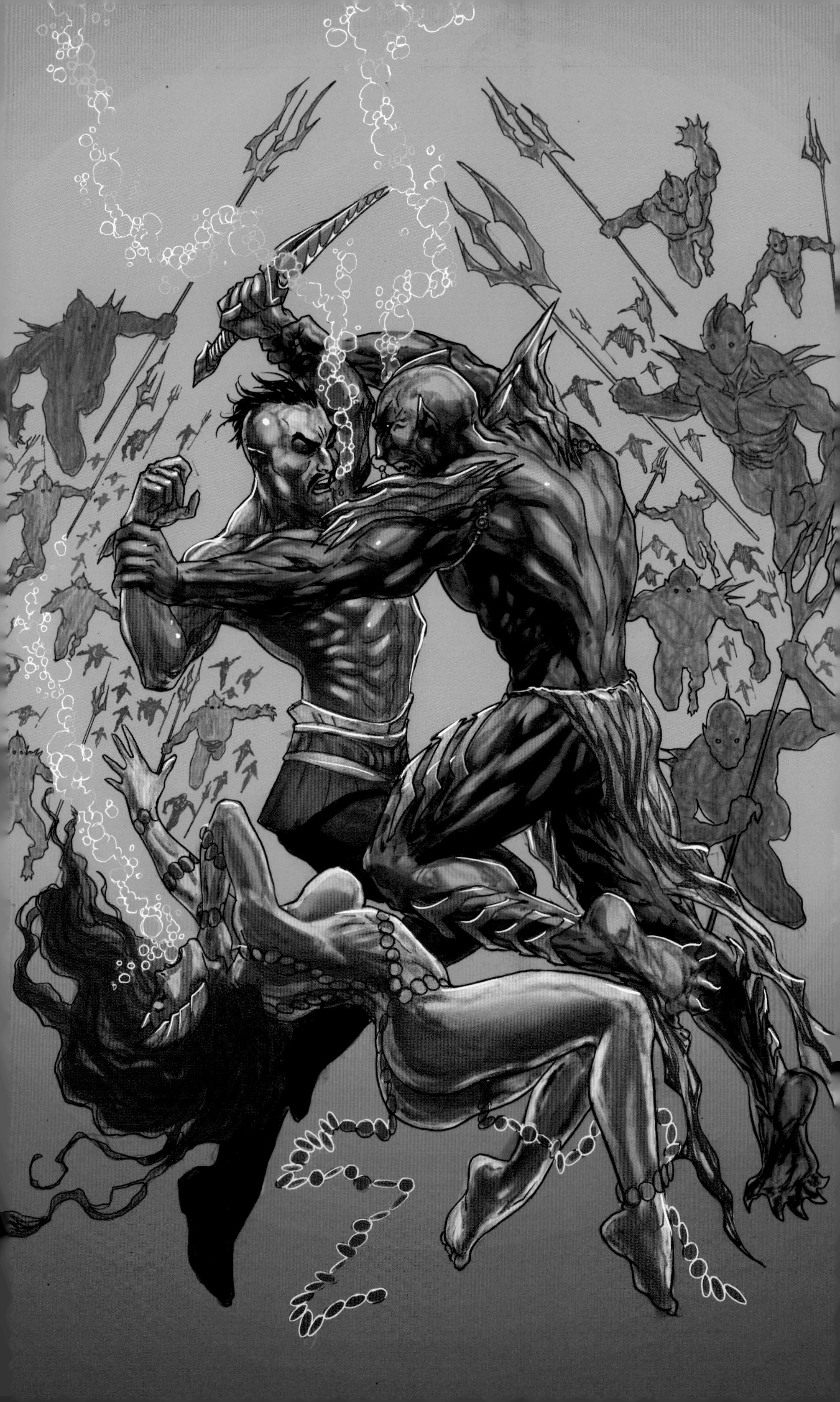

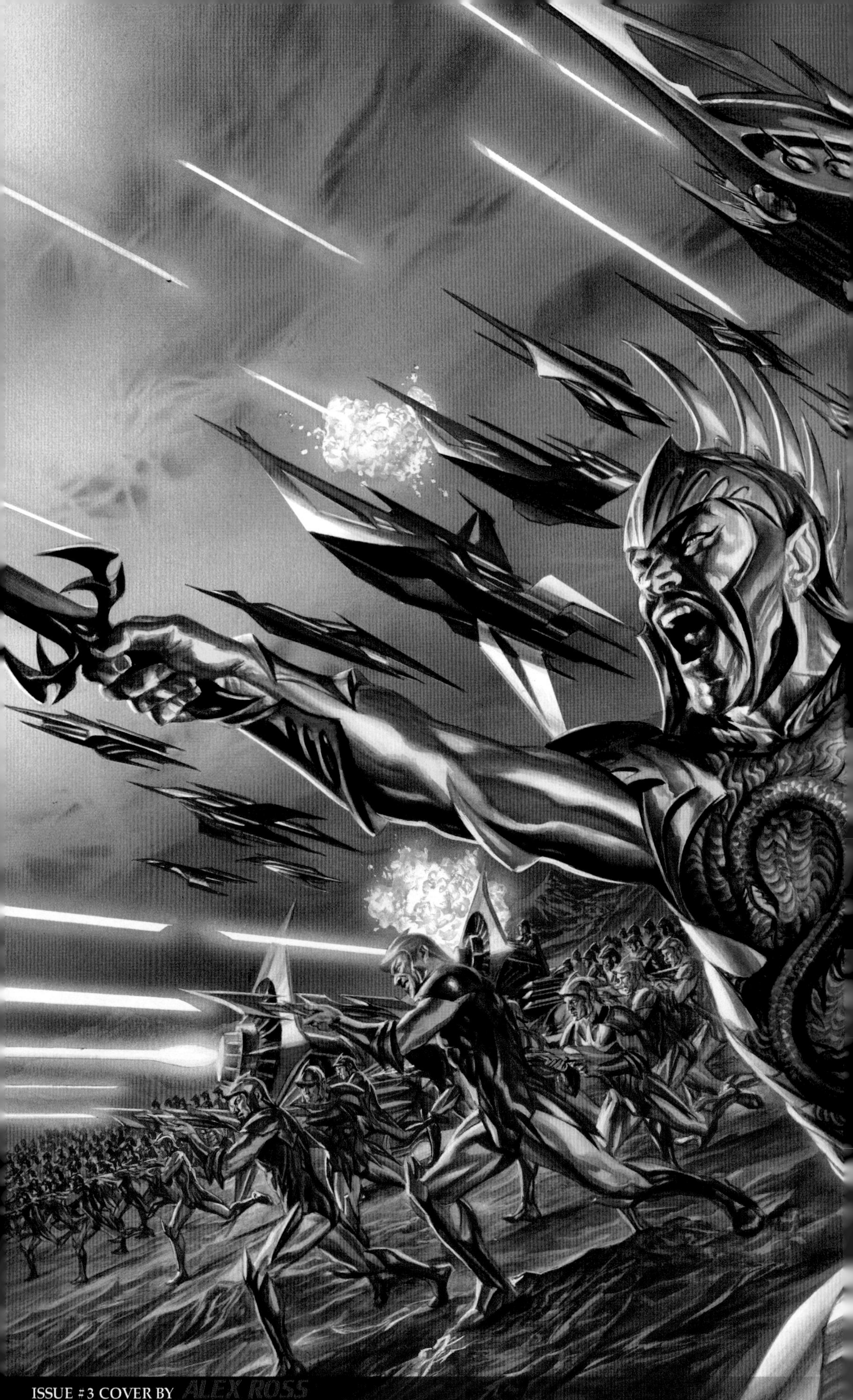

ISSUE #3 COVER BY ALEX ROSS

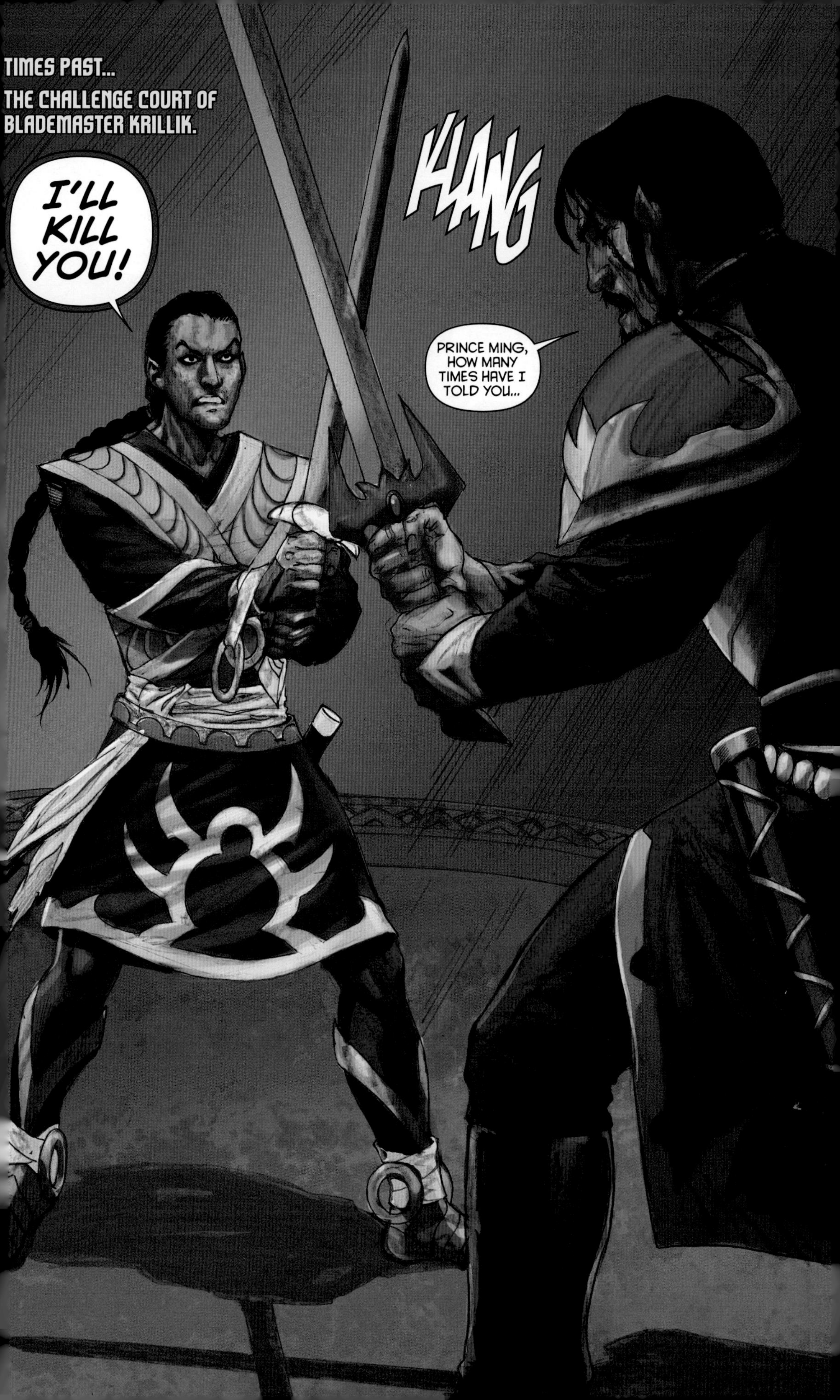
TIMES PAST...
THE CHALLENGE COURT OF BLADEMASTER KRILLIK.
I'LL KILL YOU!
KLANG
PRINCE MING, HOW MANY TIMES HAVE I TOLD YOU...

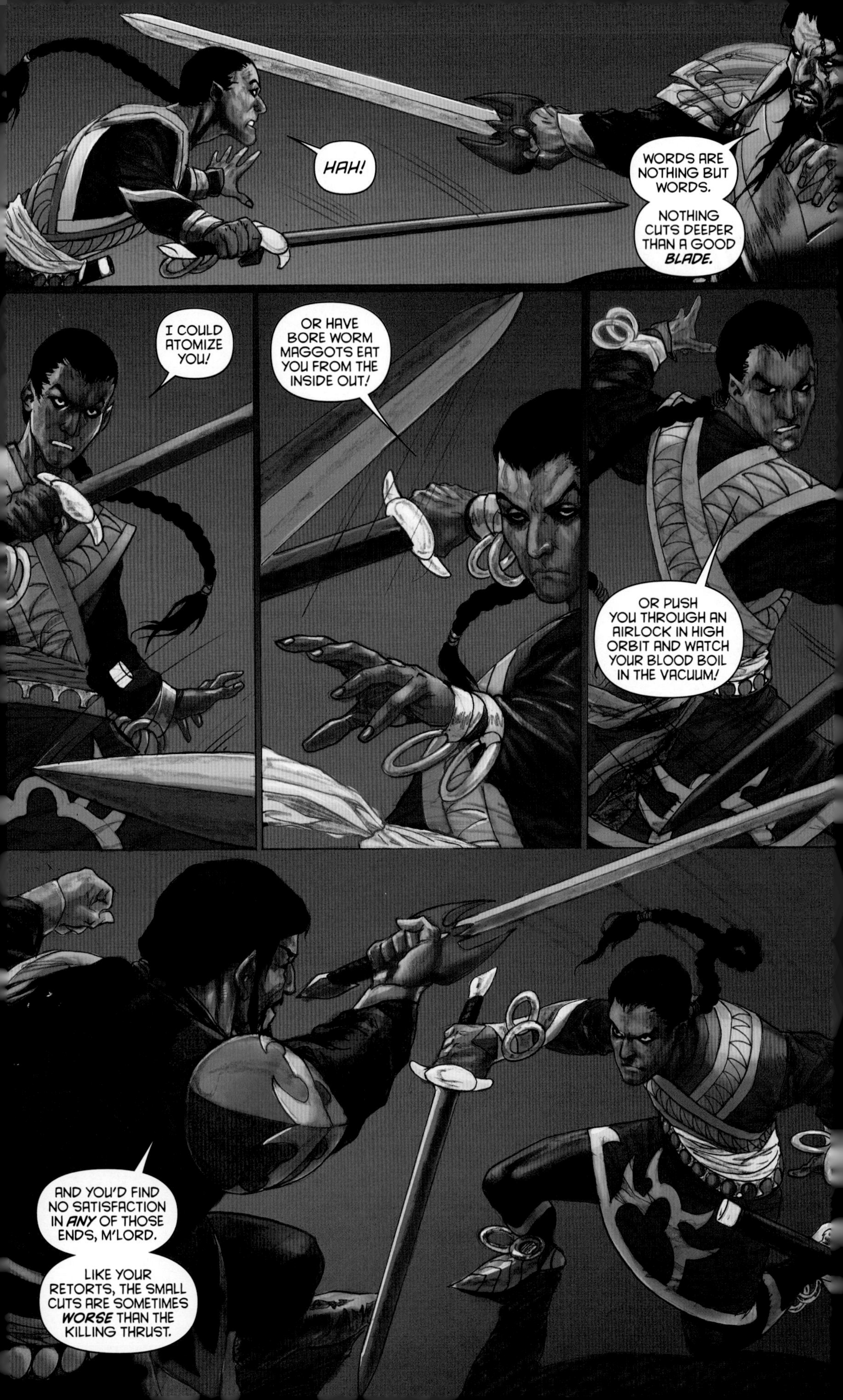
HAH!
WORDS ARE NOTHING BUT WORDS.
NOTHING CUTS DEEPER THAN A GOOD BLADE.
I COULD ATOMIZE YOU!
OR HAVE BORE WORM MAGGOTS EAT YOU FROM THE INSIDE OUT!
OR PUSH YOU THROUGH AN AIRLOCK IN HIGH ORBIT AND WATCH YOUR BLOOD BOIL IN THE VACUUM!
AND YOU'D FIND NO SATISFACTION IN ANY OF THOSE ENDS, M'LORD.
LIKE YOUR RETORTS, THE SMALL CUTS ARE SOMETIMES WORSE THAN THE KILLING THRUST.

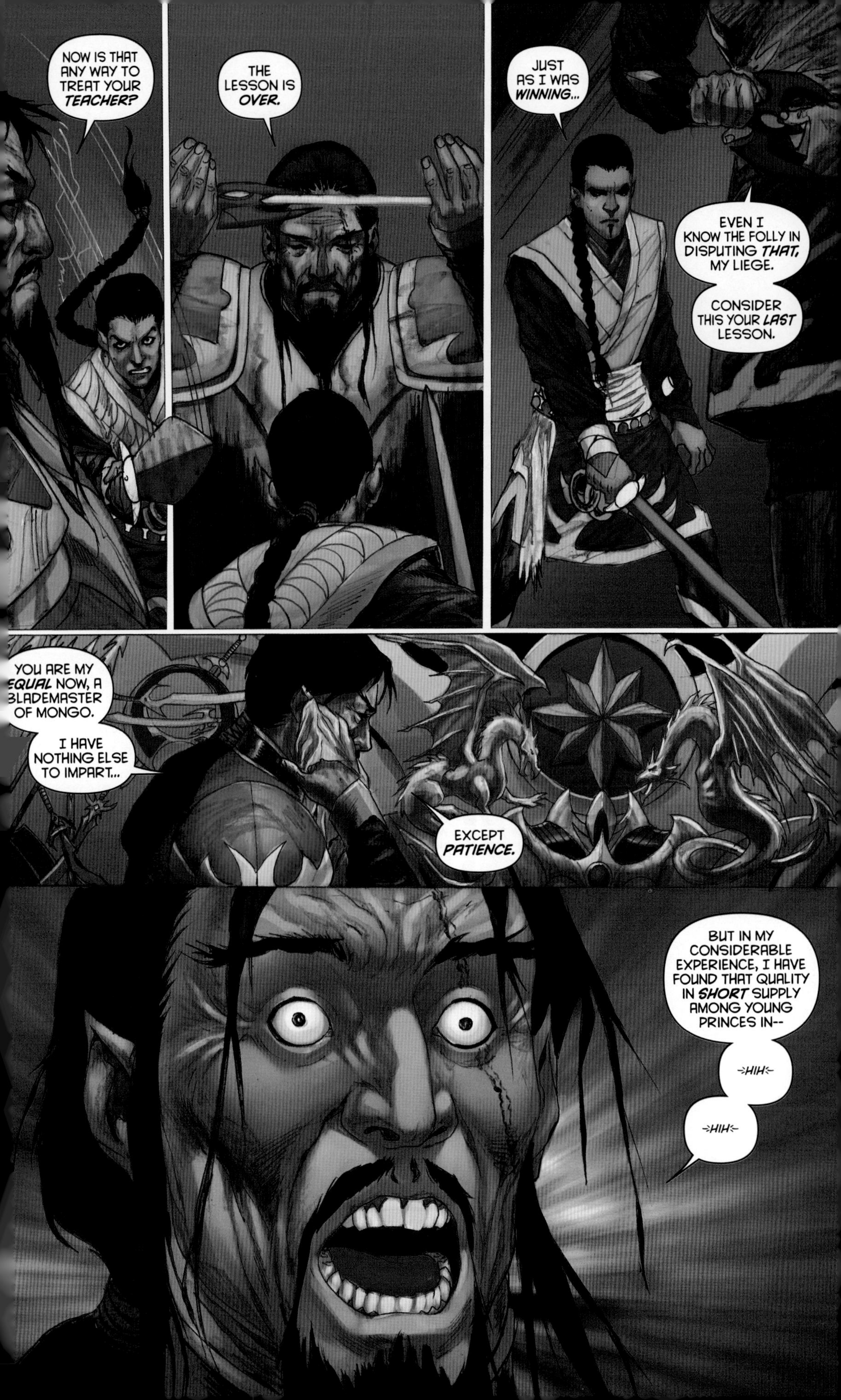

NOW IS THAT ANY WAY TO TREAT YOUR *TEACHER?*
THE LESSON IS *OVER.*
JUST AS I WAS *WINNING*...
EVEN I KNOW THE FOLLY IN DISPUTING *THAT,* MY LIEGE.
CONSIDER THIS YOUR *LAST* LESSON.
YOU ARE MY *EQUAL* NOW, A BLADEMASTER OF MONGO.
I HAVE NOTHING ELSE TO IMPART...
EXCEPT *PATIENCE.*
BUT IN MY CONSIDERABLE EXPERIENCE, I HAVE FOUND THAT QUALITY IN *SHORT* SUPPLY AMONG YOUNG PRINCES IN--
HIH
HIH

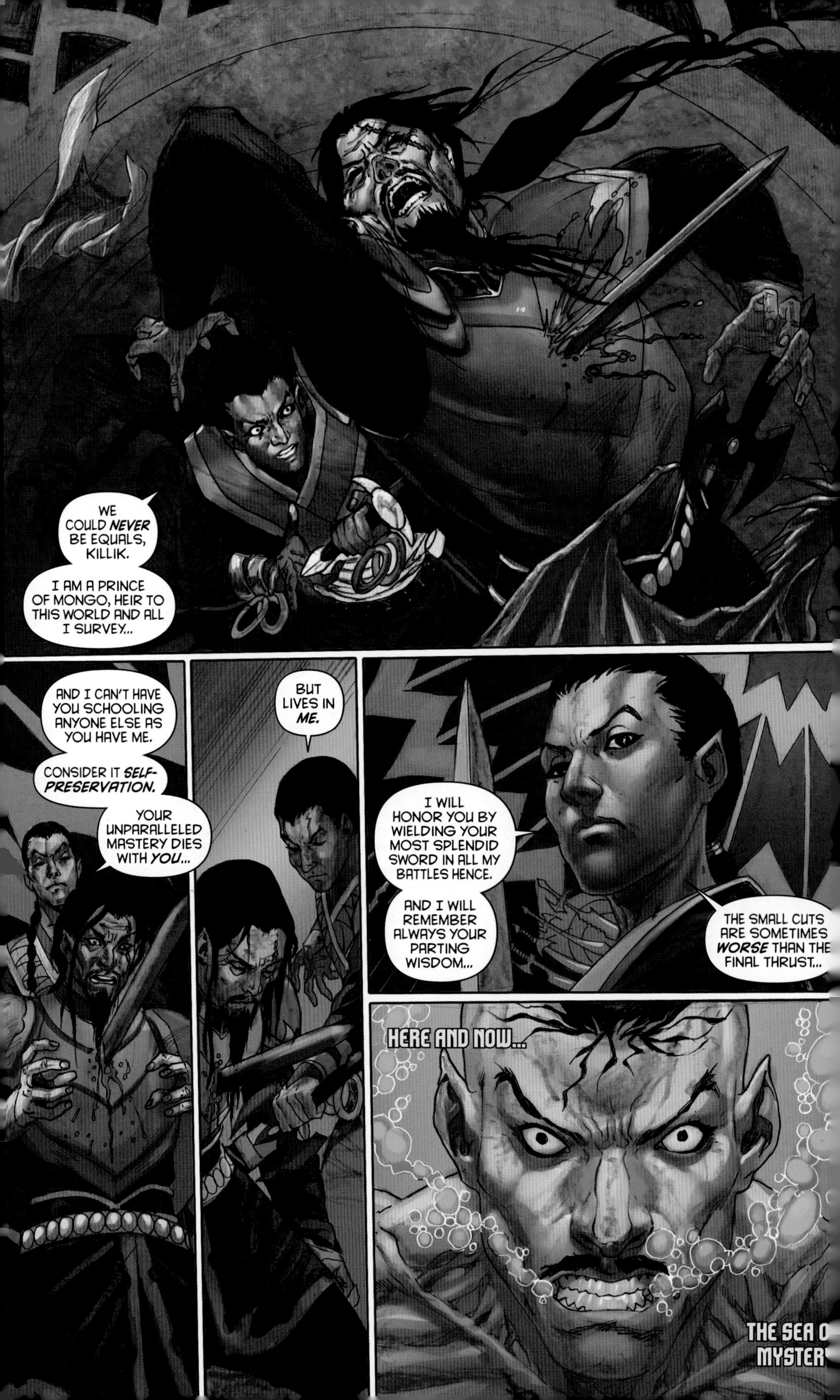
WE COULD *NEVER* BE EQUALS, KILLIK.
I AM A PRINCE OF MONGO, HEIR TO THIS WORLD AND ALL I SURVEY...
AND I CAN'T HAVE YOU SCHOOLING ANYONE ELSE AS YOU HAVE ME.
CONSIDER IT *SELF-PRESERVATION.*
YOUR UNPARALLELED MASTERY DIES WITH *YOU*...
BUT LIVES IN *ME.*
I WILL HONOR YOU BY WIELDING YOUR MOST SPLENDID SWORD IN ALL MY BATTLES HENCE.
AND I WILL REMEMBER ALWAYS YOUR PARTING WISDOM...
THE SMALL CUTS ARE SOMETIMES *WORSE* THAN THE FINAL THRUST...
HERE AND NOW...
THE SEA O
MYSTER

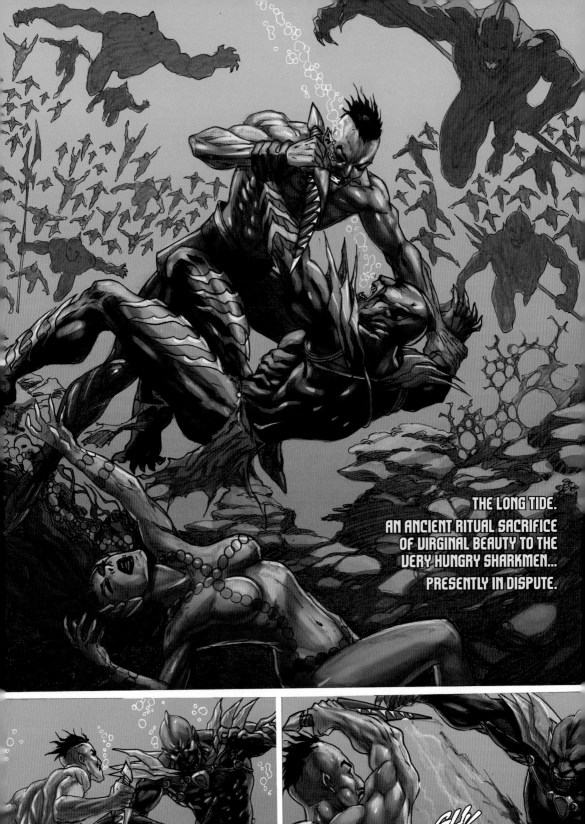

THE LONG TIDE.
AN ANCIENT RITUAL SACRIFICE OF VIRGINAL BEAUTY TO THE VERY HUNGRY SHARKMEN... PRESENTLY IN DISPUTE.

SHK

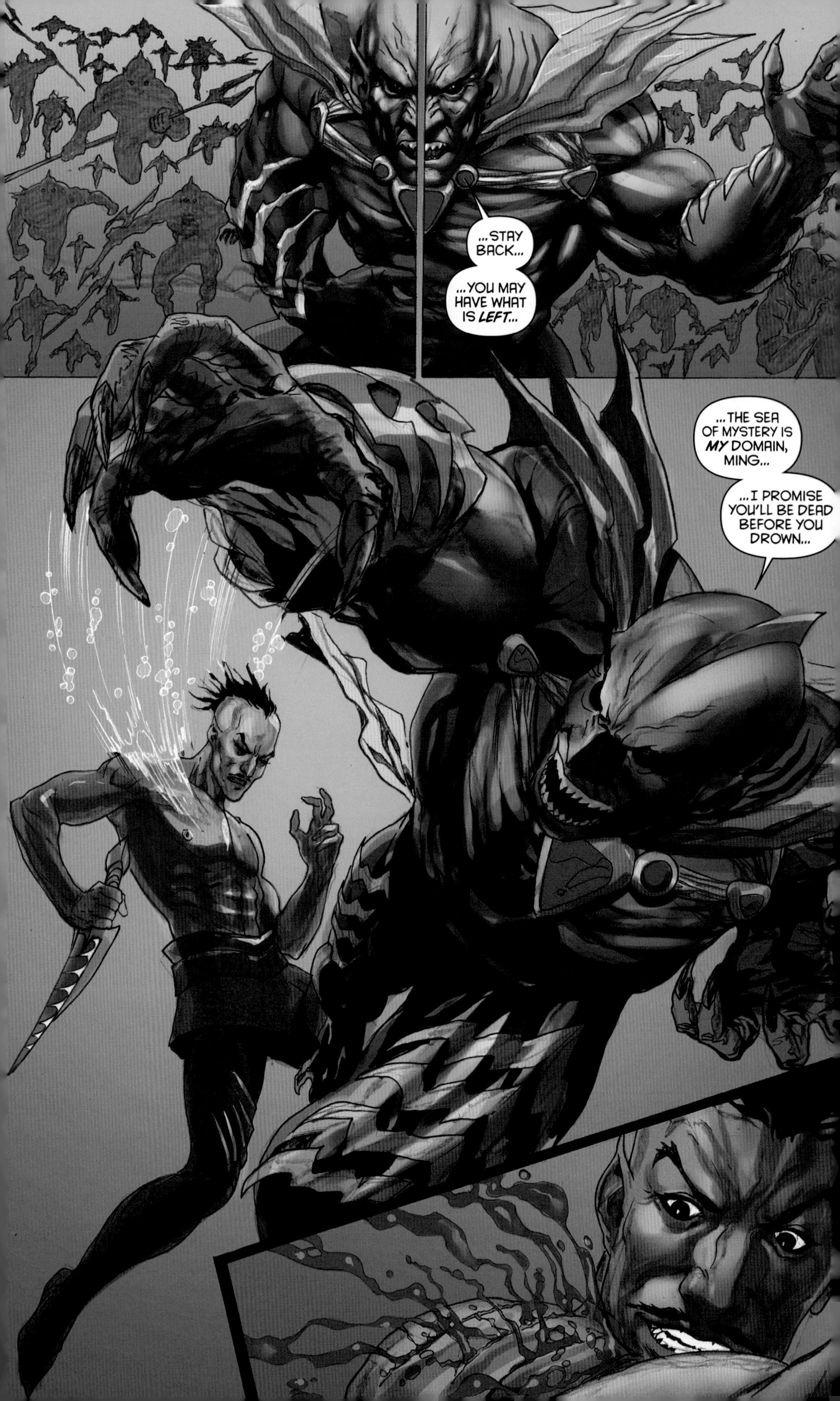
...STAY BACK...
...YOU MAY HAVE WHAT IS *LEFT*...
...THE SEA OF MYSTERY IS *MY* DOMAIN, MING...
...I PROMISE YOU'LL BE DEAD BEFORE YOU DROWN...

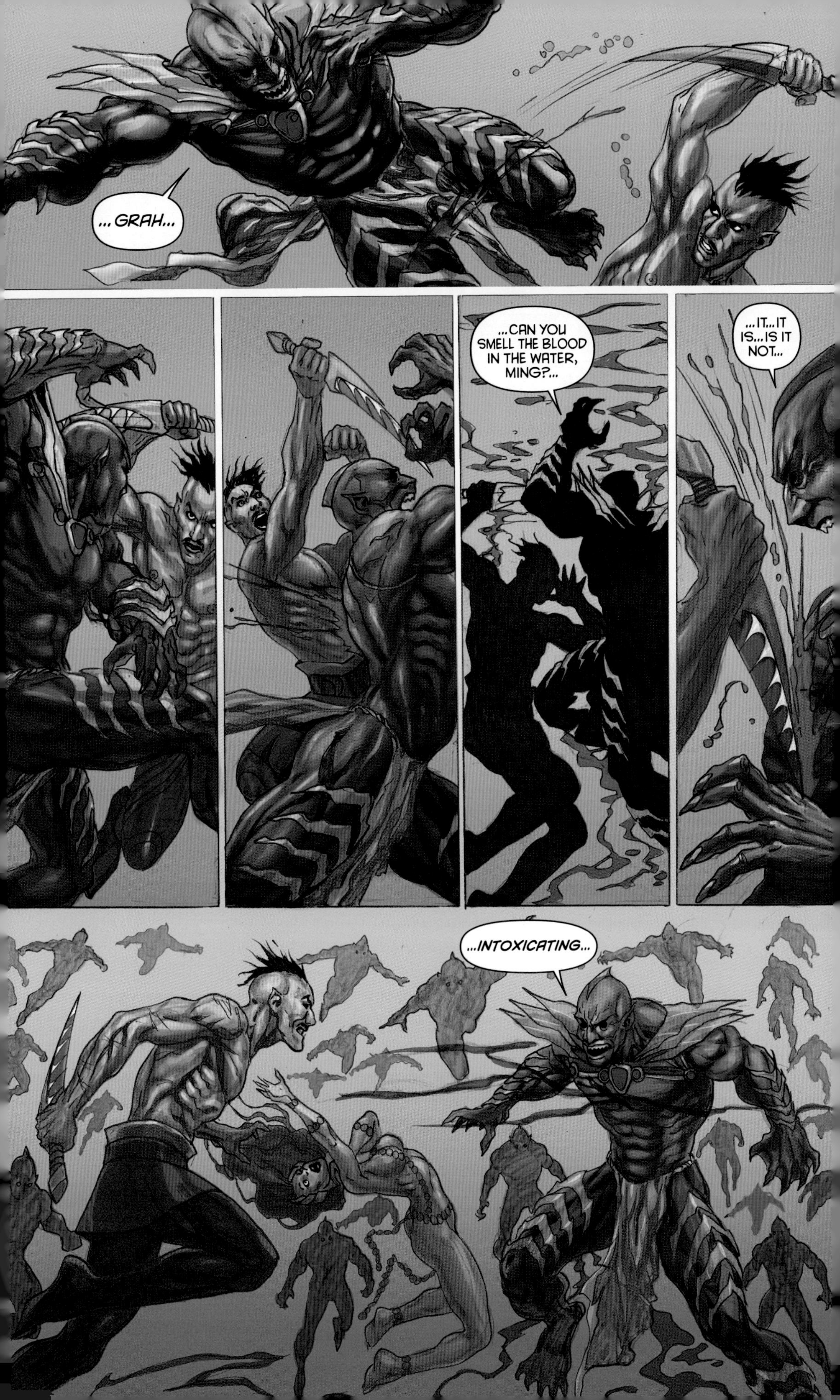

...GRAH...
...CAN YOU SMELL THE BLOOD IN THE WATER, MING?...
...IT...IT IS...IS IT NOT...
...INTOXICATING...

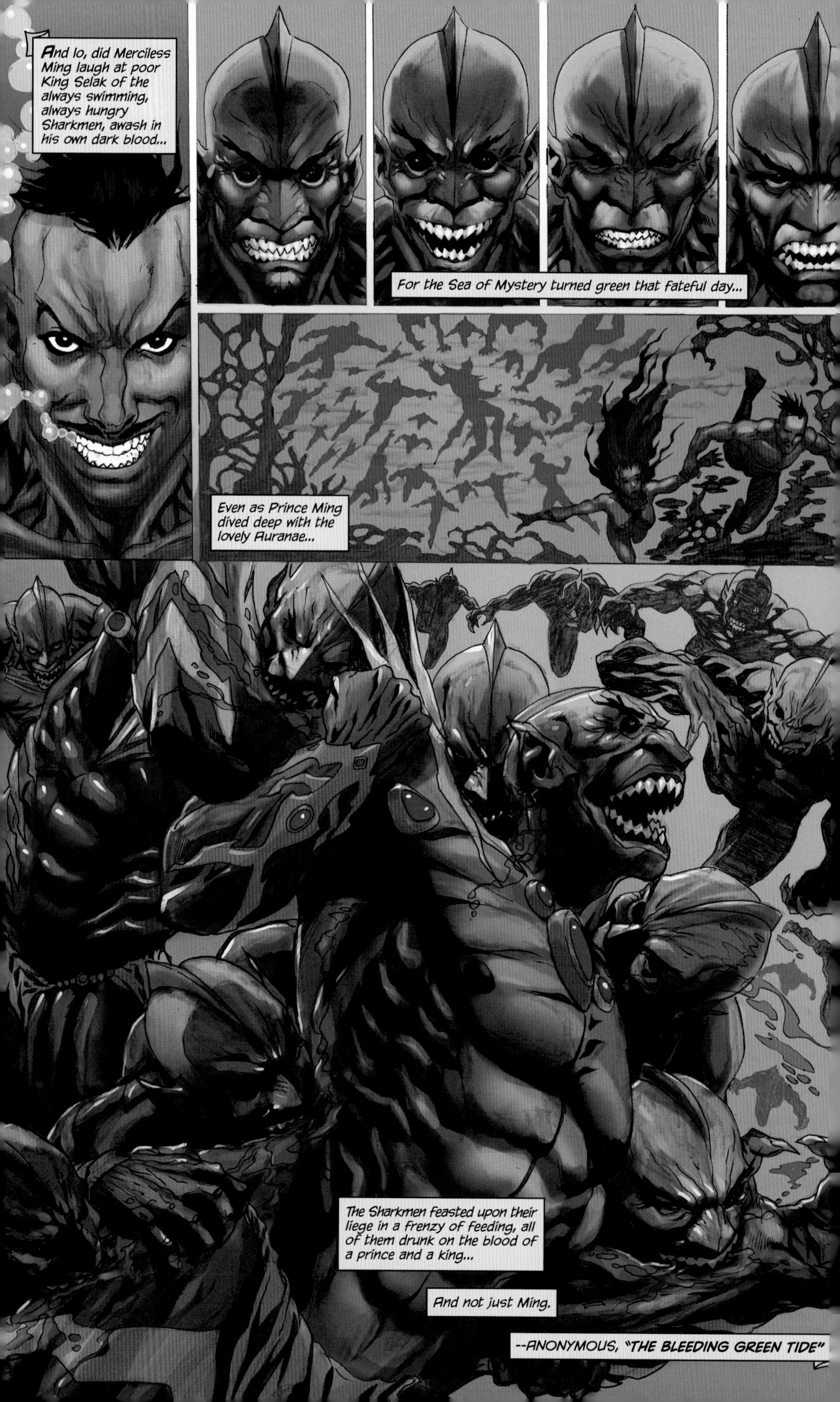
And lo, did Merciless Ming laugh at poor King Selak of the always swimming, always hungry Sharkmen, awash in his own dark blood...
For the Sea of Mystery turned green that fateful day...
Even as Prince Ming dived deep with the lovely Auranae...
The Sharkmen feasted upon their liege in a frenzy of feeding, all of them drunk on the blood of a prince and a king...
And not just Ming.
--ANONYMOUS, "THE BLEEDING GREEN TIDE"

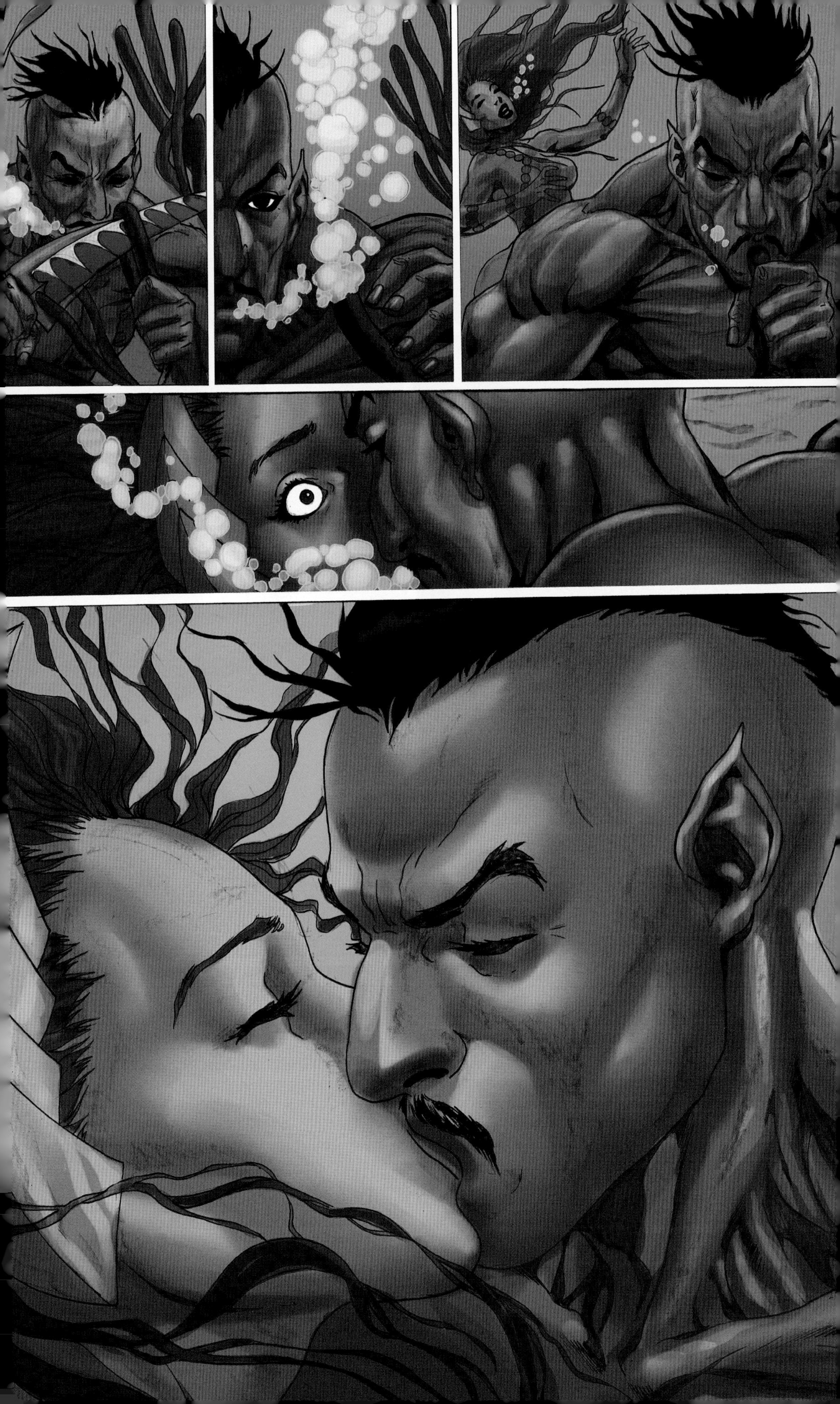

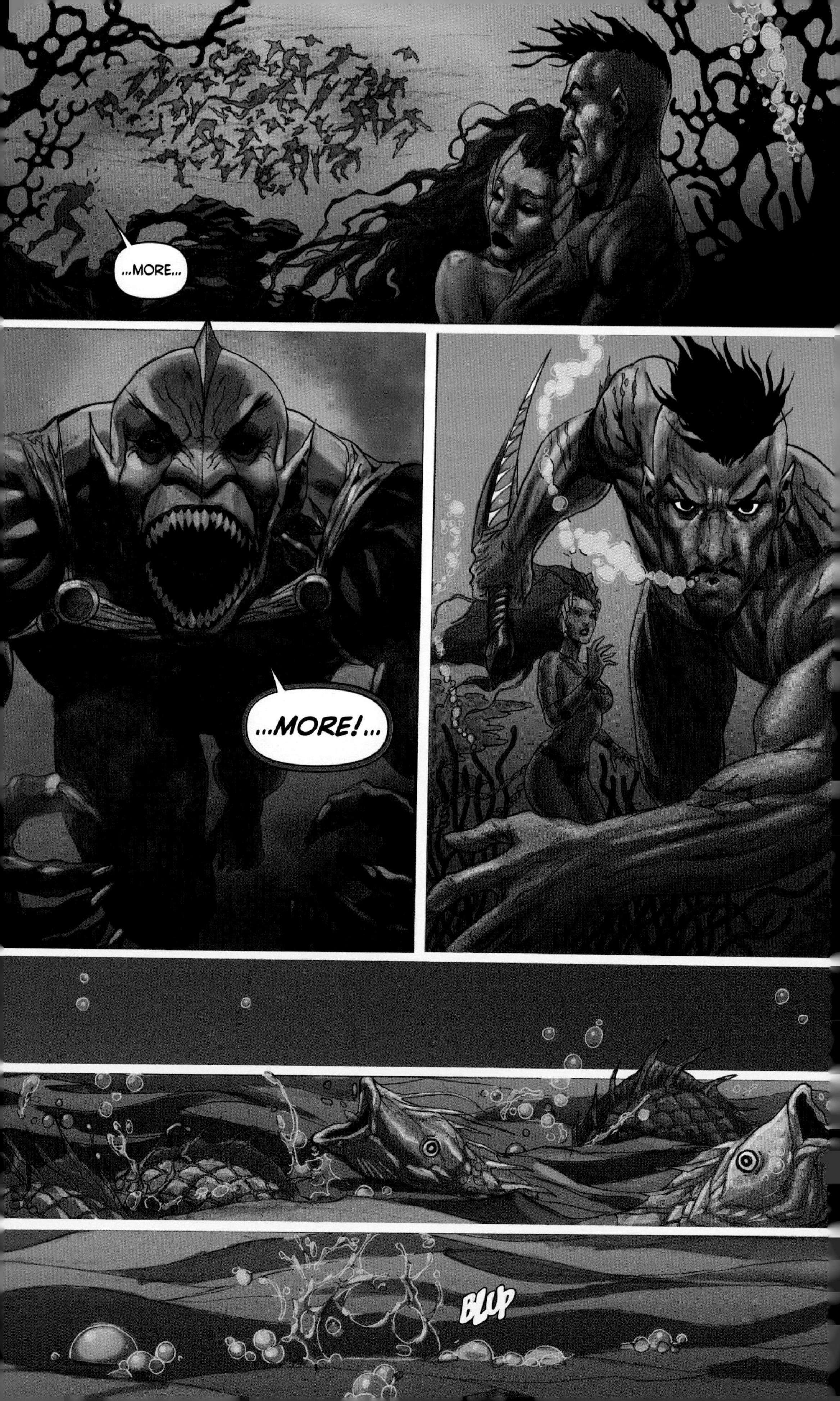
...MORE...
...MORE!...
BLUP

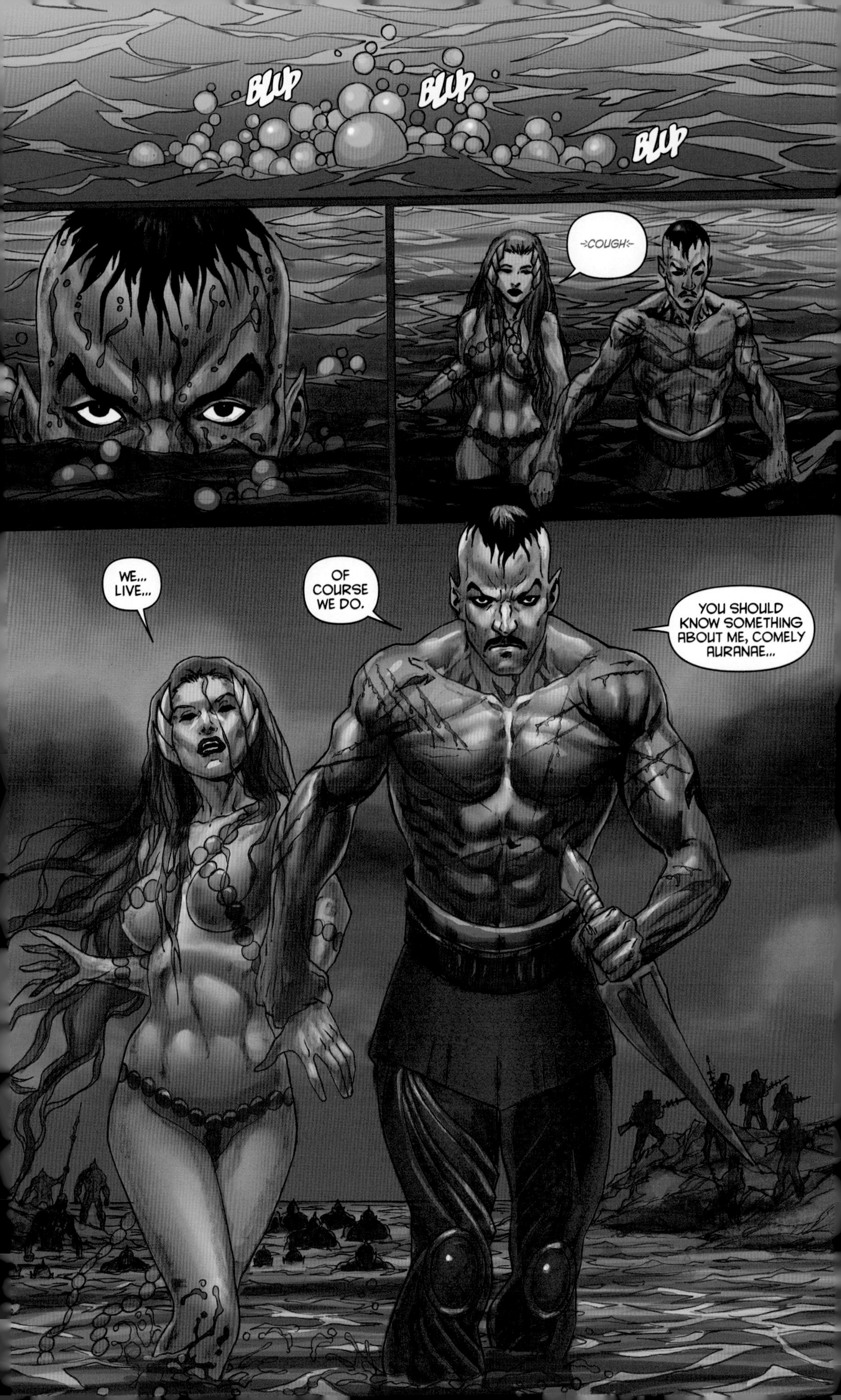
BLUP
BLUP
BLUP
COUGH
WE... LIVE...
OF COURSE WE DO.
YOU SHOULD KNOW SOMETHING ABOUT ME, COMELY AURANAE...

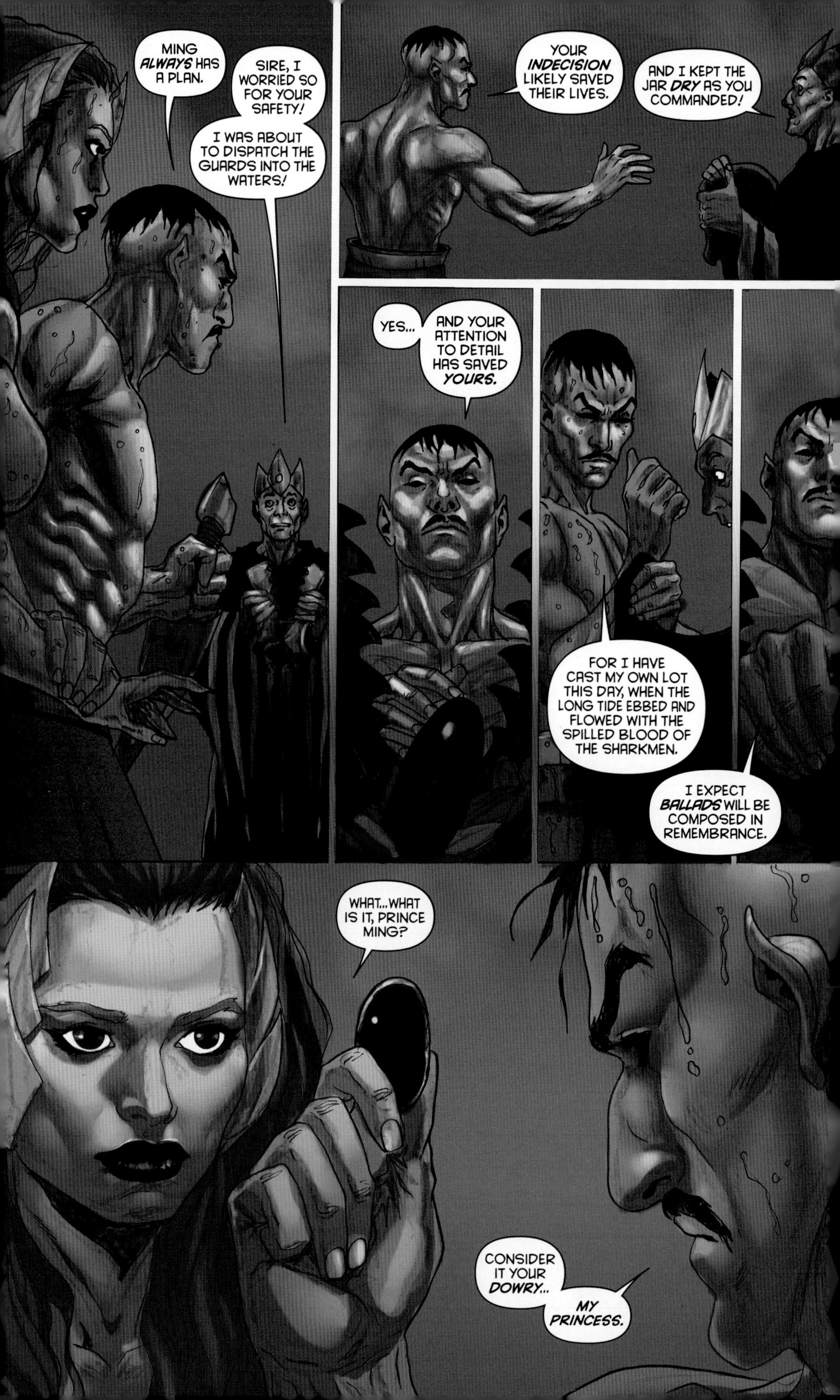
MING ALWAYS HAS A PLAN.
SIRE, I WORRIED SO FOR YOUR SAFETY!
I WAS ABOUT TO DISPATCH THE GUARDS INTO THE WATERS!
YOUR INDECISION LIKELY SAVED THEIR LIVES.
AND I KEPT THE JAR DRY AS YOU COMMANDED!
YES...
AND YOUR ATTENTION TO DETAIL HAS SAVED YOURS.
FOR I HAVE CAST MY OWN LOT THIS DAY, WHEN THE LONG TIDE EBBED AND FLOWED WITH THE SPILLED BLOOD OF THE SHARKMEN.
I EXPECT BALLADS WILL BE COMPOSED IN REMEMBRANCE.
WHAT...WHAT IS IT, PRINCE MING?
CONSIDER IT YOUR DOWRY...
MY PRINCESS.

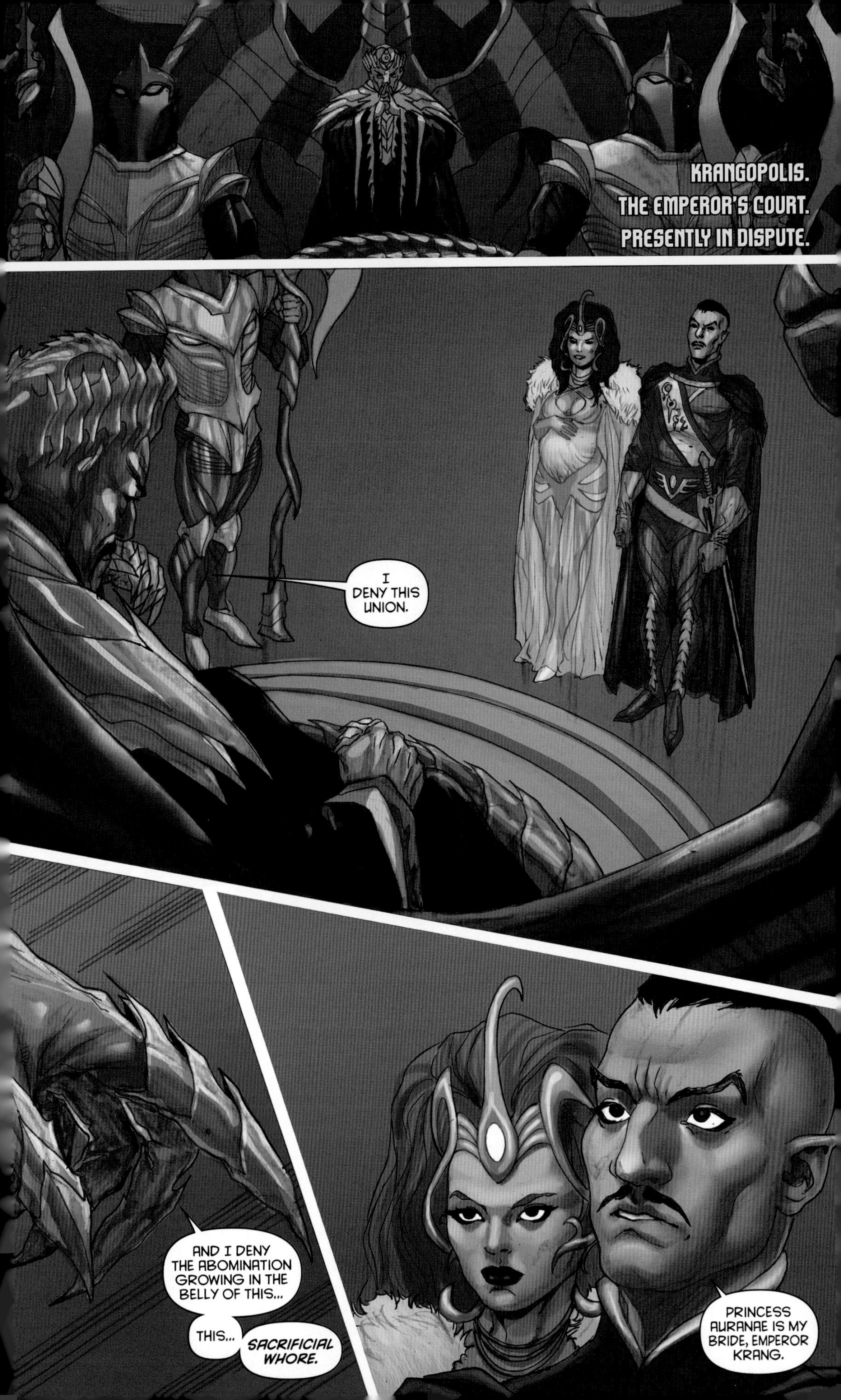
KRANGOPOLIS.
THE EMPEROR'S COURT.
PRESENTLY IN DISPUTE.
I DENY THIS UNION.
AND I DENY THE ABOMINATION GROWING IN THE BELLY OF THIS...
THIS...
SACRIFICIAL WHORE.
PRINCESS AURANAE IS MY BRIDE, EMPEROR KRANG.

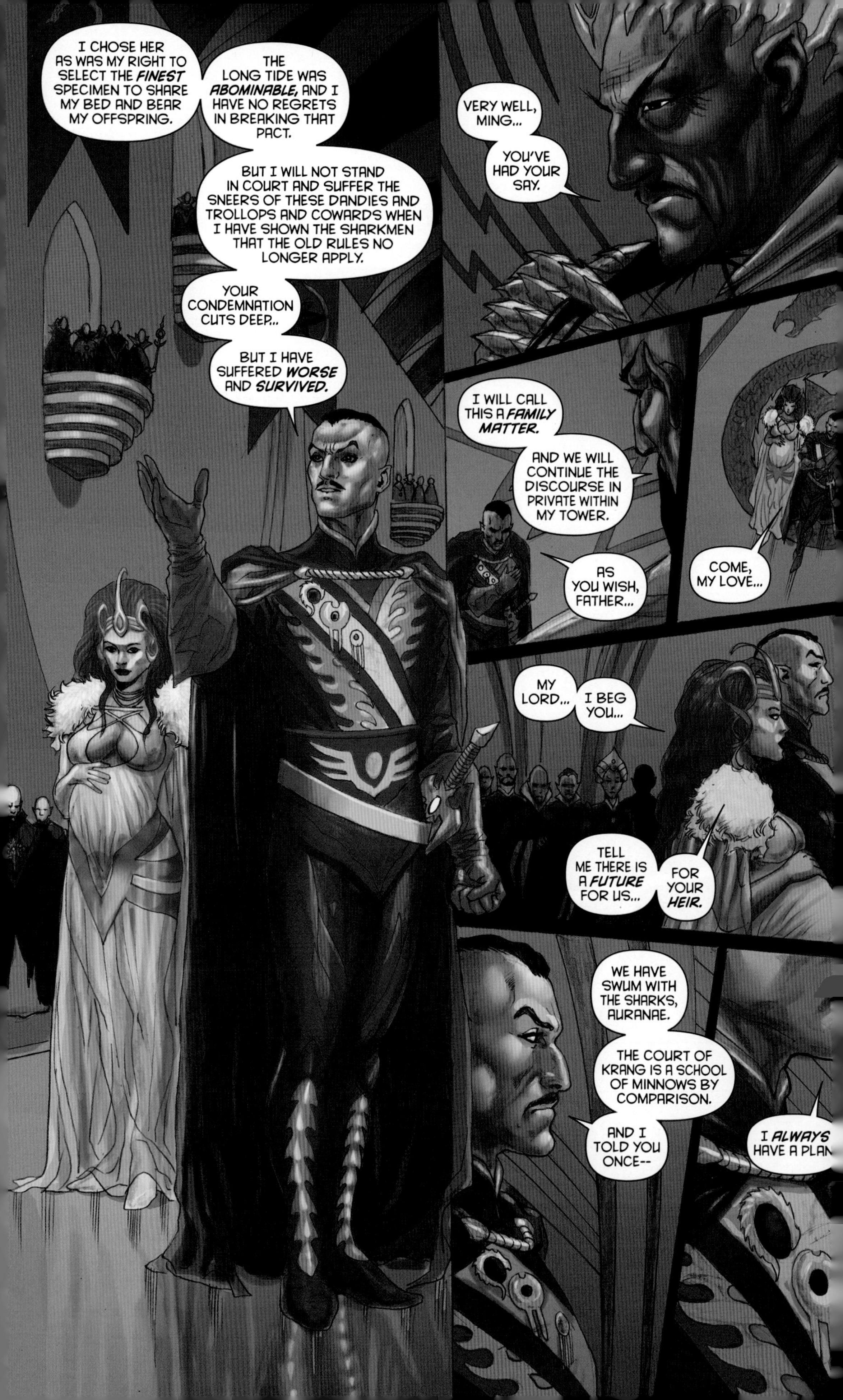
I CHOSE HER AS WAS MY RIGHT TO SELECT THE *FINEST* SPECIMEN TO SHARE MY BED AND BEAR MY OFFSPRING.
THE LONG TIDE WAS *ABOMINABLE,* AND I HAVE NO REGRETS IN BREAKING THAT PACT.
BUT I WILL NOT STAND IN COURT AND SUFFER THE SNEERS OF THESE DANDIES AND TROLLOPS AND COWARDS WHEN I HAVE SHOWN THE SHARKMEN THAT THE OLD RULES NO LONGER APPLY.
YOUR CONDEMNATION CUTS DEEP...
BUT I HAVE SUFFERED *WORSE* AND *SURVIVED.*
VERY WELL, MING...
YOU'VE HAD YOUR SAY.
I WILL CALL THIS A *FAMILY MATTER.*
AND WE WILL CONTINUE THE DISCOURSE IN PRIVATE WITHIN MY TOWER.
AS YOU WISH, FATHER...
COME, MY LOVE...
MY LORD...
I BEG YOU...
TELL ME THERE IS A *FUTURE* FOR US...
FOR YOUR *HEIR.*
WE HAVE SWUM WITH THE SHARKS, AURANAE.
THE COURT OF KRANG IS A SCHOOL OF MINNOWS BY COMPARISON.
AND I TOLD YOU ONCE--
I *ALWAYS* HAVE A PLAN

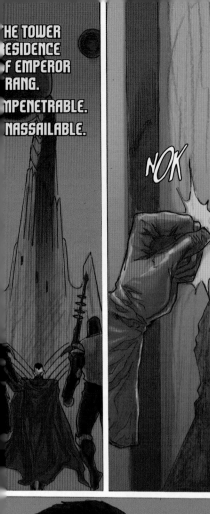

THE TOWER RESIDENCE OF EMPEROR RANG.

IMPENETRABLE.

UNASSAILABLE.

NOK

GUARDS, LEAVE US...

POUR US WINE. YOU'RE ONLY PUNCTUAL WHEN IT'S ABOUT *YOU*, MING.

IT *IS* ABOUT ME, FATHER.

AS A MONARCH-IN-WAITING, ALL ROADS LEAD TO *ME*...

LIKE THE INEXORABLE TUG OF *GRAVITY*...

THIS DISCUSSION WAS A LONG TIME COMING--

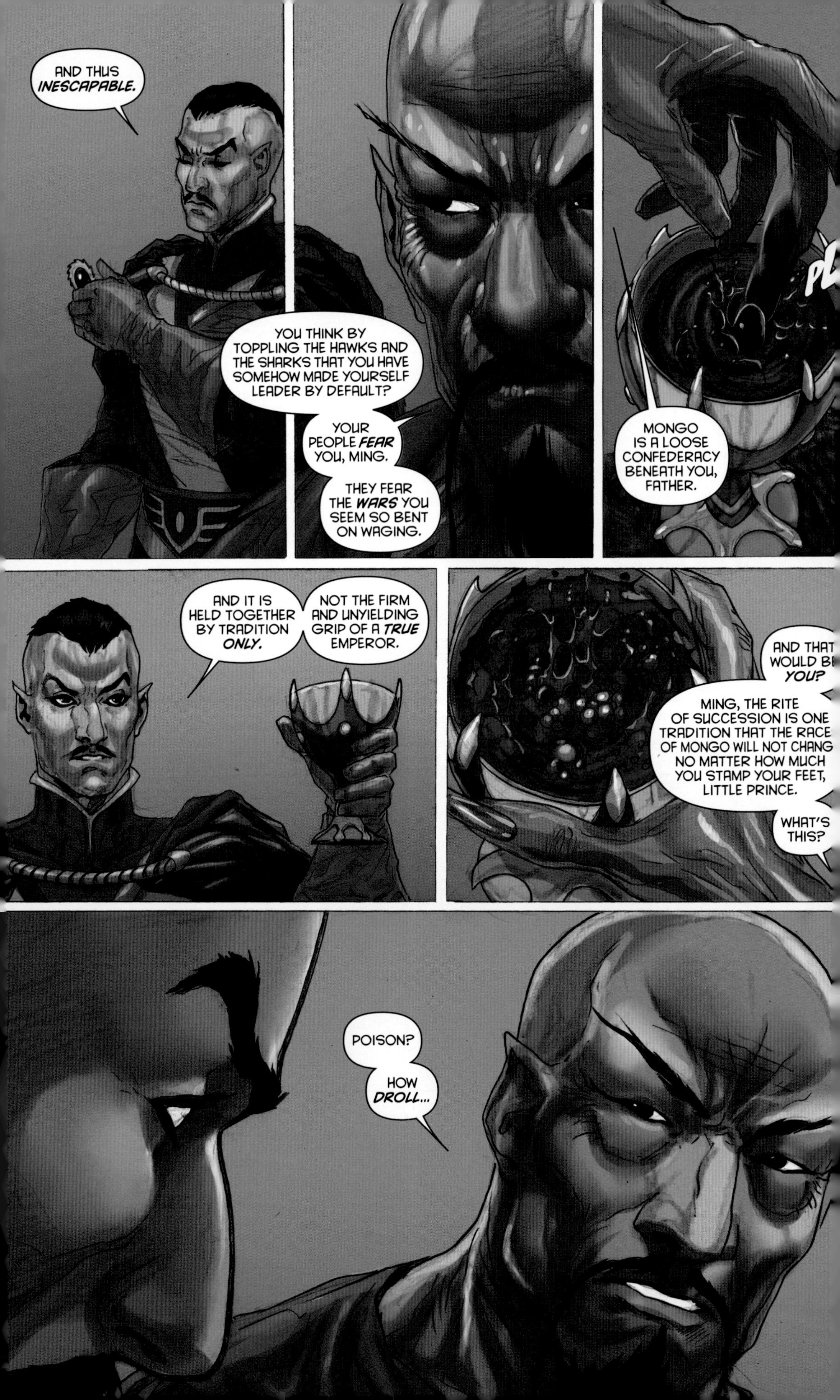
AND THUS *INESCAPABLE.*
YOU THINK BY TOPPLING THE HAWKS AND THE SHARKS THAT YOU HAVE SOMEHOW MADE YOURSELF LEADER BY DEFAULT?
YOUR PEOPLE *FEAR* YOU, MING.
THEY FEAR THE *WARS* YOU SEEM SO BENT ON WAGING.
MONGO IS A LOOSE CONFEDERACY BENEATH YOU, FATHER.
AND IT IS HELD TOGETHER BY TRADITION *ONLY.*
NOT THE FIRM AND UNYIELDING GRIP OF A *TRUE* EMPEROR.
AND THAT WOULD B *YOU?*
MING, THE RITE OF SUCCESSION IS ONE TRADITION THAT THE RACE OF MONGO WILL NOT CHANG NO MATTER HOW MUCH YOU STAMP YOUR FEET, LITTLE PRINCE.
WHAT'S THIS?
POISON?
HOW *DROLL...*

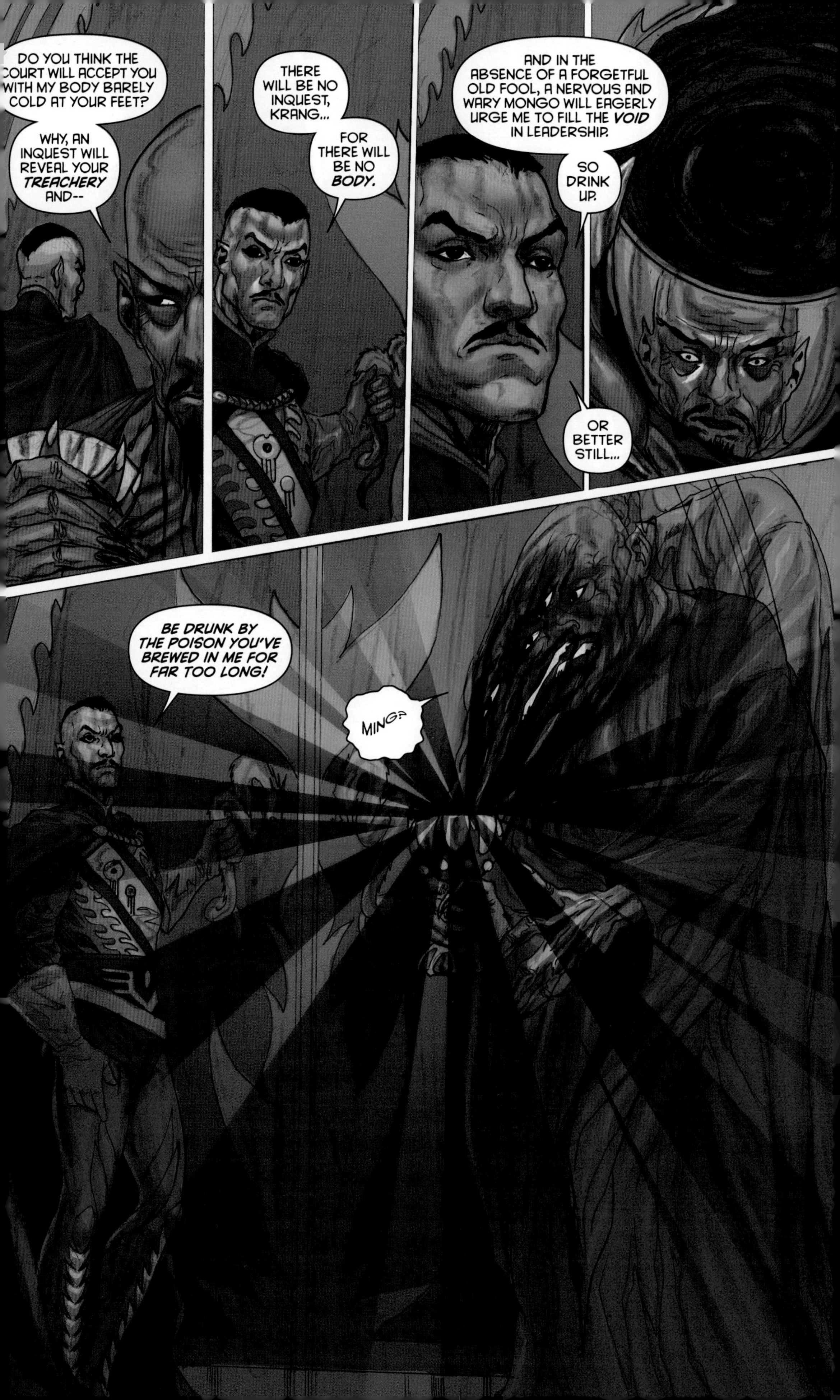
DO YOU THINK THE COURT WILL ACCEPT YOU WITH MY BODY BARELY COLD AT YOUR FEET?
WHY, AN INQUEST WILL REVEAL YOUR *TREACHERY* AND--
THERE WILL BE NO INQUEST, KRANG...
FOR THERE WILL BE NO *BODY.*
AND IN THE ABSENCE OF A FORGETFUL OLD FOOL, A NERVOUS AND WARY MONGO WILL EAGERLY URGE ME TO FILL THE *VOID* IN LEADERSHIP.
SO DRINK UP.
OR BETTER STILL...
BE DRUNK BY THE POISON YOU'VE BREWED IN ME FOR FAR TOO LONG!
MING?

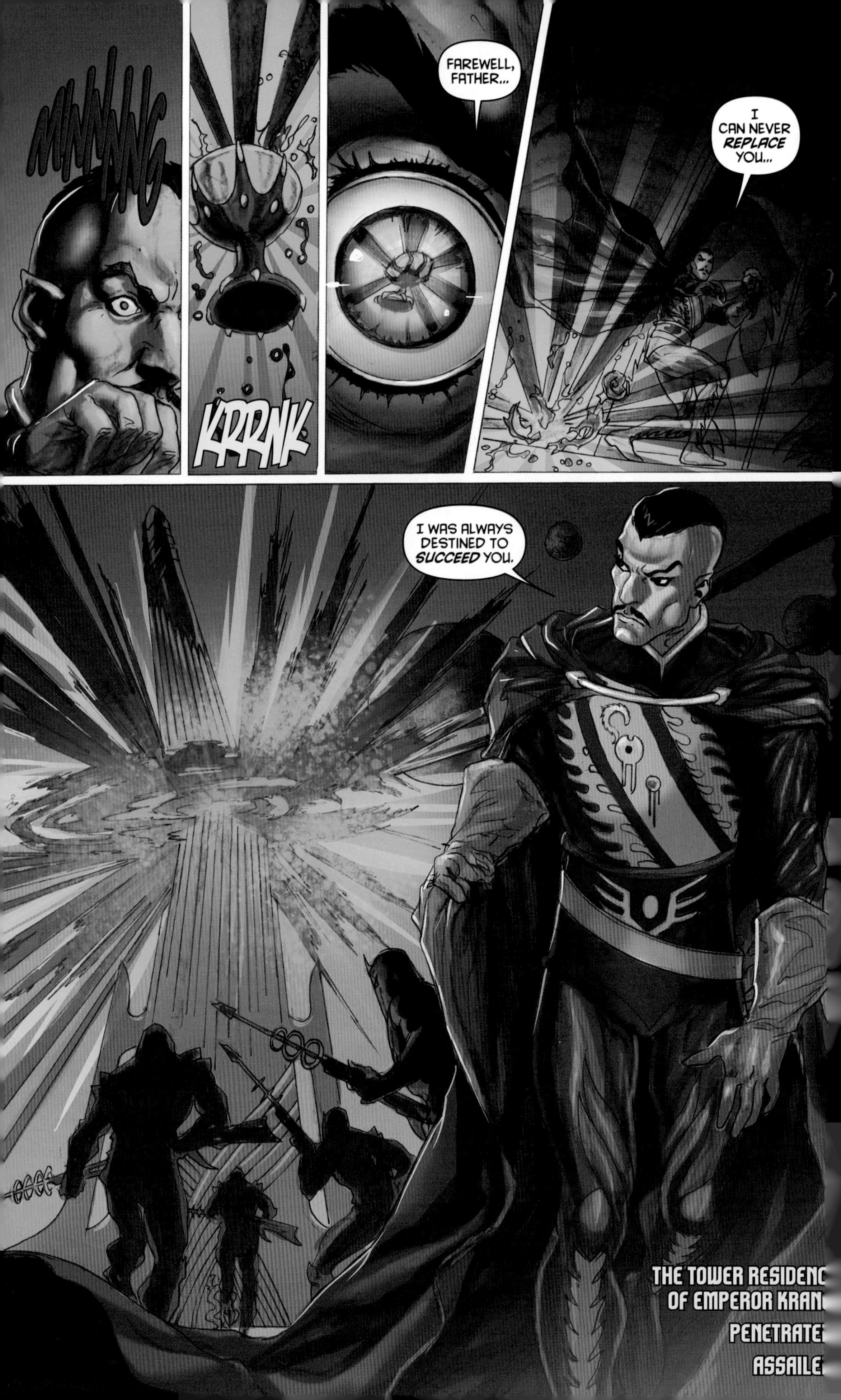

MNNNNG
KRRNK
FAREWELL, FATHER...
I CAN NEVER REPLACE YOU...
I WAS ALWAYS DESTINED TO SUCCEED YOU.
THE TOWER RESIDENC
OF EMPEROR KRAN
PENETRATE
ASSAILE

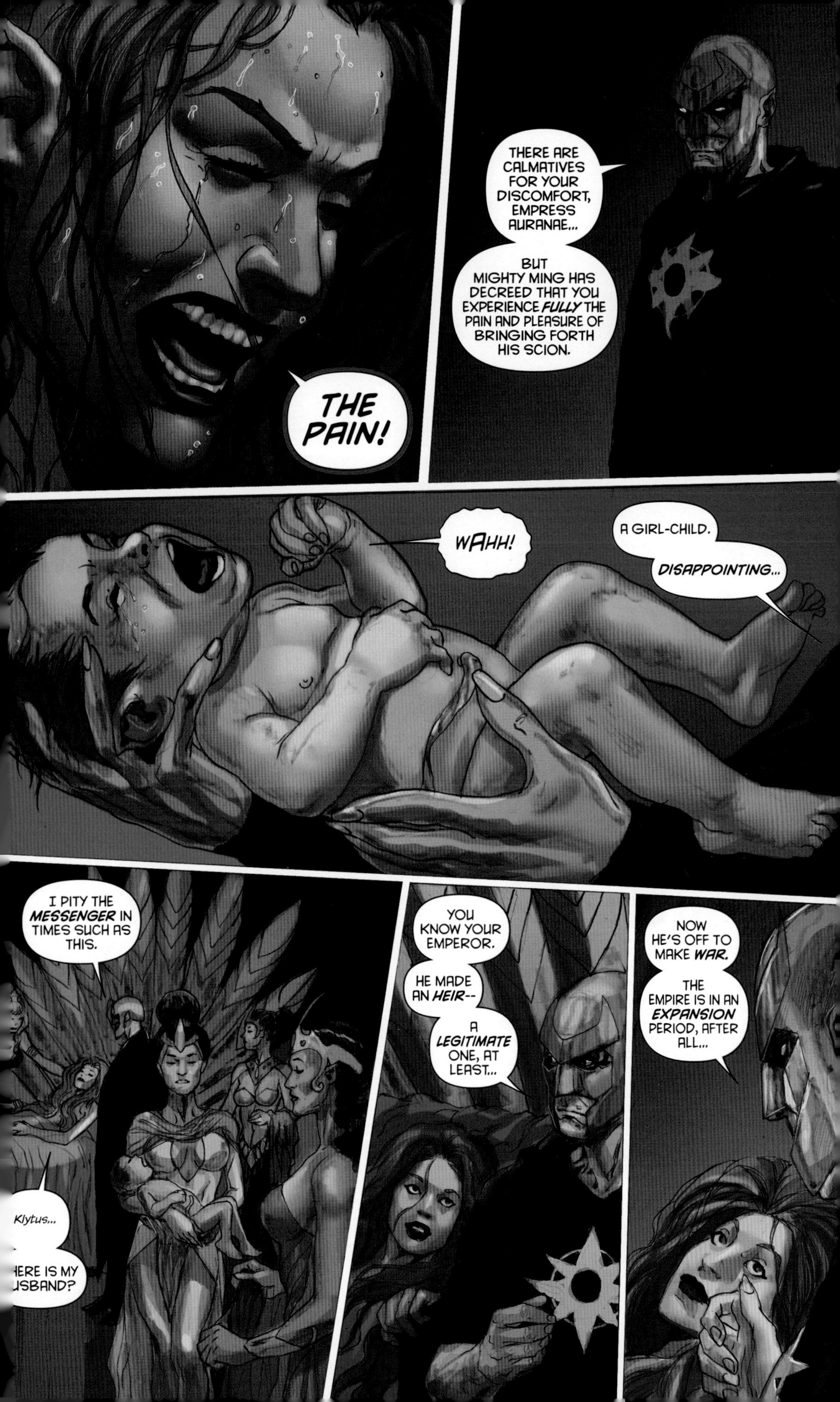
THE PAIN!
THERE ARE CALMATIVES FOR YOUR DISCOMFORT, EMPRESS AURANAE...
BUT MIGHTY MING HAS DECREED THAT YOU EXPERIENCE *FULLY* THE PAIN AND PLEASURE OF BRINGING FORTH HIS SCION.
WAHH!
A GIRL-CHILD.
DISAPPOINTING...
I PITY THE *MESSENGER* IN TIMES SUCH AS THIS.
Klytus...
HERE IS MY USBAND?
YOU KNOW YOUR EMPEROR.
HE MADE AN *HEIR*--
A *LEGITIMATE* ONE, AT LEAST...
NOW HE'S OFF TO MAKE *WAR.*
THE EMPIRE IS IN AN *EXPANSION* PERIOD, AFTER ALL...

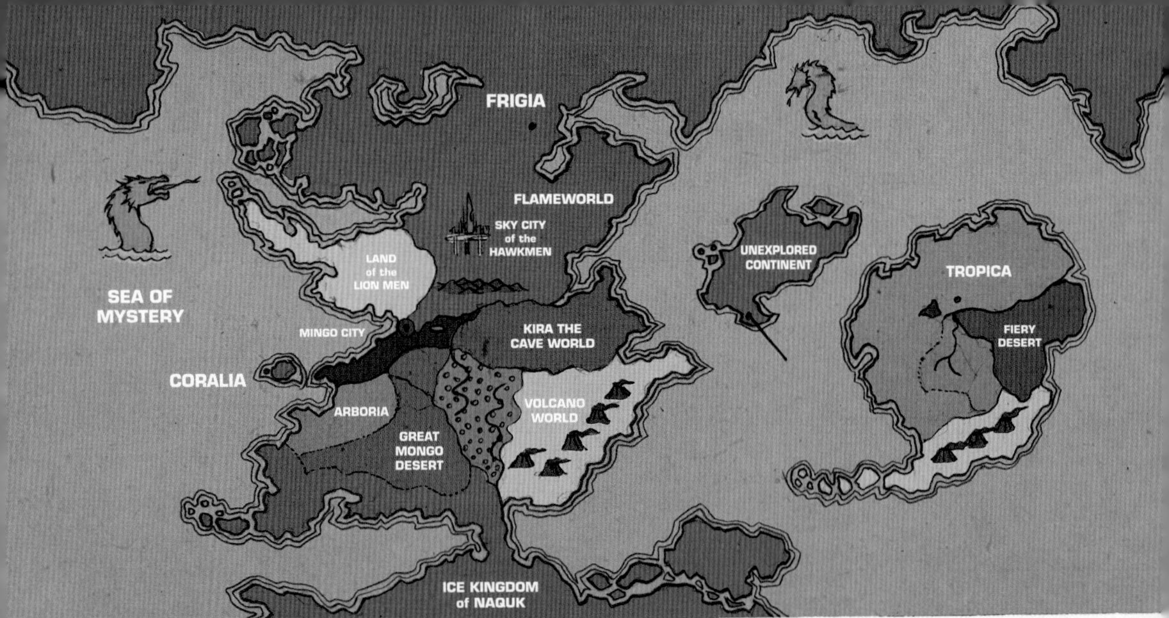
FRIGIA
FLAMEWORLD
SKY CITY of the HAWKMEN
LAND of the LION MEN
SEA OF MYSTERY
MINGO CITY
CORALIA
KIRA THE CAVE WORLD
ARBORIA
GREAT MONGO DESERT
VOLCANO WORLD
UNEXPLORED CONTINENT
TROPICA
FIERY DESERT
ICE KINGDOM of NAQUK

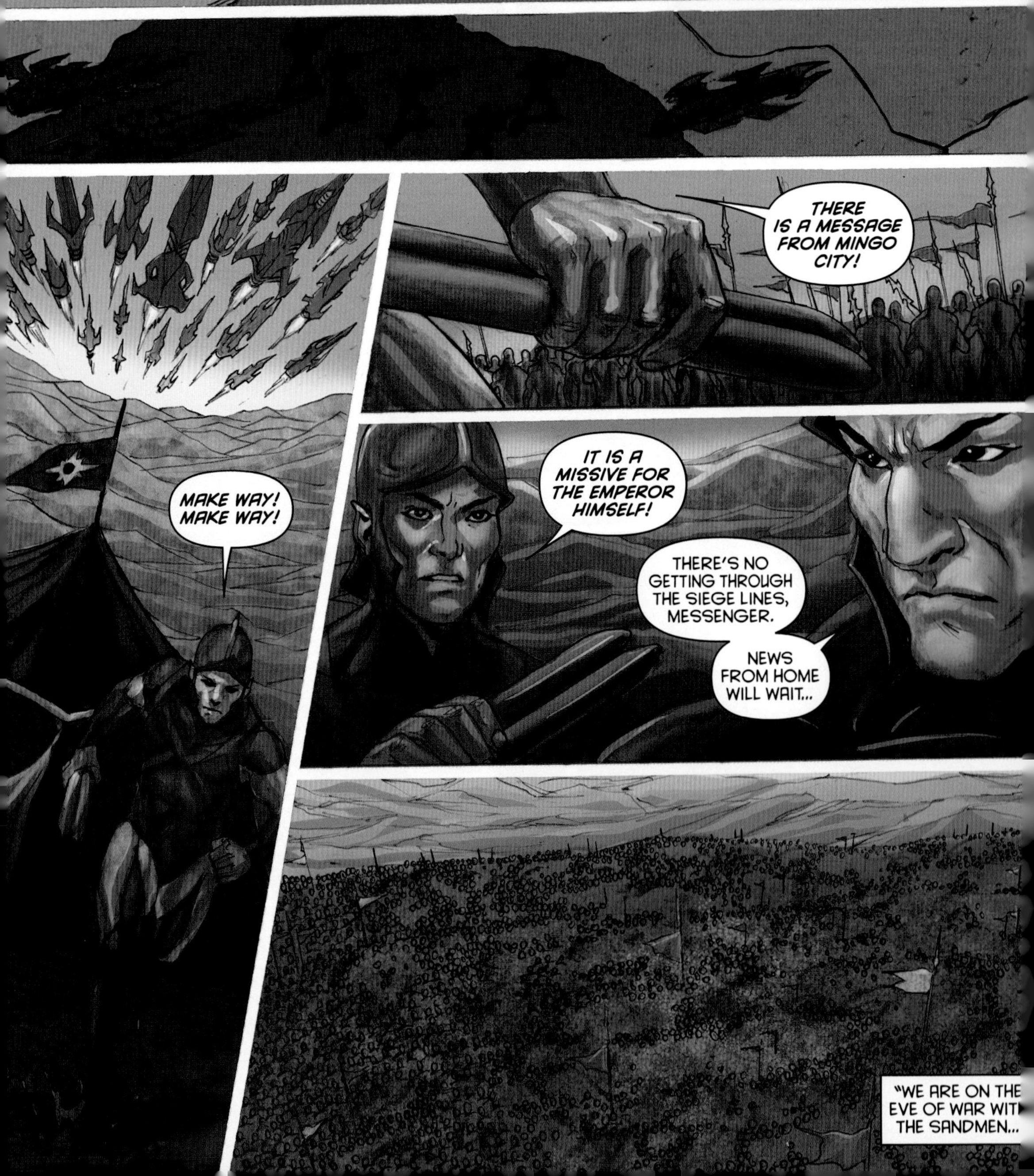
MAKE WAY! MAKE WAY!
THERE IS A MESSAGE FROM MINGO CITY!
IT IS A MISSIVE FOR THE EMPEROR HIMSELF!
THERE'S NO GETTING THROUGH THE SIEGE LINES, MESSENGER.
NEWS FROM HOME WILL WAIT...
"WE ARE ON THE EVE OF WAR WITH THE SANDMEN...

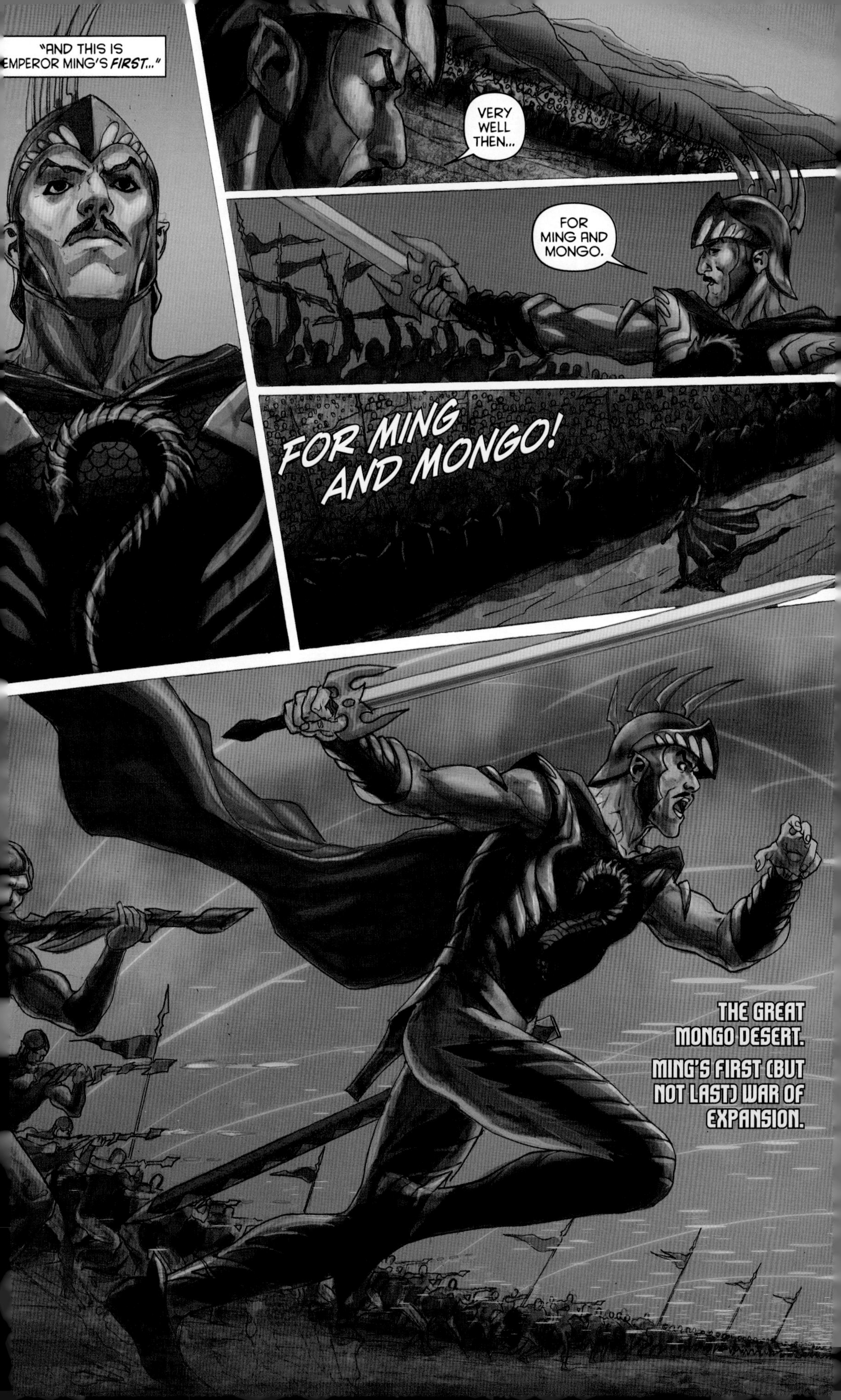
"AND THIS IS
EMPEROR MING'S *FIRST*..."
VERY WELL THEN...
FOR MING AND MONGO.
FOR MING AND MONGO!
THE GREAT MONGO DESERT.
MING'S FIRST (BUT NOT LAST) WAR OF EXPANSION.

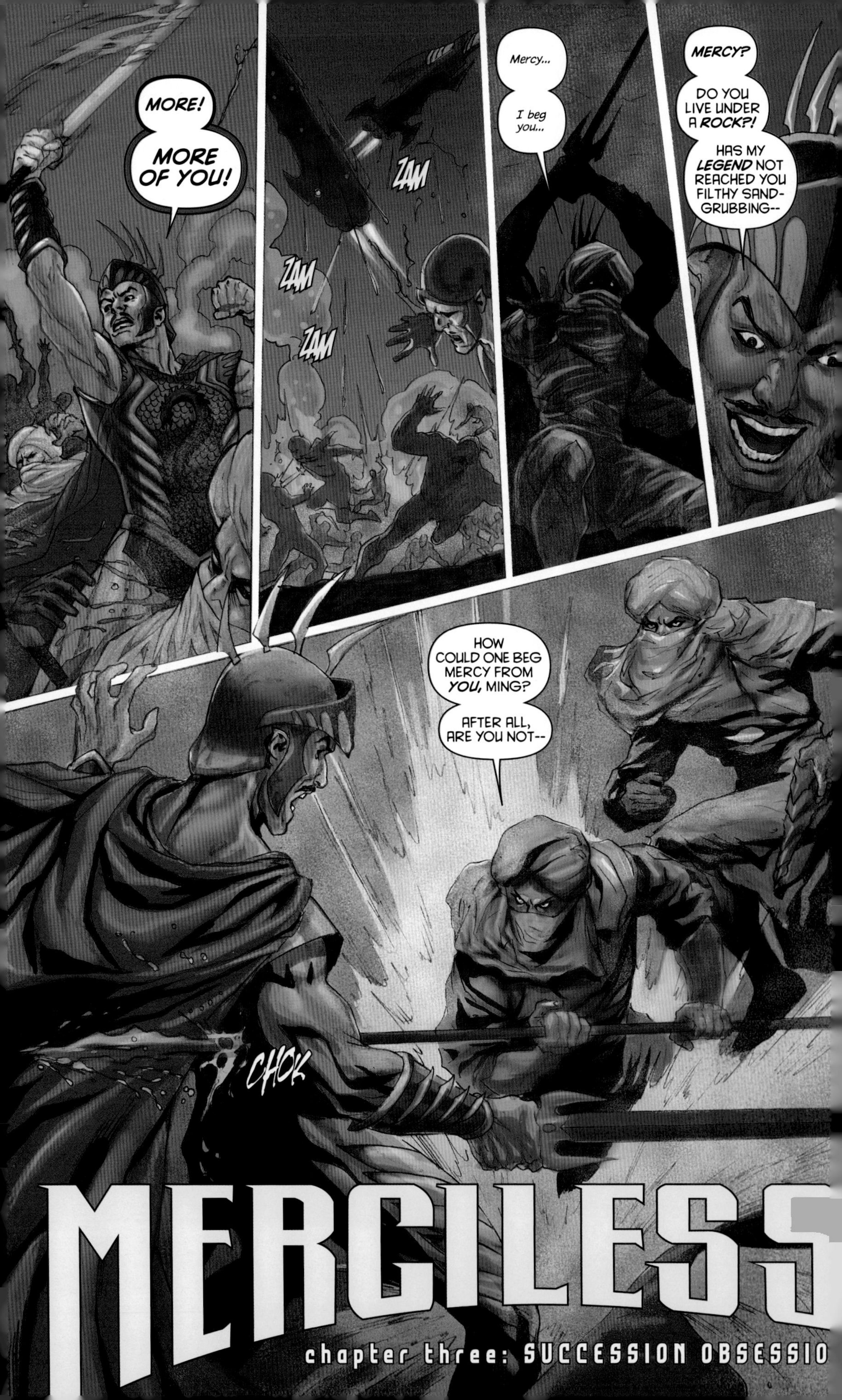
MORE!
MORE OF YOU!
ZAM
ZAM
ZAM
Mercy...
I beg you...
MERCY?
DO YOU LIVE UNDER A ROCK?!
HAS MY LEGEND NOT REACHED YOU FILTHY SAND-GRUBBING--
HOW COULD ONE BEG MERCY FROM YOU, MING?
AFTER ALL, ARE YOU NOT--
CHOK
MERCILESS
chapter three: SUCCESSION OBSESSIO

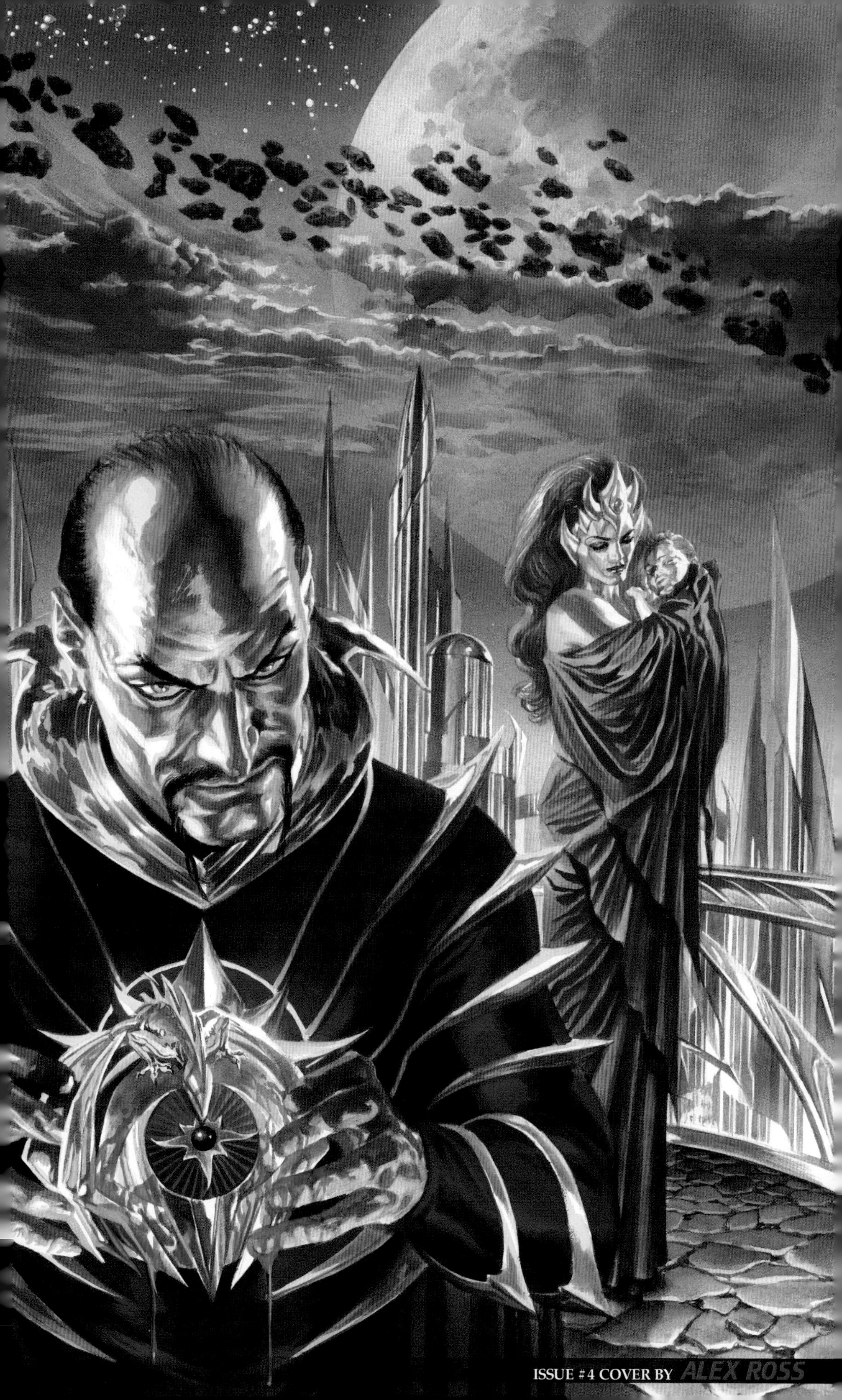

ISSUE #4 COVER BY ALEX ROSS

chapter four: ABSOLUTION
MERCILESS
THIS DAY YOU DIE, MING!
THE GREAT MONGO DESERT.
WAR IS HELL.
EVEN ON MONGO.

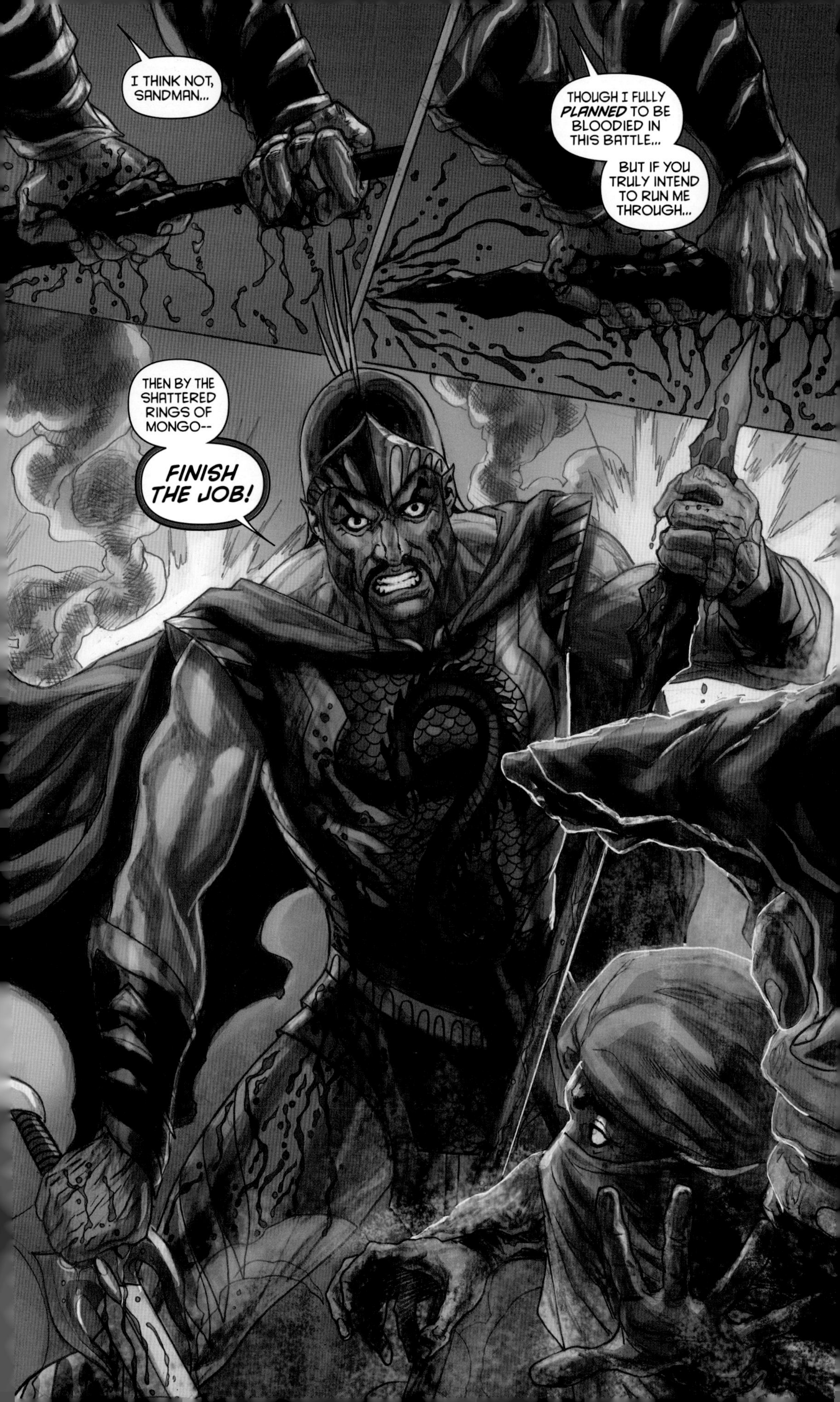
I THINK NOT, SANDMAN...
THOUGH I FULLY *PLANNED* TO BE BLOODIED IN THIS BATTLE...
BUT IF YOU TRULY INTEND TO RUN ME THROUGH...
THEN BY THE SHATTERED RINGS OF MONGO--
FINISH THE JOB!

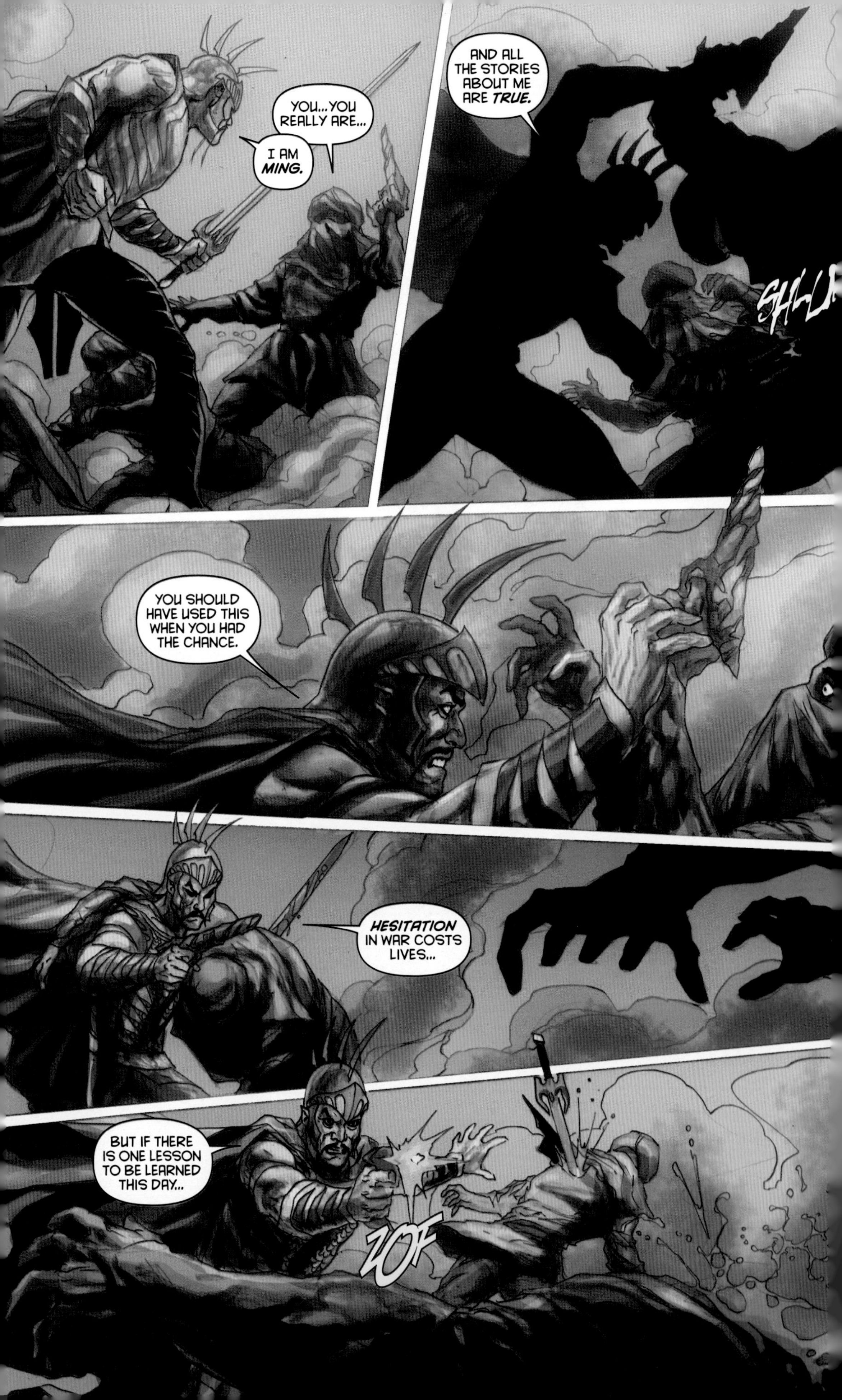
YOU...YOU REALLY ARE...
I AM MING.
AND ALL THE STORIES ABOUT ME ARE TRUE.
SHLURK
YOU SHOULD HAVE USED THIS WHEN YOU HAD THE CHANCE.
HESITATION IN WAR COSTS LIVES...
BUT IF THERE IS ONE LESSON TO BE LEARNED THIS DAY...
ZOF

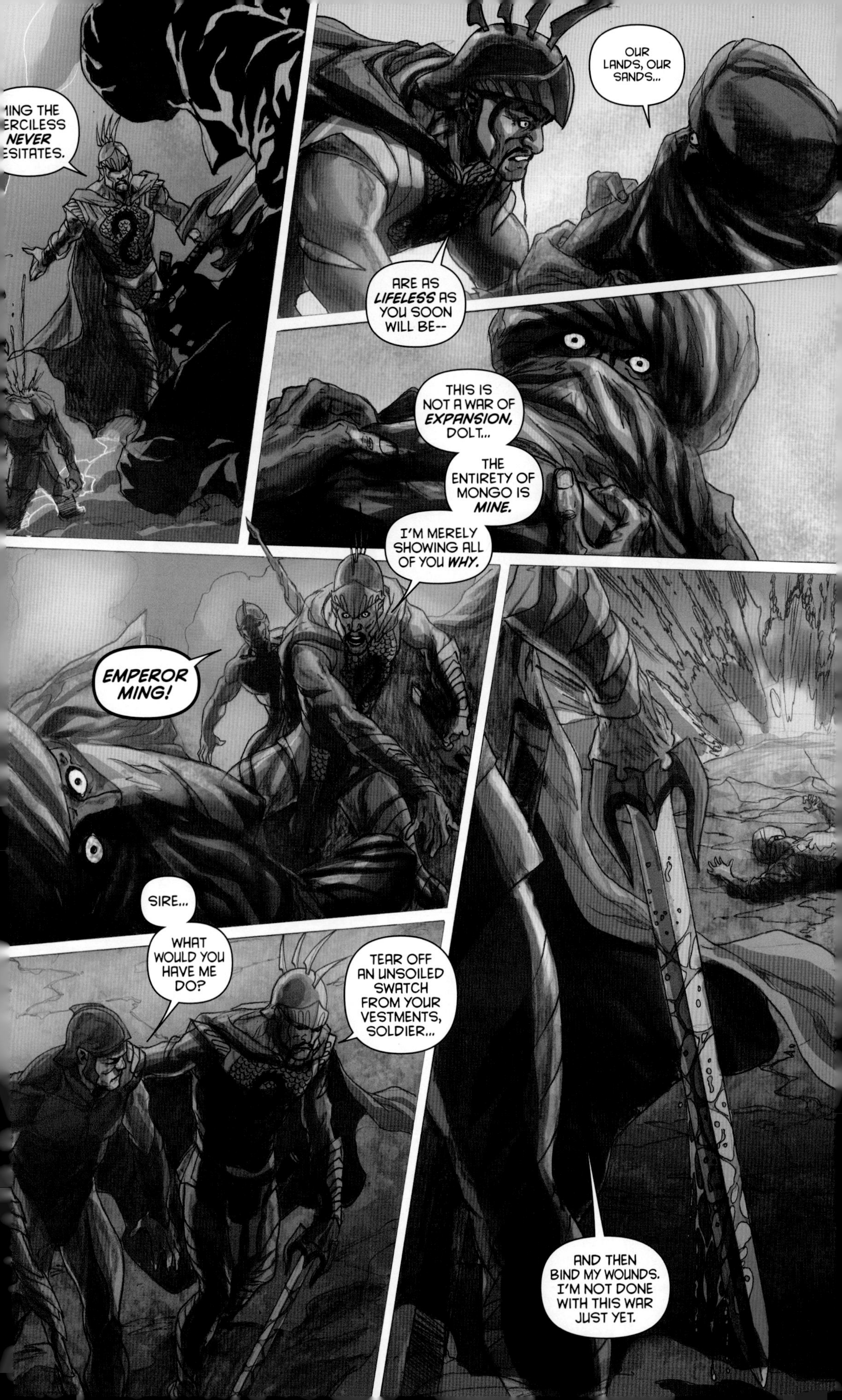

ING THE
ERCILESS
NEVER
ESITATES.
OUR LANDS, OUR SANDS...
ARE AS LIFELESS AS YOU SOON WILL BE--
THIS IS NOT A WAR OF EXPANSION, DOLT...
THE ENTIRETY OF MONGO IS MINE.
I'M MERELY SHOWING ALL OF YOU WHY.
EMPEROR MING!
SIRE...
WHAT WOULD YOU HAVE ME DO?
TEAR OFF AN UNSOILED SWATCH FROM YOUR VESTMENTS, SOLDIER...
AND THEN BIND MY WOUNDS. I'M NOT DONE WITH THIS WAR JUST YET.

THE GREAT MONGO DESERT.

BEHIND THE LINE

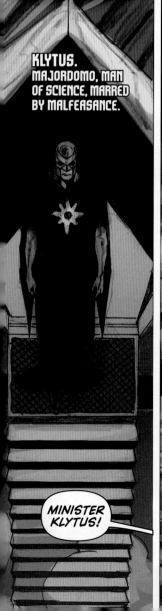

KLYTUS.
MAJORDOMO, MAN OF SCIENCE, MARRED BY MALFEASANCE.

MINISTER KLYTUS!

WHERE IS GLORIOUS MING, CENTURION?

AT THE FRONT, MINISTER...

THE EMPEROR LED THE FIRST CHARGE *HIMSELF*--

BUT THERE IS WORD TRICKLING BACK THROUGH THE LINES THAT OUR GLORIOUS LIEGE HAS BEEN WOUNDED...

PERHAPS *MORTALLY.*

CURIOUS...

LOOK THERE!

HE LIVES!

H DO LIV

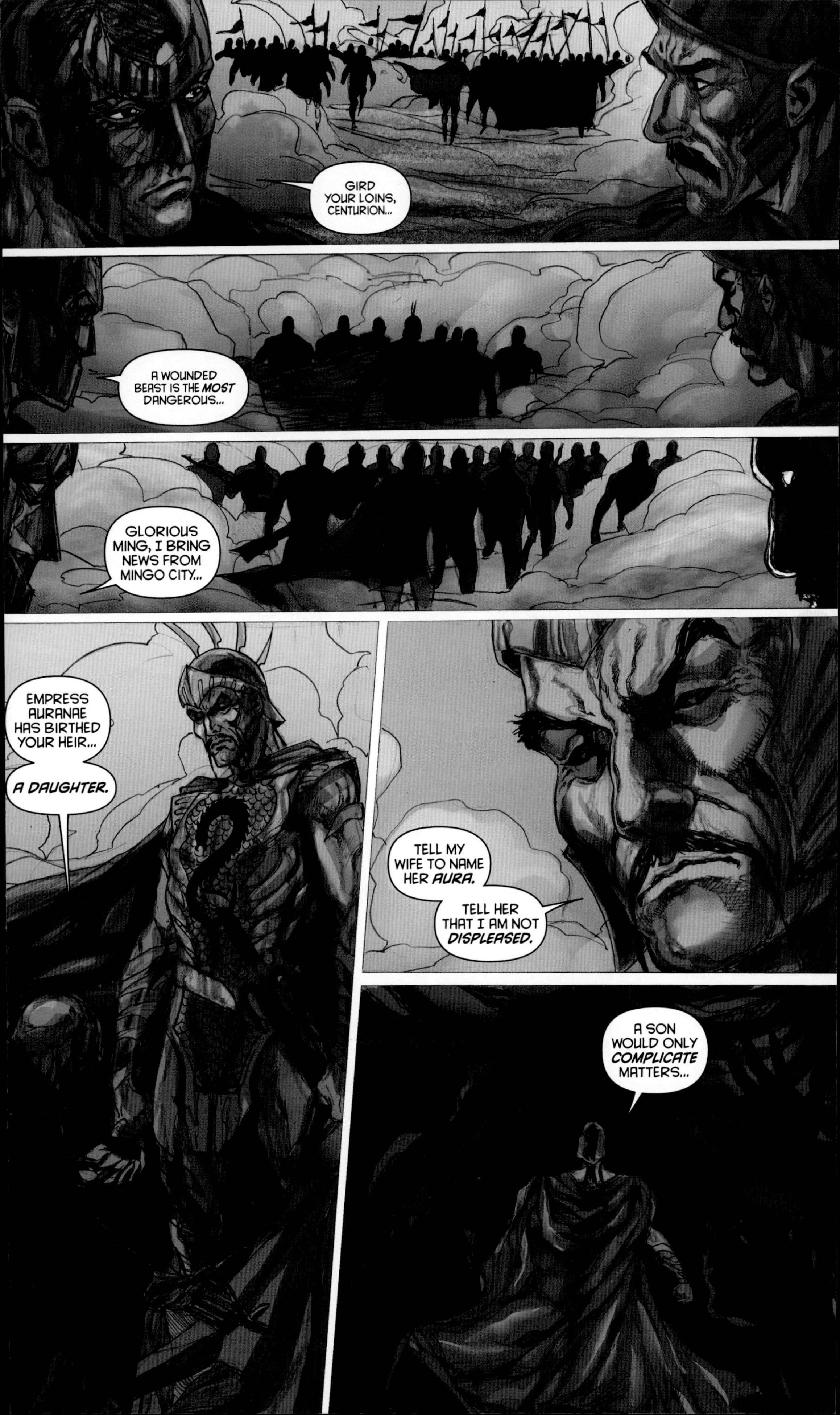
GIRD YOUR LOINS, CENTURION...
A WOUNDED BEAST IS THE *MOST* DANGEROUS...
GLORIOUS MING, I BRING NEWS FROM MINGO CITY...
EMPRESS AURANAE HAS BIRTHED YOUR HEIR...
A DAUGHTER.
TELL MY WIFE TO NAME HER *AURA.*
TELL HER THAT I AM NOT *DISPLEASED.*
A SON WOULD ONLY *COMPLICATE* MATTERS...

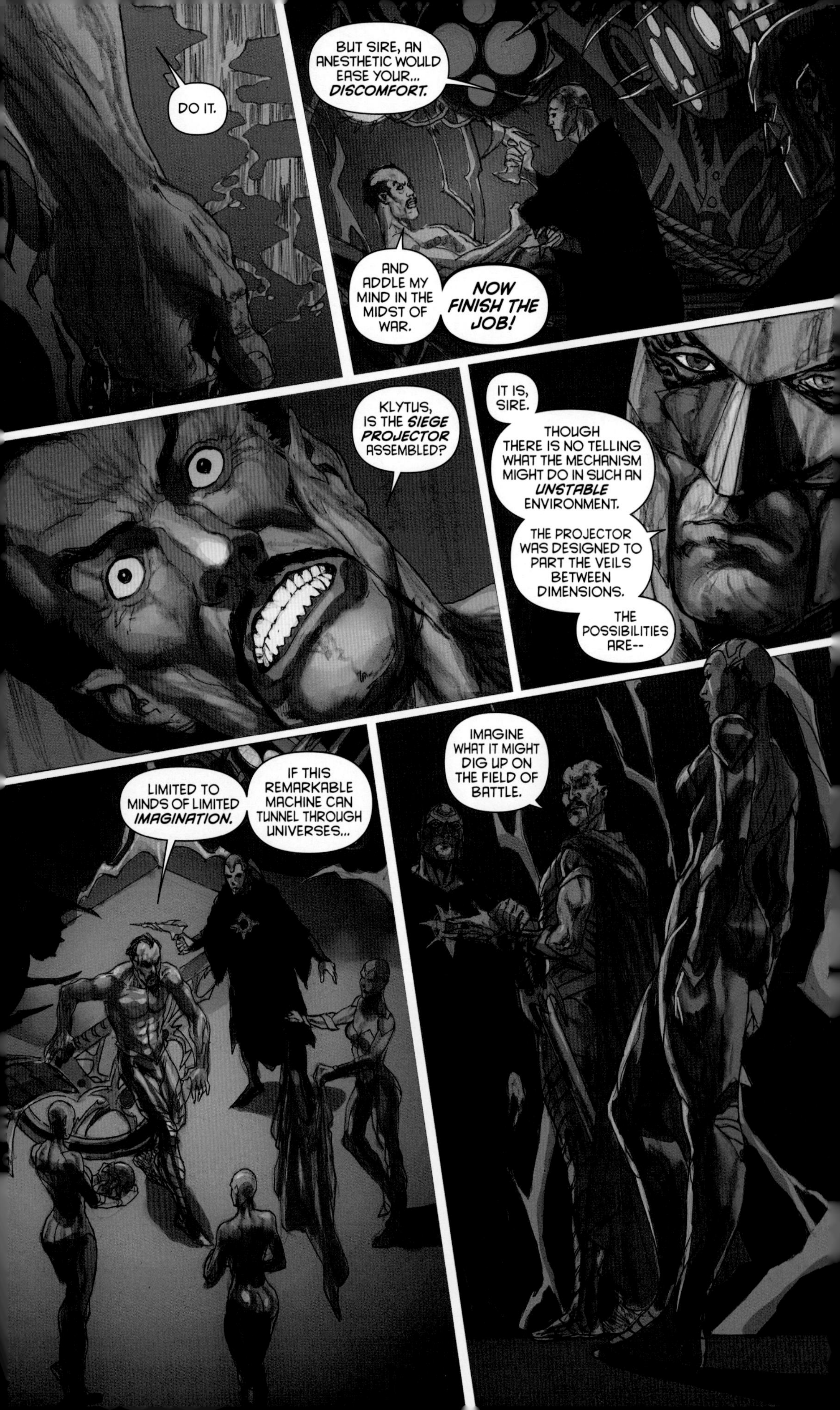

DO IT.
BUT SIRE, AN ANESTHETIC WOULD EASE YOUR... DISCOMFORT.
AND ADDLE MY MIND IN THE MIDST OF WAR.
NOW FINISH THE JOB!
KLYTUS, IS THE SIEGE PROJECTOR ASSEMBLED?
IT IS, SIRE.
THOUGH THERE IS NO TELLING WHAT THE MECHANISM MIGHT DO IN SUCH AN UNSTABLE ENVIRONMENT.
THE PROJECTOR WAS DESIGNED TO PART THE VEILS BETWEEN DIMENSIONS.
THE POSSIBILITIES ARE--
LIMITED TO MINDS OF LIMITED IMAGINATION.
IF THIS REMARKABLE MACHINE CAN TUNNEL THROUGH UNIVERSES...
IMAGINE WHAT IT MIGHT DIG UP ON THE FIELD OF BATTLE.

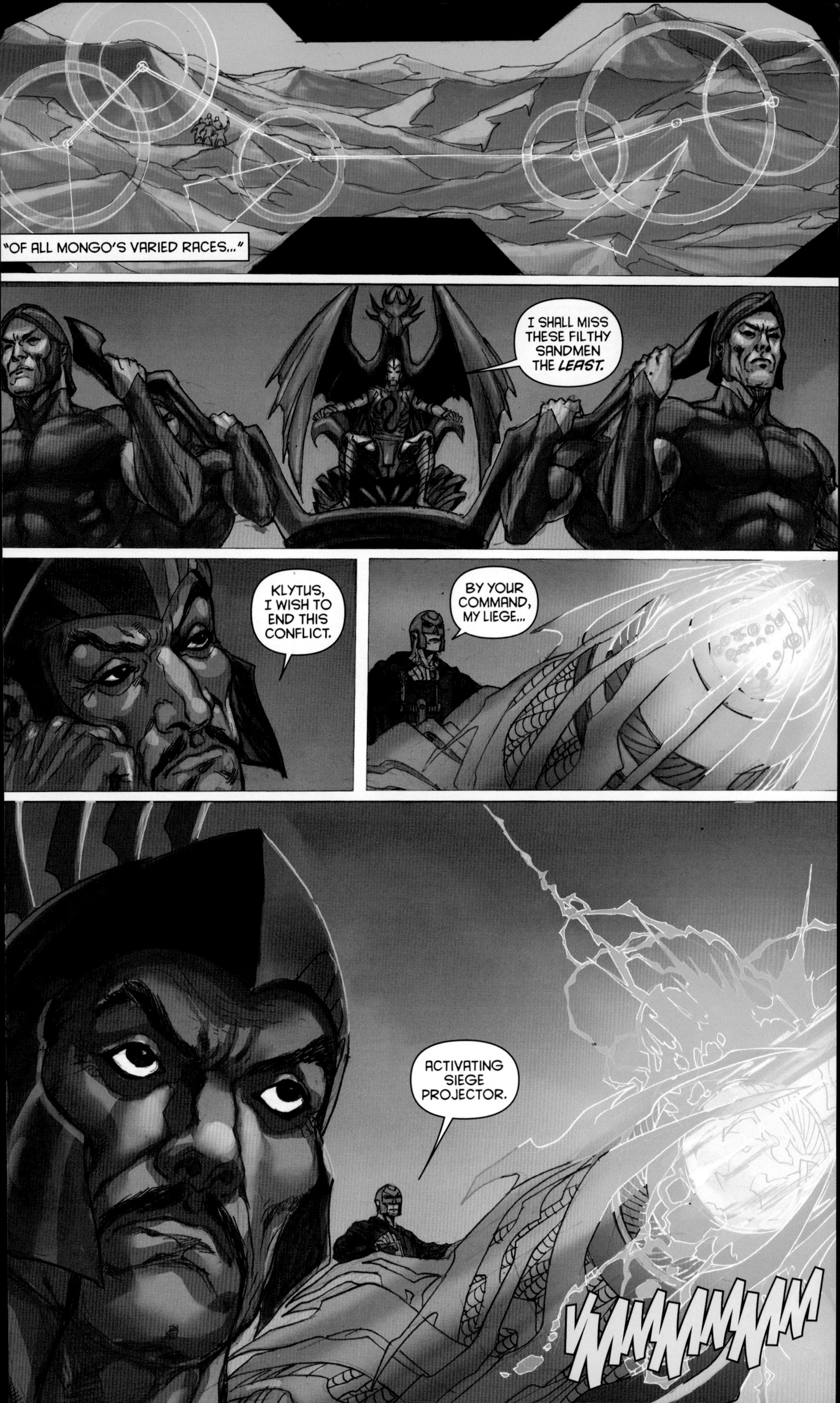
"OF ALL MONGO'S VARIED RACES..."
I SHALL MISS THESE FILTHY SANDMEN THE LEAST.
KLYTUS, I WISH TO END THIS CONFLICT.
BY YOUR COMMAND, MY LIEGE...
ACTIVATING SIEGE PROJECTOR.
VMMMMMM

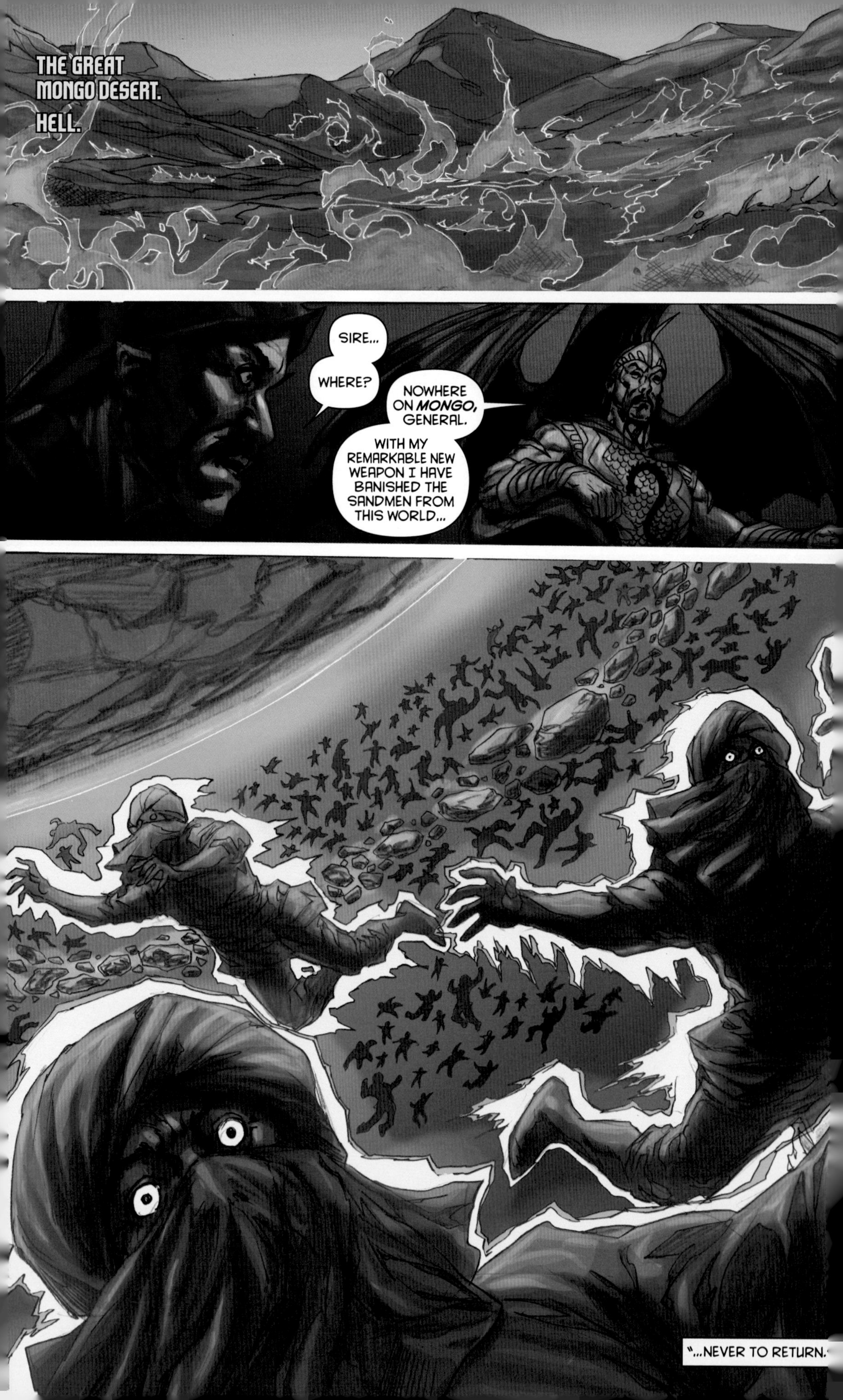
THE GREAT MONGO DESERT.
HELL.
SIRE...
WHERE?
NOWHERE ON MONGO, GENERAL.
WITH MY REMARKABLE NEW WEAPON I HAVE BANISHED THE SANDMEN FROM THIS WORLD...
"...NEVER TO RETURN."

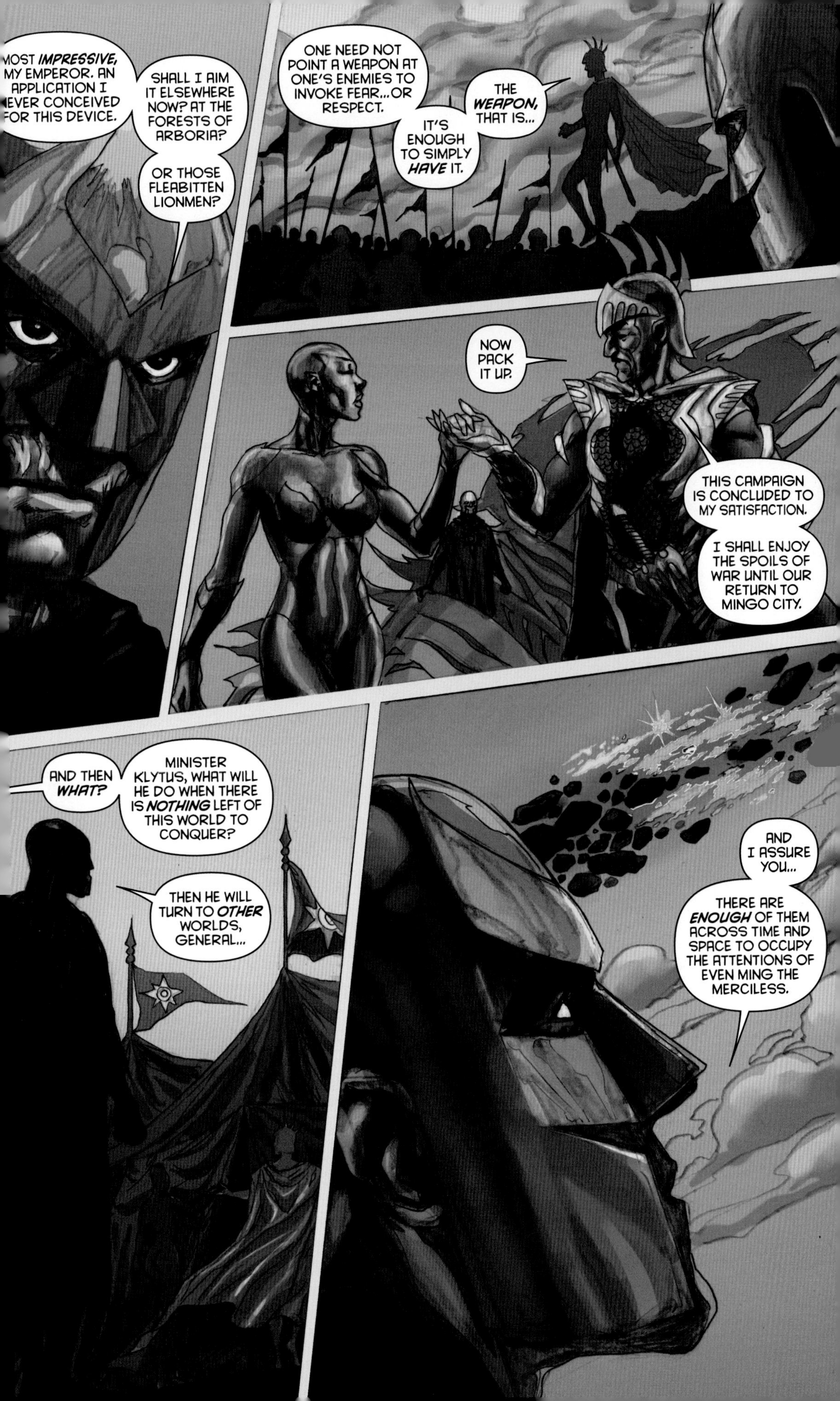

MOST IMPRESSIVE, MY EMPEROR. AN APPLICATION I NEVER CONCEIVED FOR THIS DEVICE.
SHALL I AIM IT ELSEWHERE NOW? AT THE FORESTS OF ARBORIA?
OR THOSE FLEABITTEN LIONMEN?
ONE NEED NOT POINT A WEAPON AT ONE'S ENEMIES TO INVOKE FEAR...OR RESPECT.
IT'S ENOUGH TO SIMPLY HAVE IT.
THE WEAPON, THAT IS...
NOW PACK IT UP.
THIS CAMPAIGN IS CONCLUDED TO MY SATISFACTION.
I SHALL ENJOY THE SPOILS OF WAR UNTIL OUR RETURN TO MINGO CITY.
AND THEN WHAT?
MINISTER KLYTUS, WHAT WILL HE DO WHEN THERE IS NOTHING LEFT OF THIS WORLD TO CONQUER?
THEN HE WILL TURN TO OTHER WORLDS, GENERAL...
AND I ASSURE YOU...
THERE ARE ENOUGH OF THEM ACROSS TIME AND SPACE TO OCCUPY THE ATTENTIONS OF EVEN MING THE MERCILESS.

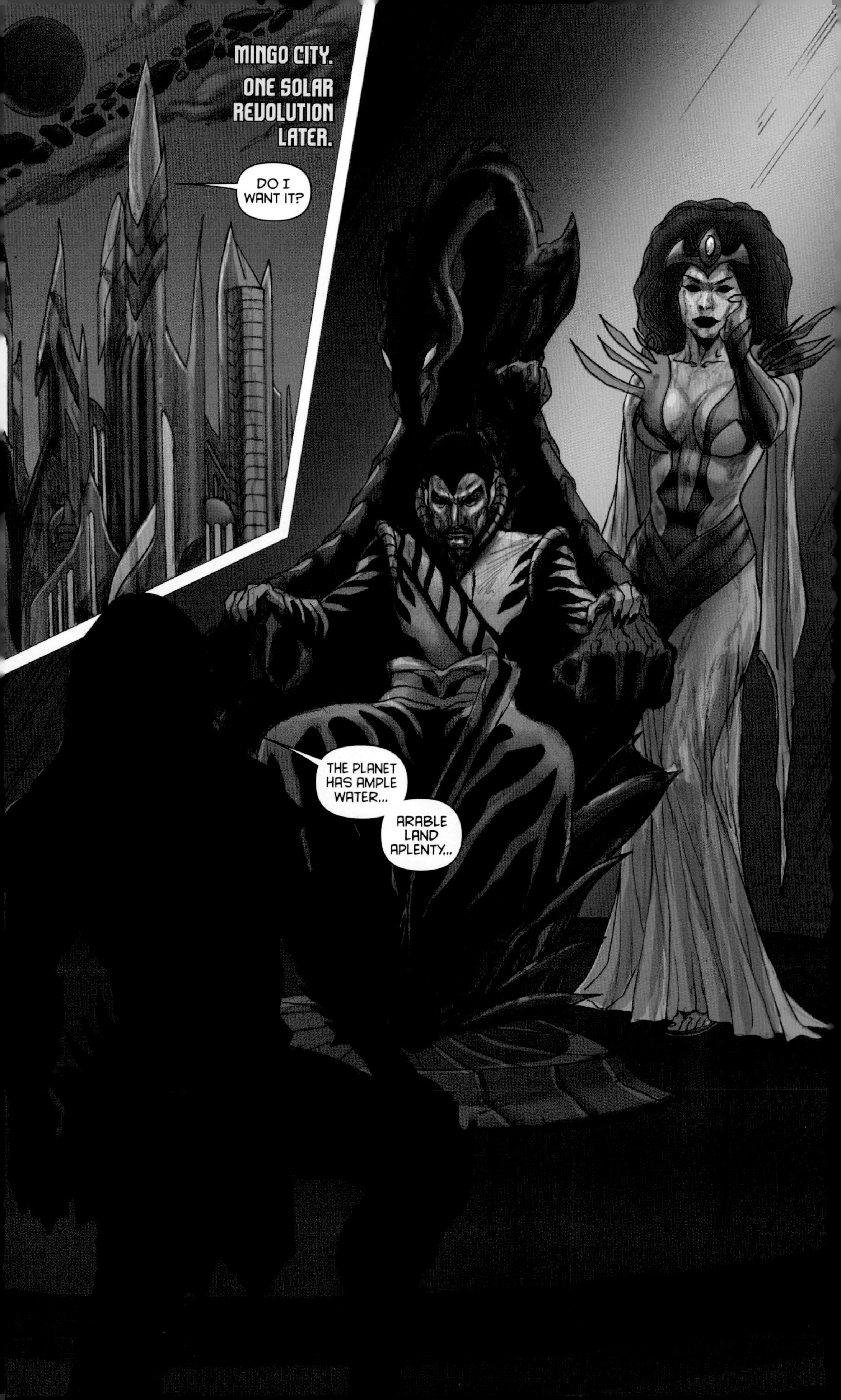
MINGO CITY.
ONE SOLAR REVOLUTION LATER.
DO I WANT IT?
THE PLANET HAS AMPLE WATER...
ARABLE LAND APLENTY...

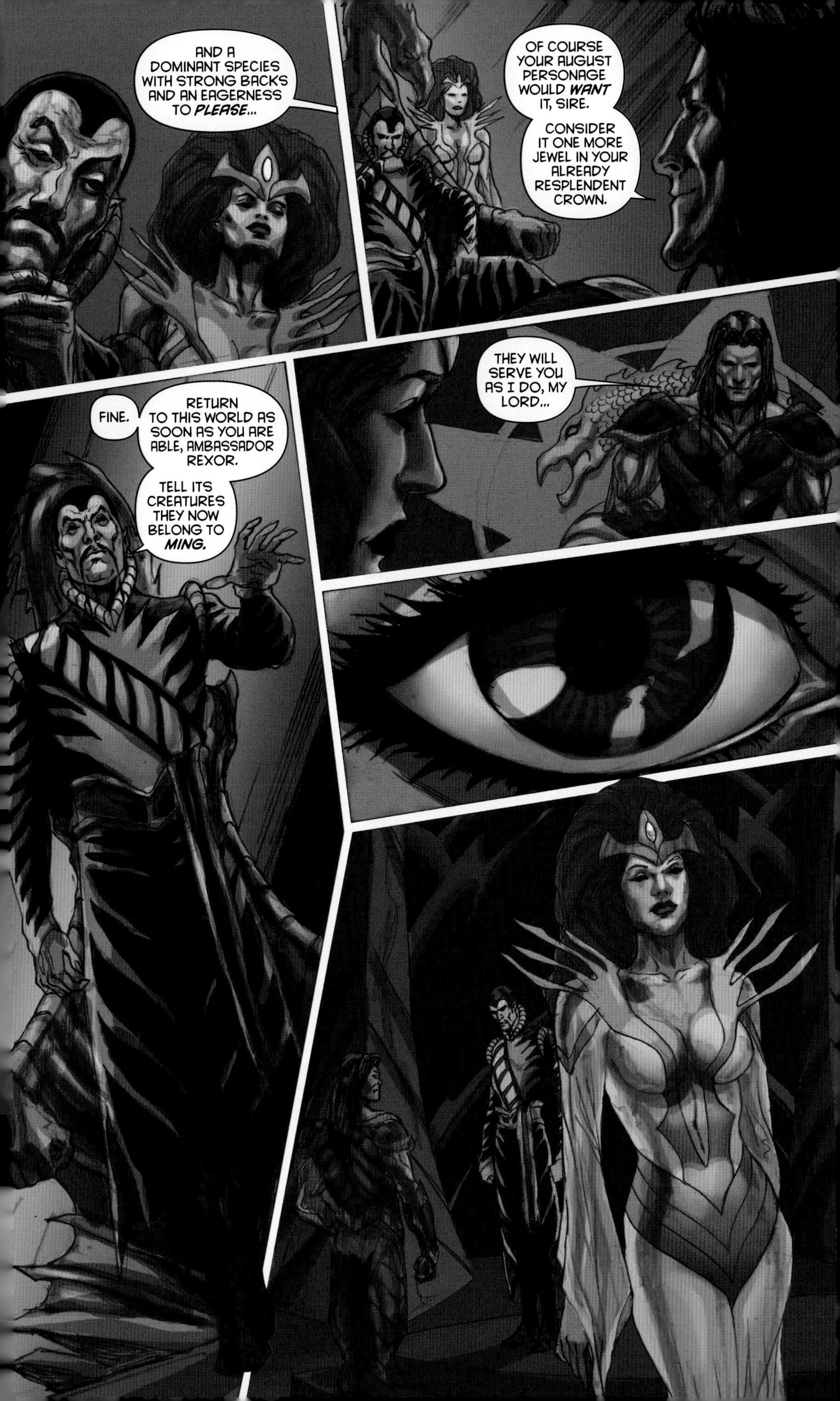
AND A DOMINANT SPECIES WITH STRONG BACKS AND AN EAGERNESS TO *PLEASE*...
OF COURSE YOUR AUGUST PERSONAGE WOULD *WANT* IT, SIRE.
CONSIDER IT ONE MORE JEWEL IN YOUR ALREADY RESPLENDENT CROWN.
FINE.
RETURN TO THIS WORLD AS SOON AS YOU ARE ABLE, AMBASSADOR REXOR.
TELL ITS CREATURES THEY NOW BELONG TO *MING.*
THEY WILL SERVE YOU AS I DO, MY LORD...

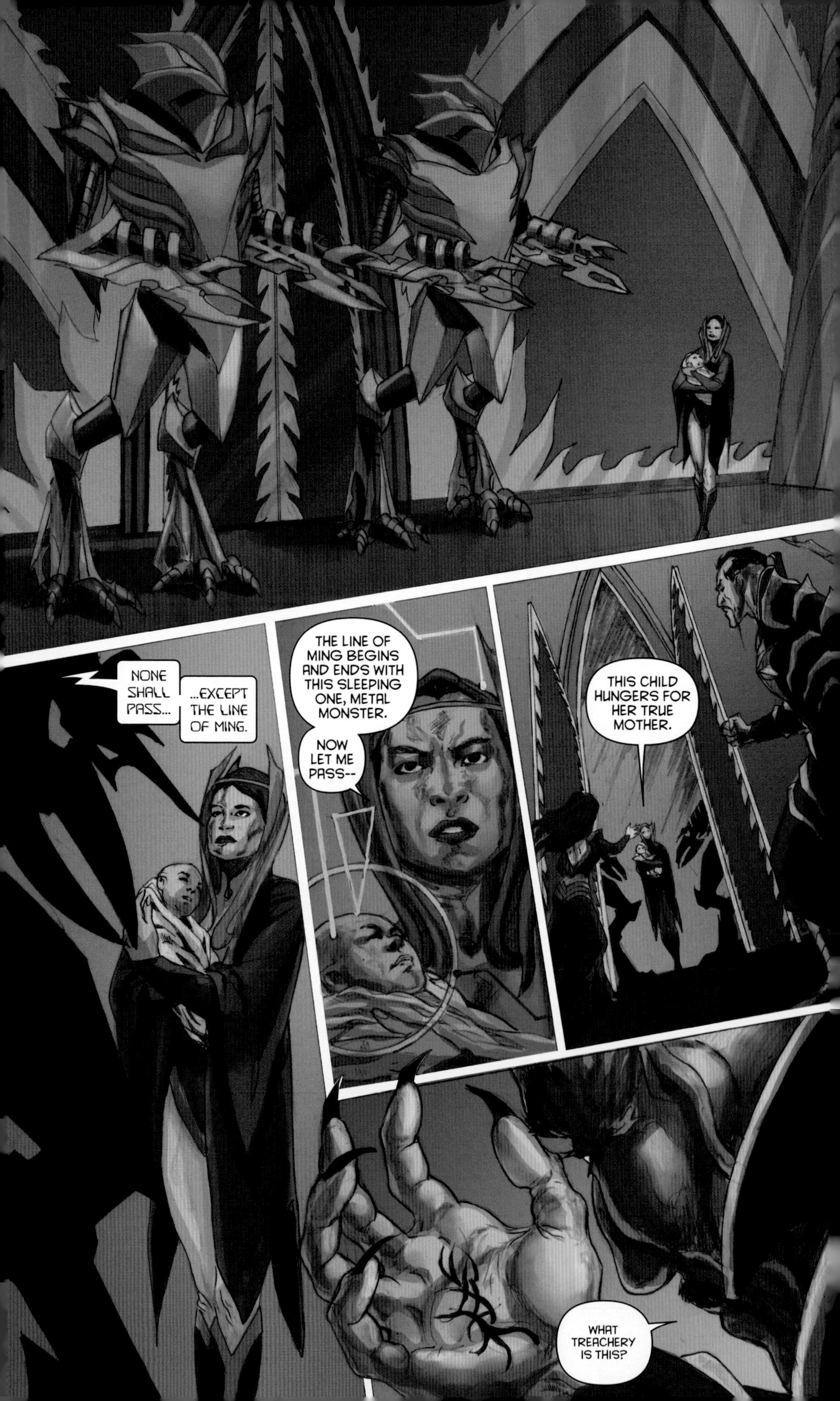
NONE SHALL PASS...
...EXCEPT THE LINE OF MING.
THE LINE OF MING BEGINS AND ENDS WITH THIS SLEEPING ONE, METAL MONSTER.
NOW LET ME PASS--
THIS CHILD HUNGERS FOR HER TRUE MOTHER.
WHAT TREACHERY IS THIS?

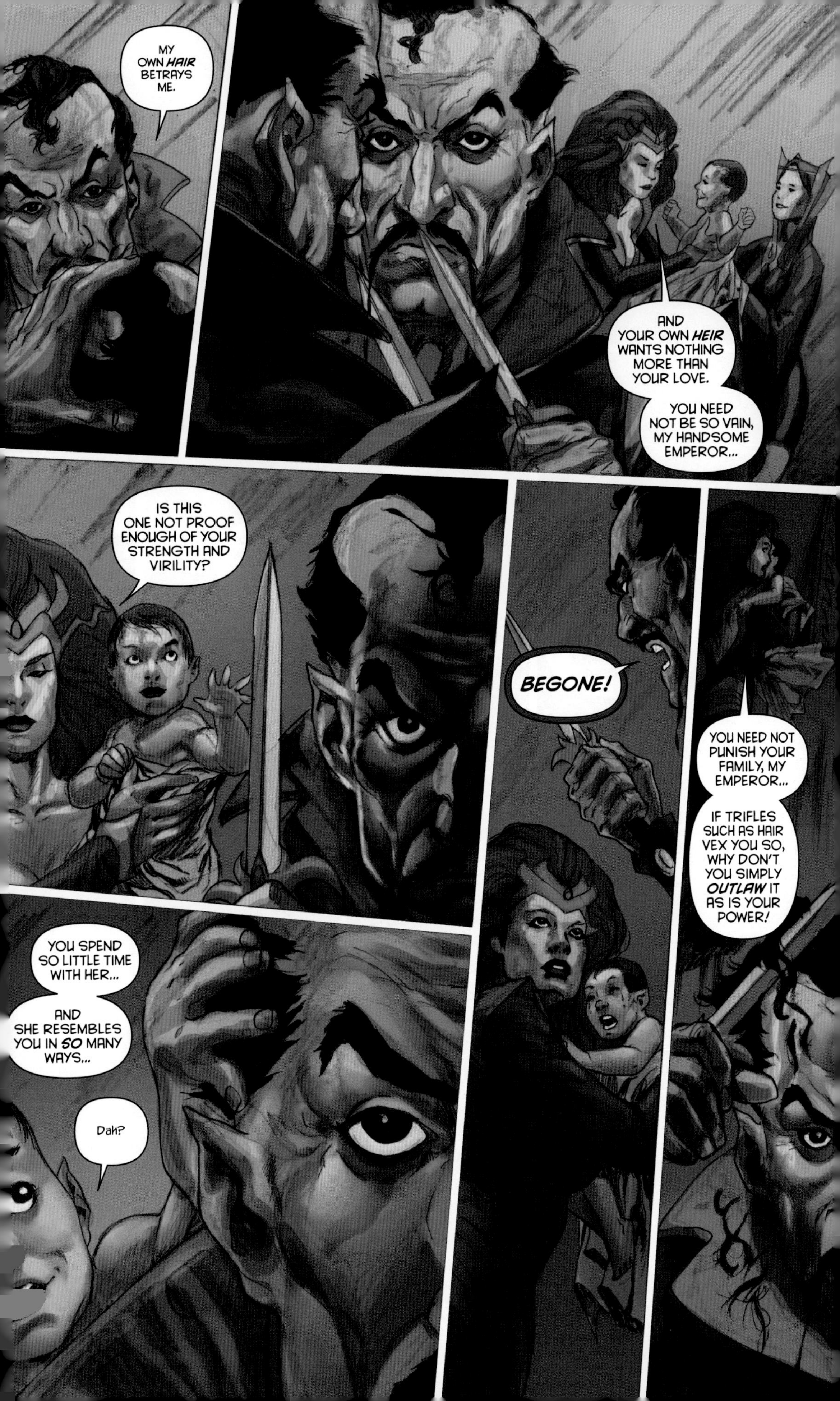
MY OWN HAIR BETRAYS ME.
AND YOUR OWN HEIR WANTS NOTHING MORE THAN YOUR LOVE.
YOU NEED NOT BE SO VAIN, MY HANDSOME EMPEROR...
IS THIS ONE NOT PROOF ENOUGH OF YOUR STRENGTH AND VIRILITY?
BEGONE!
YOU NEED NOT PUNISH YOUR FAMILY, MY EMPEROR...
IF TRIFLES SUCH AS HAIR VEX YOU SO, WHY DON'T YOU SIMPLY OUTLAW IT AS IS YOUR POWER!
YOU SPEND SO LITTLE TIME WITH HER...
AND SHE RESEMBLES YOU IN SO MANY WAYS...
Dah?

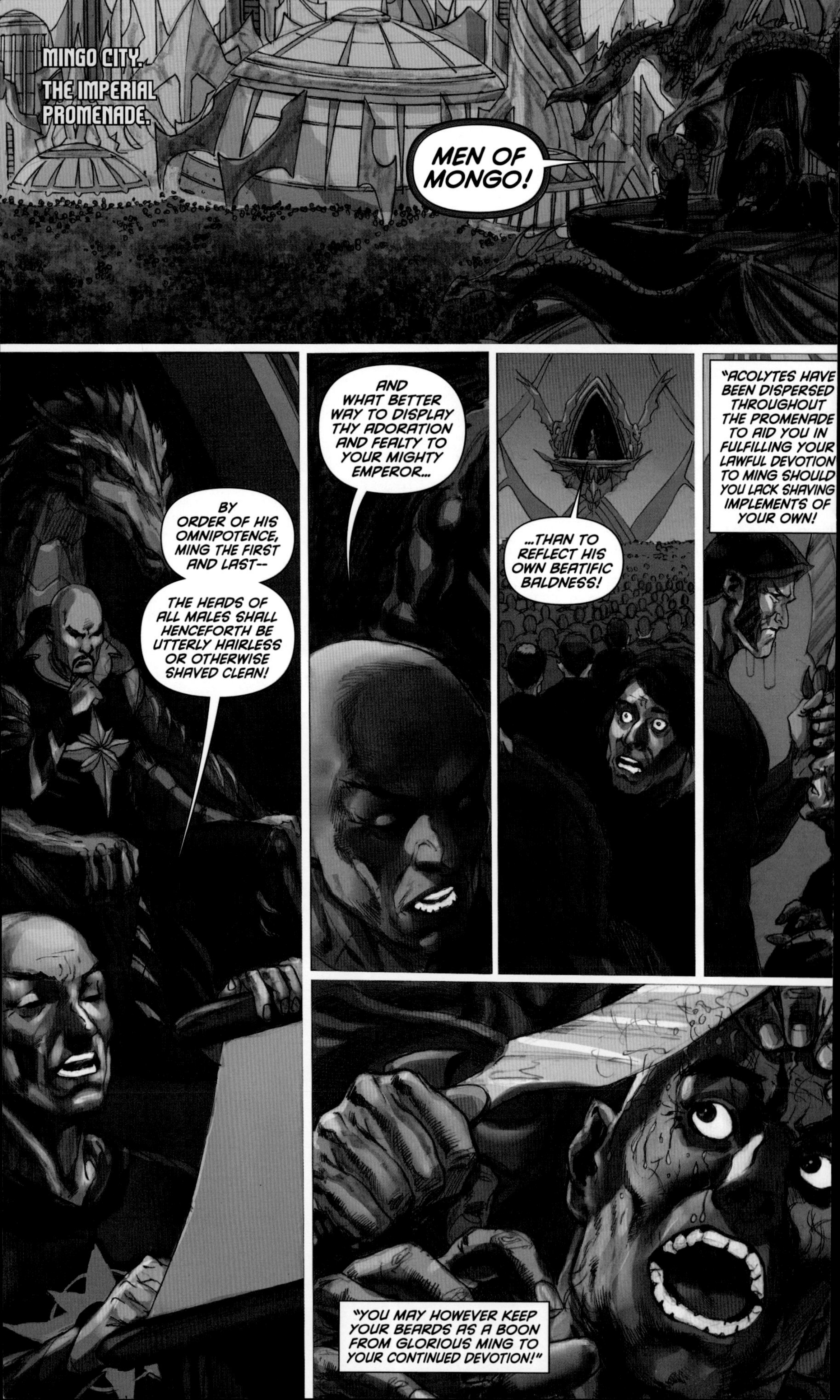

MINGO CITY.
THE IMPERIAL PROMENADE.
MEN OF MONGO!
BY ORDER OF HIS OMNIPOTENCE, MING THE FIRST AND LAST--
THE HEADS OF ALL MALES SHALL HENCEFORTH BE UTTERLY HAIRLESS OR OTHERWISE SHAVED CLEAN!
AND WHAT BETTER WAY TO DISPLAY THY ADORATION AND FEALTY TO YOUR MIGHTY EMPEROR...
...THAN TO REFLECT HIS OWN BEATIFIC BALDNESS!
"ACOLYTES HAVE BEEN DISPERSED THROUGHOUT THE PROMENADE TO AID YOU IN FULFILLING YOUR LAWFUL DEVOTION TO MING SHOULD YOU LACK SHAVING IMPLEMENTS OF YOUR OWN!
"YOU MAY HOWEVER KEEP YOUR BEARDS AS A BOON FROM GLORIOUS MING TO YOUR CONTINUED DEVOTION!"

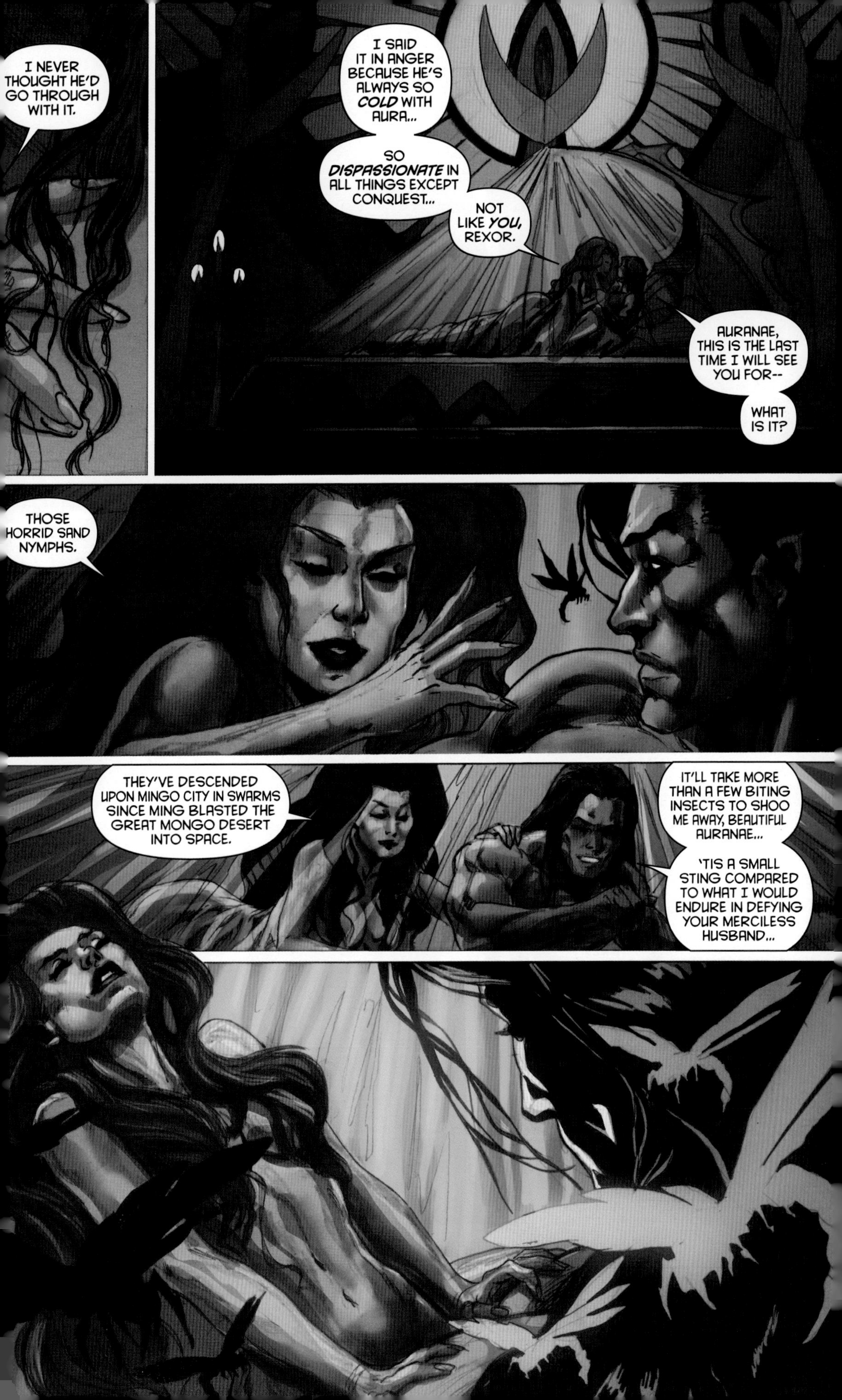
I NEVER THOUGHT HE'D GO THROUGH WITH IT.
I SAID IT IN ANGER BECAUSE HE'S ALWAYS SO COLD WITH AURA...
SO DISPASSIONATE IN ALL THINGS EXCEPT CONQUEST...
NOT LIKE YOU, REXOR.
AURANAE, THIS IS THE LAST TIME I WILL SEE YOU FOR--
WHAT IS IT?
THOSE HORRID SAND NYMPHS.
THEY'VE DESCENDED UPON MINGO CITY IN SWARMS SINCE MING BLASTED THE GREAT MONGO DESERT INTO SPACE.
IT'LL TAKE MORE THAN A FEW BITING INSECTS TO SHOO ME AWAY, BEAUTIFUL AURANAE...
'TIS A SMALL STING COMPARED TO WHAT I WOULD ENDURE IN DEFYING YOUR MERCILESS HUSBAND...

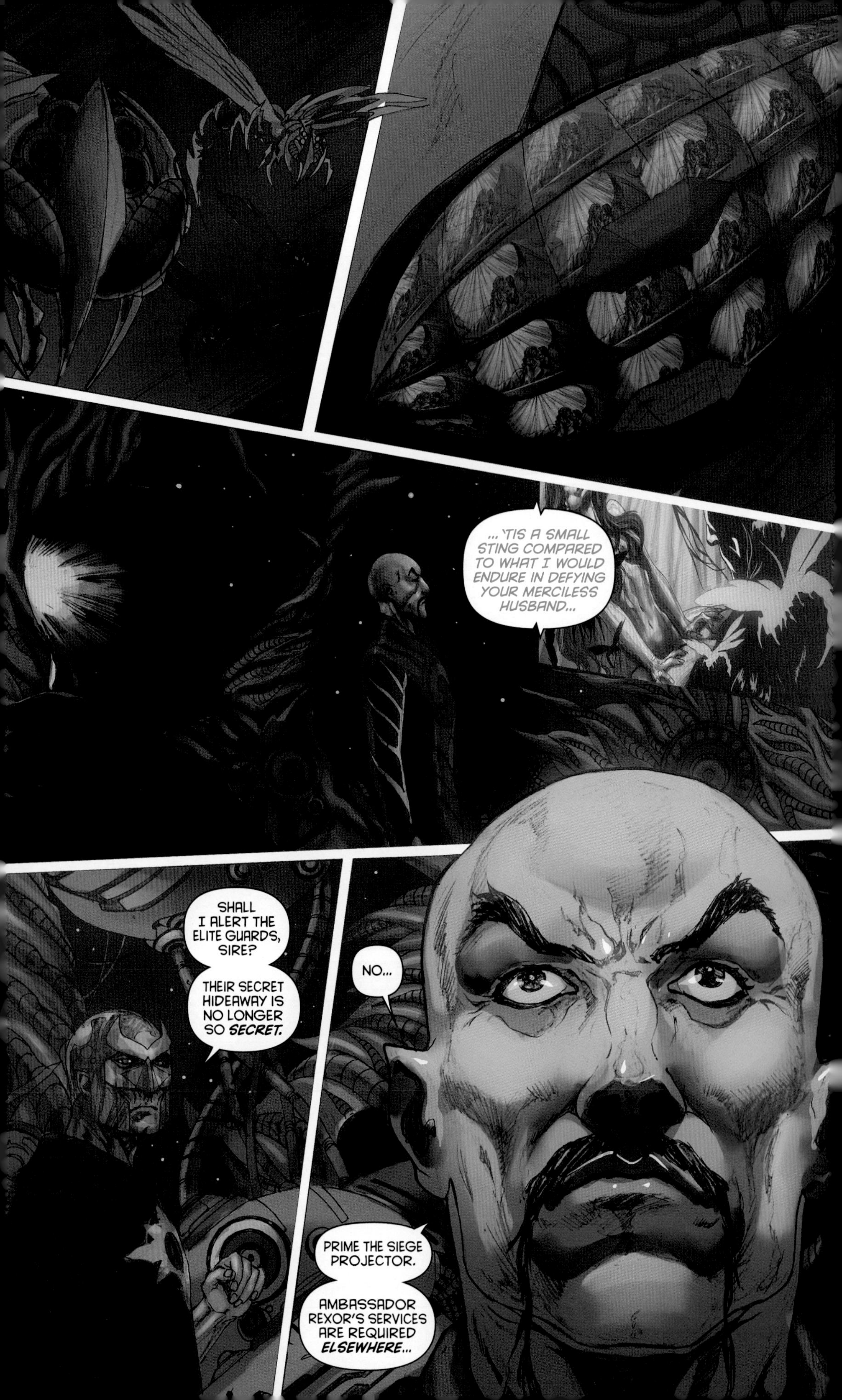
...'TIS A SMALL STING COMPARED TO WHAT I WOULD ENDURE IN DEFYING YOUR MERCILESS HUSBAND...
SHALL I ALERT THE ELITE GUARDS, SIRE?
THEIR SECRET HIDEAWAY IS NO LONGER SO *SECRET.*
NO...
PRIME THE SIEGE PROJECTOR.
AMBASSADOR REXOR'S SERVICES ARE REQUIRED *ELSEWHERE*...

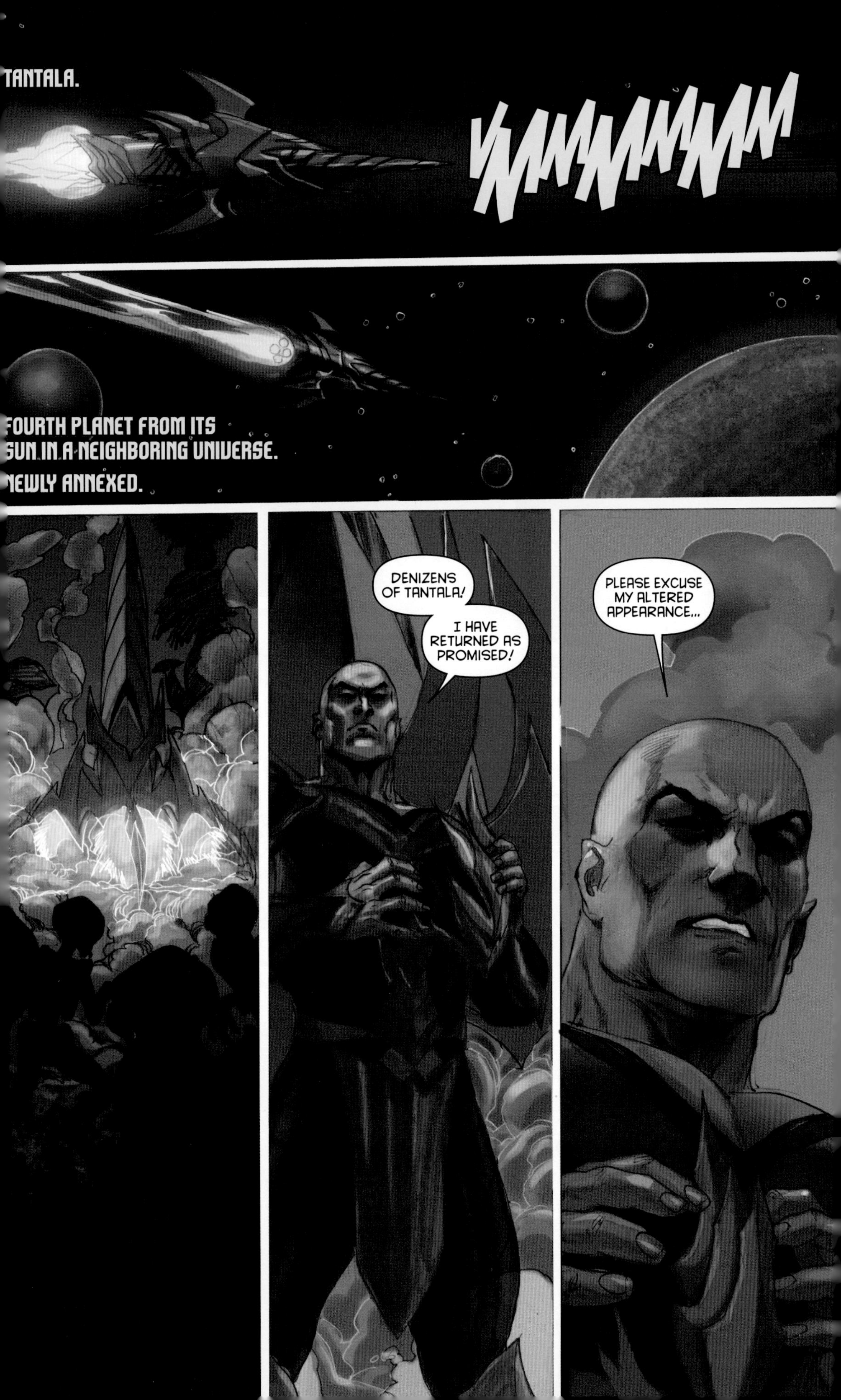

TANTALA.
VWAWAWAWAWAM
FOURTH PLANET FROM ITS SUN IN A NEIGHBORING UNIVERSE.
NEWLY ANNEXED.
DENIZENS OF TANTALA!
I HAVE RETURNED AS PROMISED!
PLEASE EXCUSE MY ALTERED APPEARANCE...

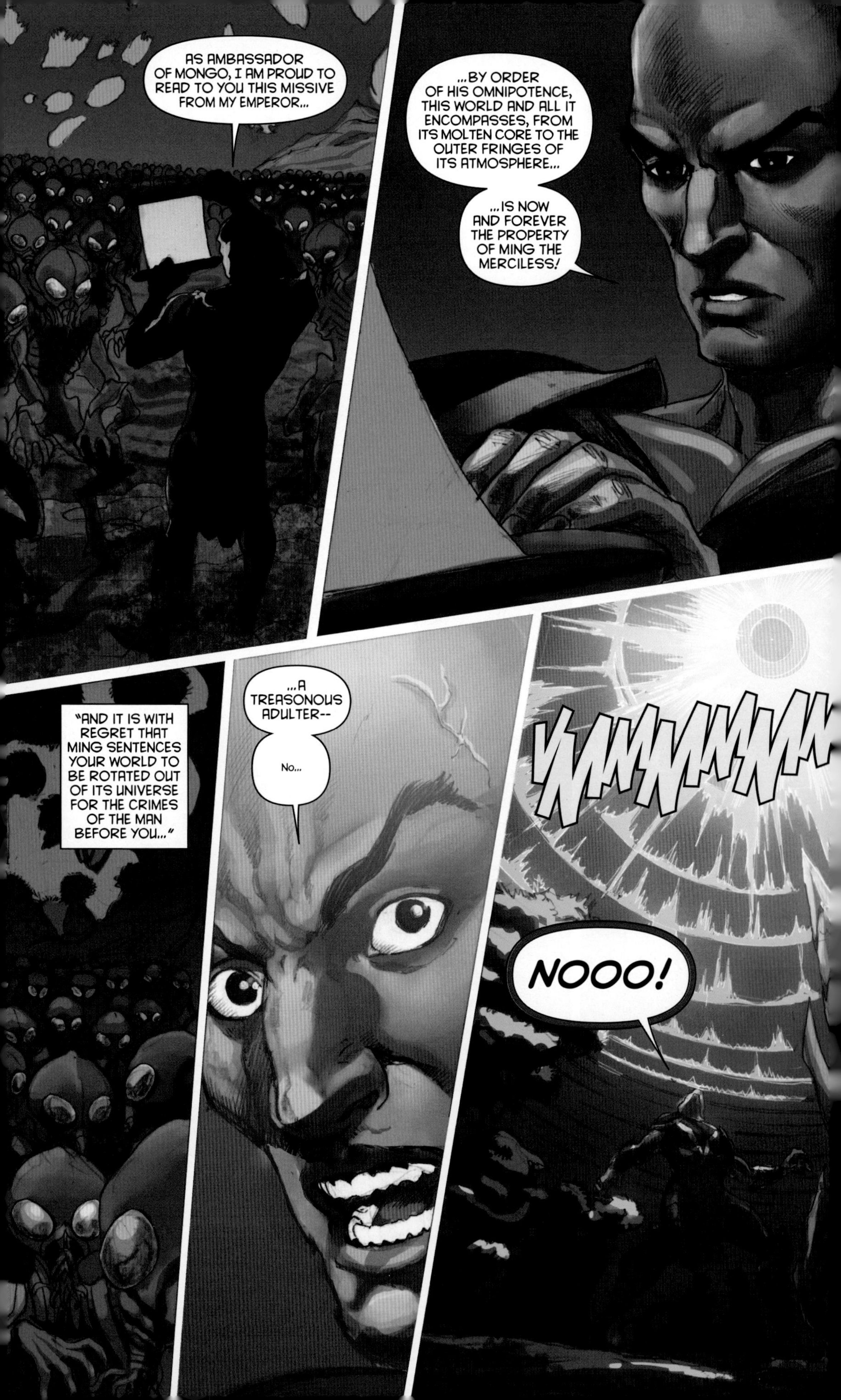
AS AMBASSADOR OF MONGO, I AM PROUD TO READ TO YOU THIS MISSIVE FROM MY EMPEROR...
...BY ORDER OF HIS OMNIPOTENCE, THIS WORLD AND ALL IT ENCOMPASSES, FROM ITS MOLTEN CORE TO THE OUTER FRINGES OF ITS ATMOSPHERE...
...IS NOW AND FOREVER THE PROPERTY OF MING THE MERCILESS!
"AND IT IS WITH REGRET THAT MING SENTENCES YOUR WORLD TO BE ROTATED OUT OF ITS UNIVERSE FOR THE CRIMES OF THE MAN BEFORE YOU..."
...A TREASONOUS ADULTER--
No...
VMMMMMMMM
NOOO!

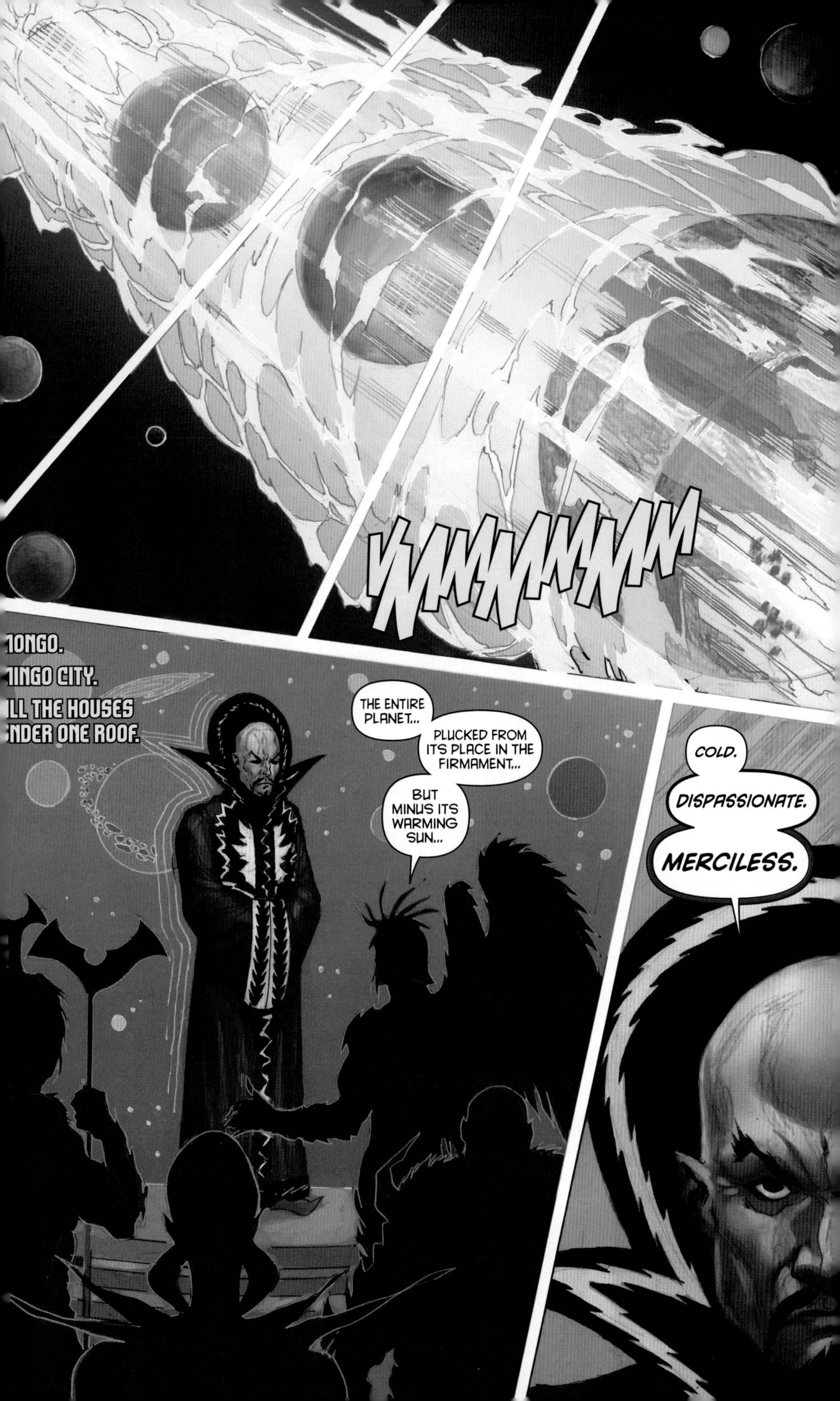
VMMMMMMM
ʼIONGO.
ʼIINGO CITY.
LL THE HOUSES
NDER ONE ROOF.
THE ENTIRE PLANET...
PLUCKED FROM ITS PLACE IN THE FIRMAMENT...
BUT MINUS ITS WARMING SUN...
COLD.
DISPASSIONATE.
MERCILESS.

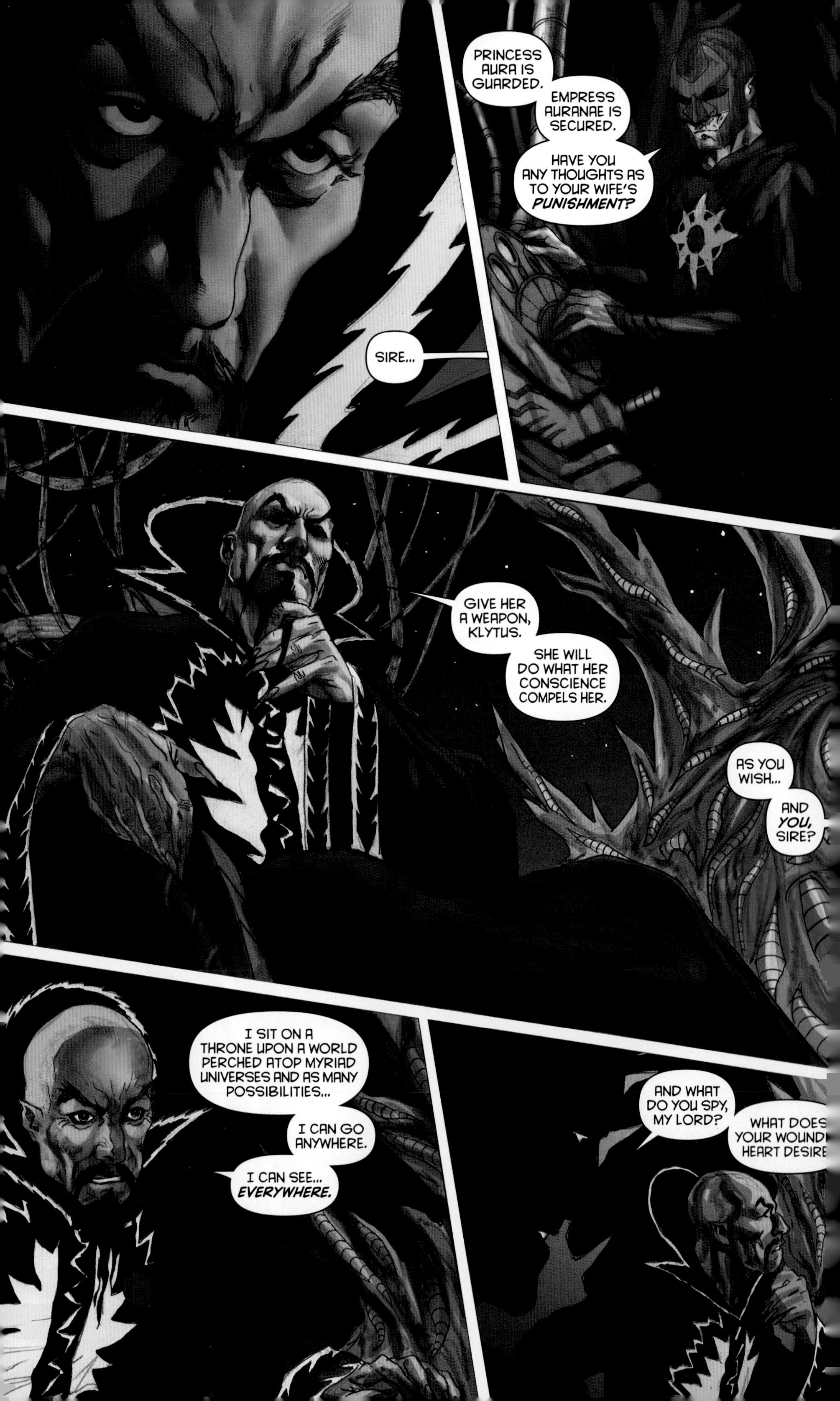
SIRE...
PRINCESS AURA IS GUARDED.
EMPRESS AURANAE IS SECURED.
HAVE YOU ANY THOUGHTS AS TO YOUR WIFE'S *PUNISHMENT?*
GIVE HER A WEAPON, KLYTUS.
SHE WILL DO WHAT HER CONSCIENCE COMPELS HER.
AS YOU WISH...
AND *YOU,* SIRE?
I SIT ON A THRONE UPON A WORLD PERCHED ATOP MYRIAD UNIVERSES AND AS MANY POSSIBILITIES...
I CAN GO ANYWHERE.
I CAN SEE... *EVERYWHERE.*
AND WHAT DO YOU SPY, MY LORD?
WHAT DOES YOUR WOUND HEART DESIRE

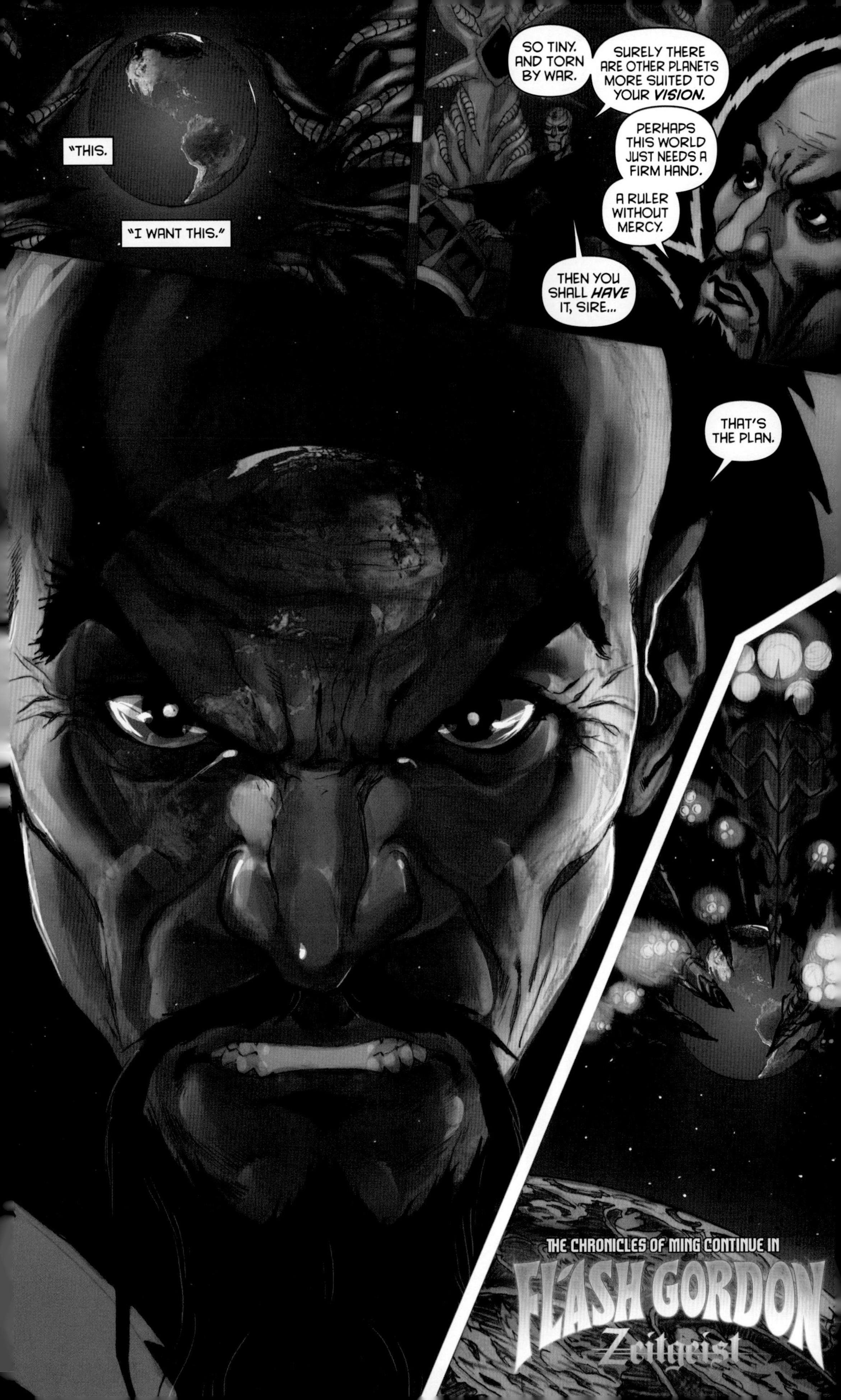

"THIS.
"I WANT THIS."
SO TINY. AND TORN BY WAR.
SURELY THERE ARE OTHER PLANETS MORE SUITED TO YOUR VISION.
PERHAPS THIS WORLD JUST NEEDS A FIRM HAND.
A RULER WITHOUT MERCY.
THEN YOU SHALL HAVE IT, SIRE...
THAT'S THE PLAN.
THE CHRONICLES OF MING CONTINUE IN
FLASH GORDON
Zeitgeist

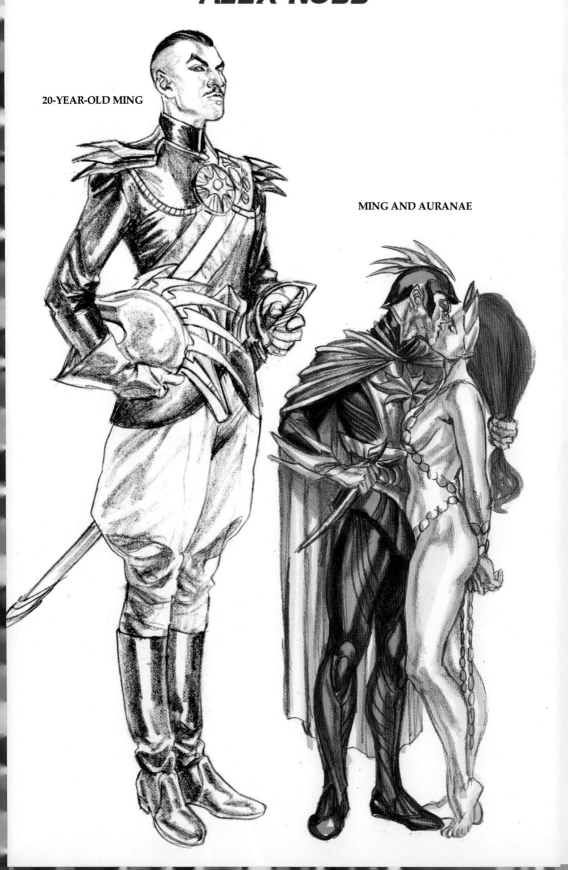

CHARACTER DESIGNS AND SKETCHES BY

ALEX ROSS

20-YEAR-OLD MING

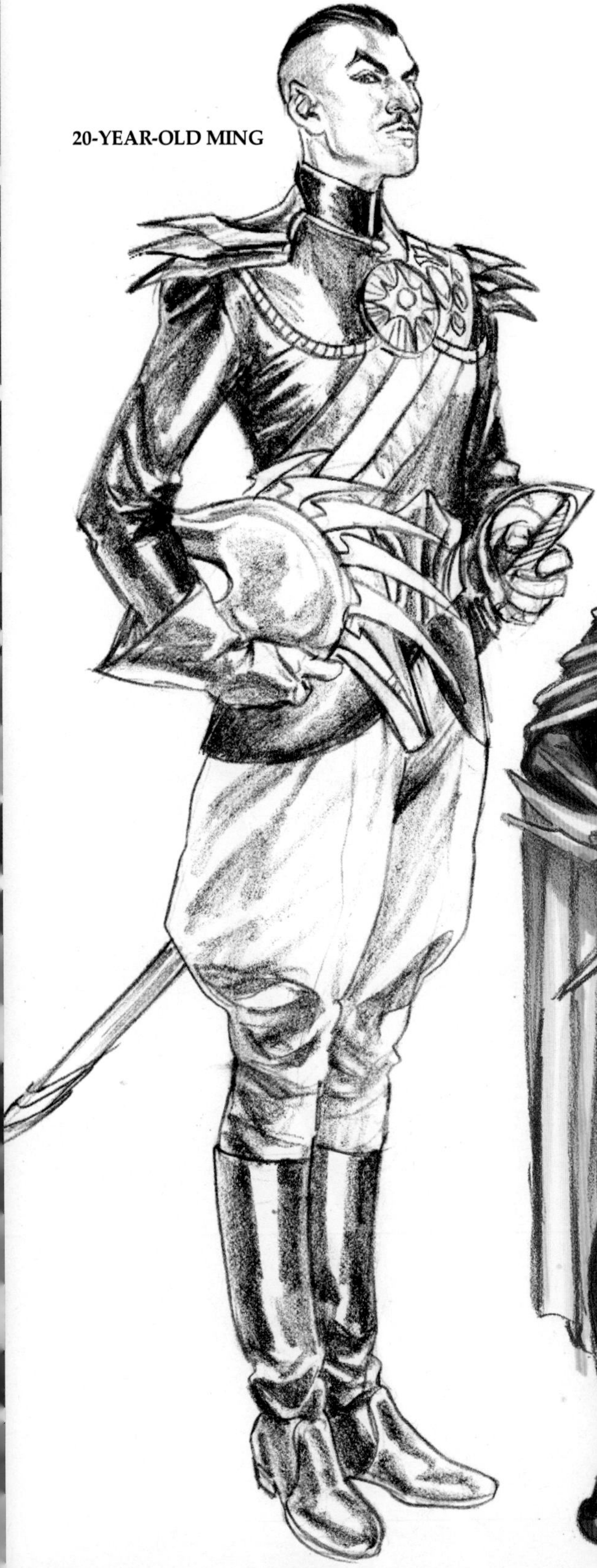

MING AND AURANAE

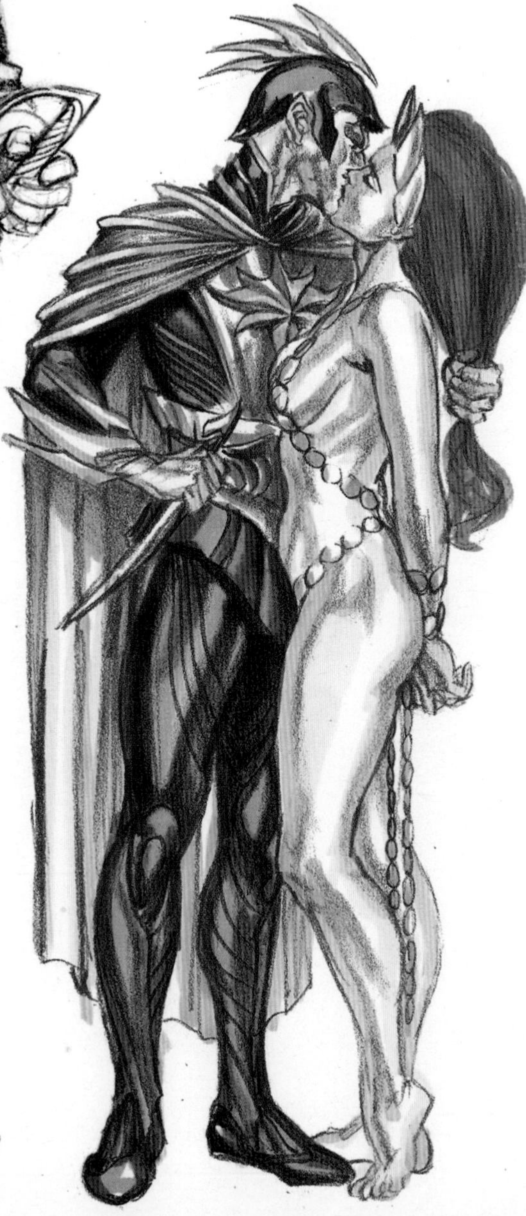

MING'S DRAGON ARMOR

ARMOR FOR MING'S SOLDIERS

THE SANDMEN

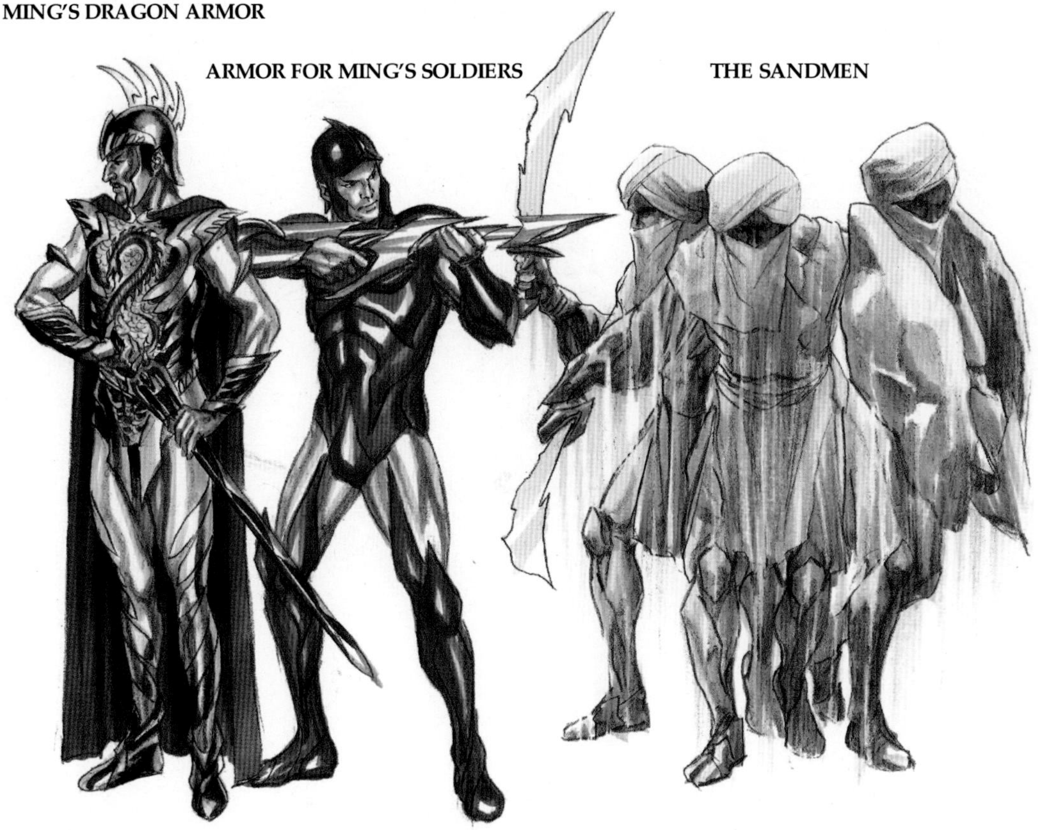

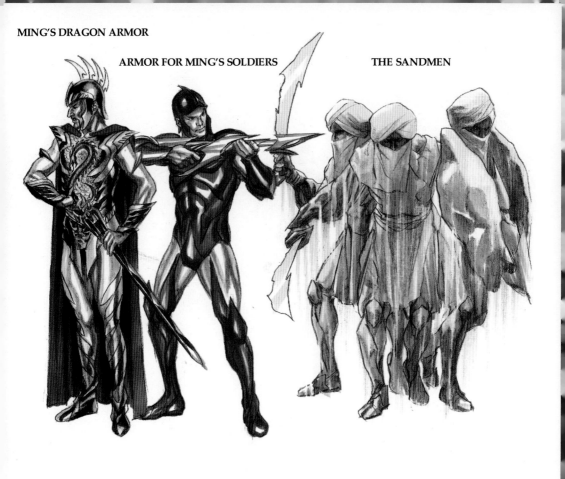

MING AND AURANAE (PREGNANT)

KRANG'S NIGHTCLOTHES

KLYTUS WITH NEW HELMET

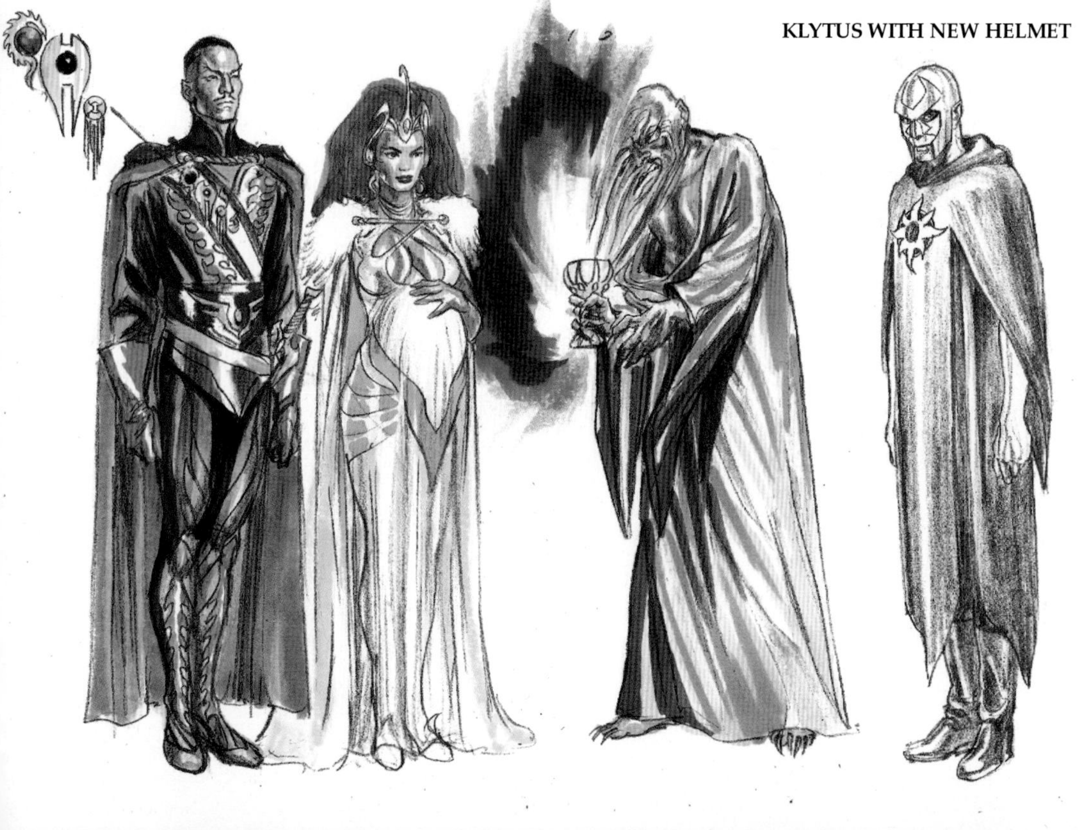

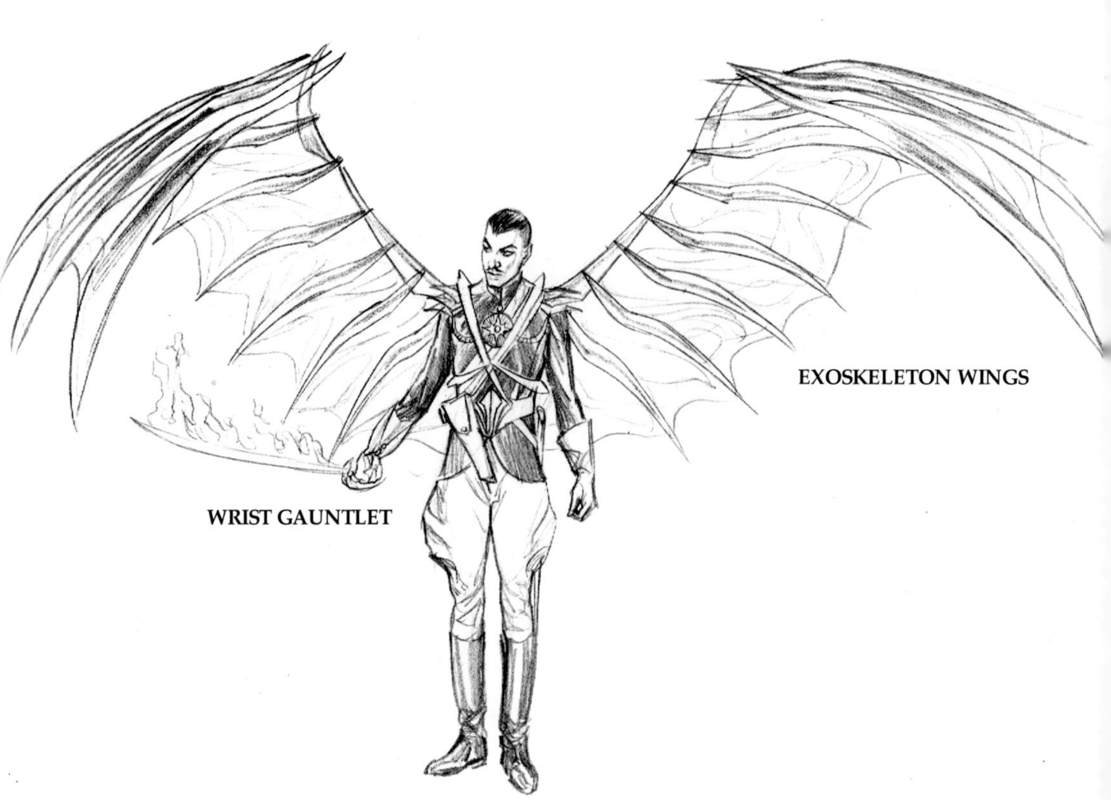
EXOSKELETON WINGS
WRIST GAUNTLET

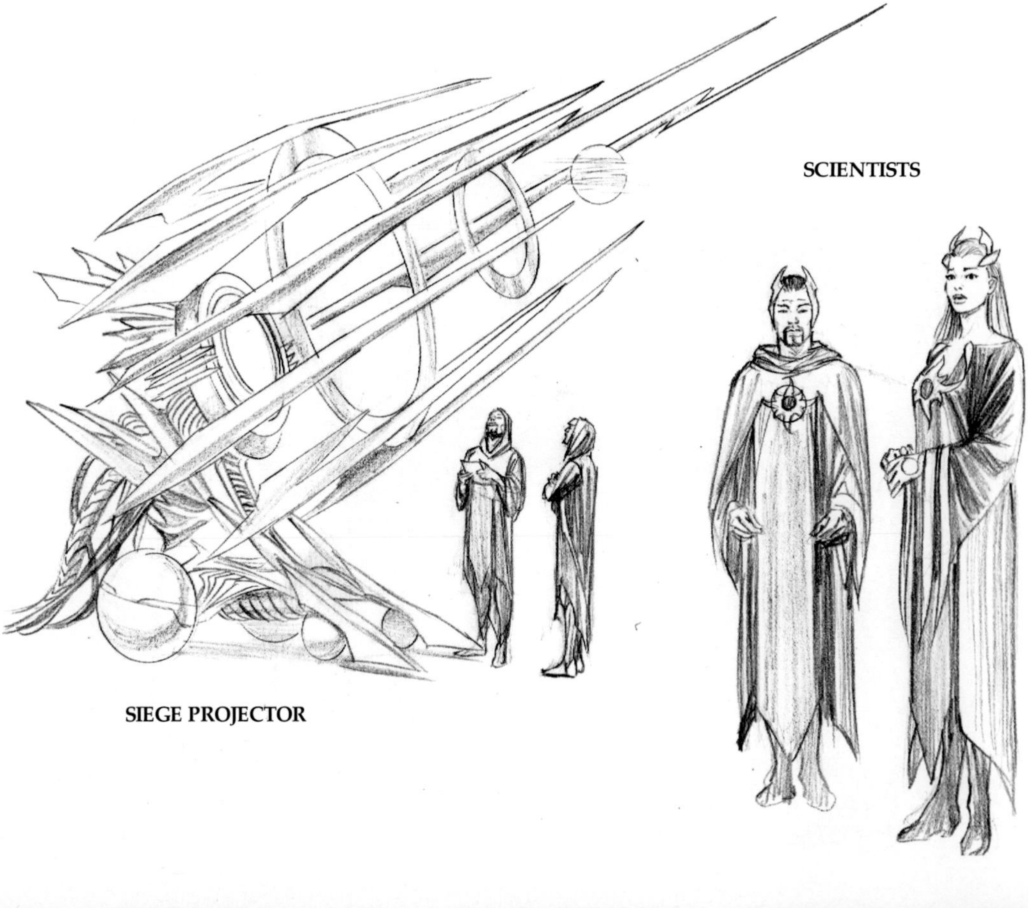
SCIENTISTS
SIEGE PROJECTOR

EARLY MING ROUGHS

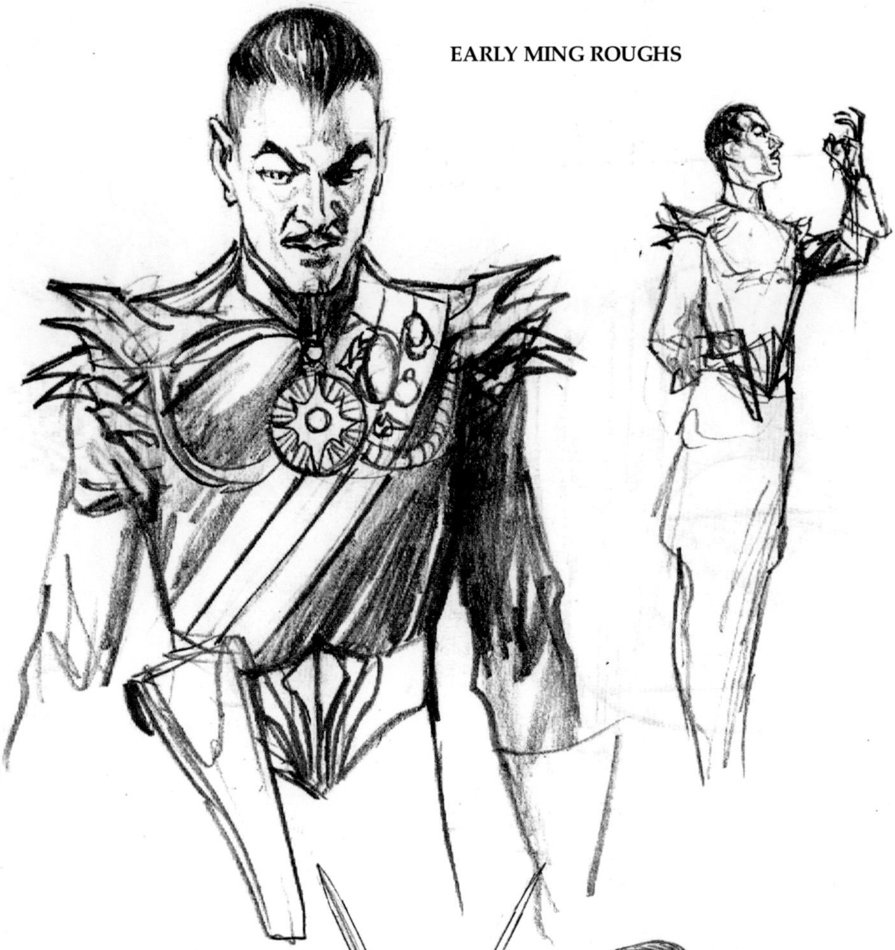

12-YEAR-OLD MING
WITH LONG BRAID

KILLIK

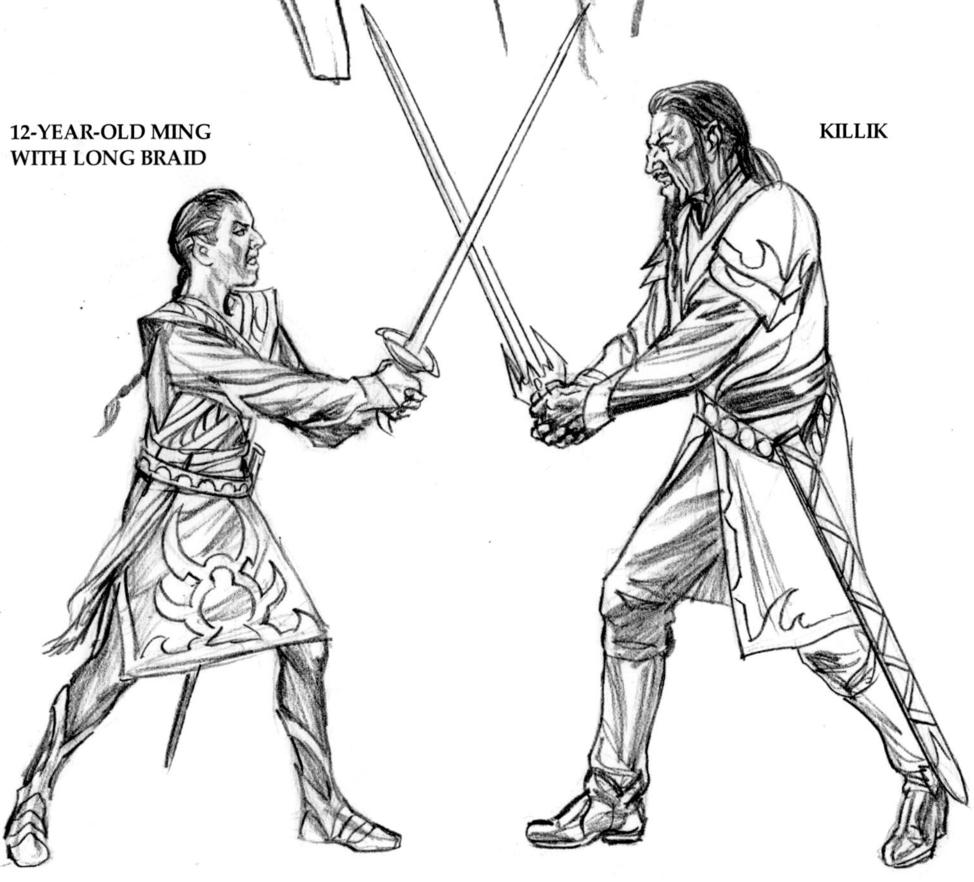

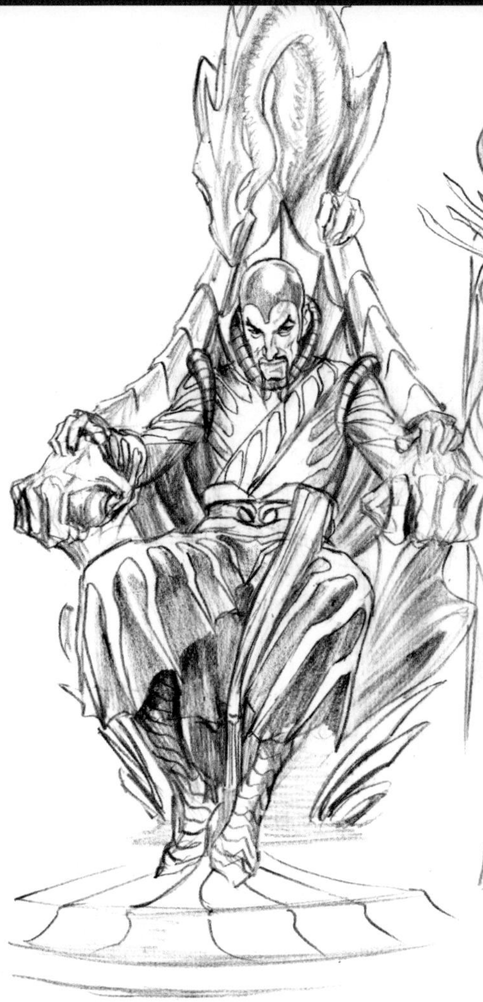

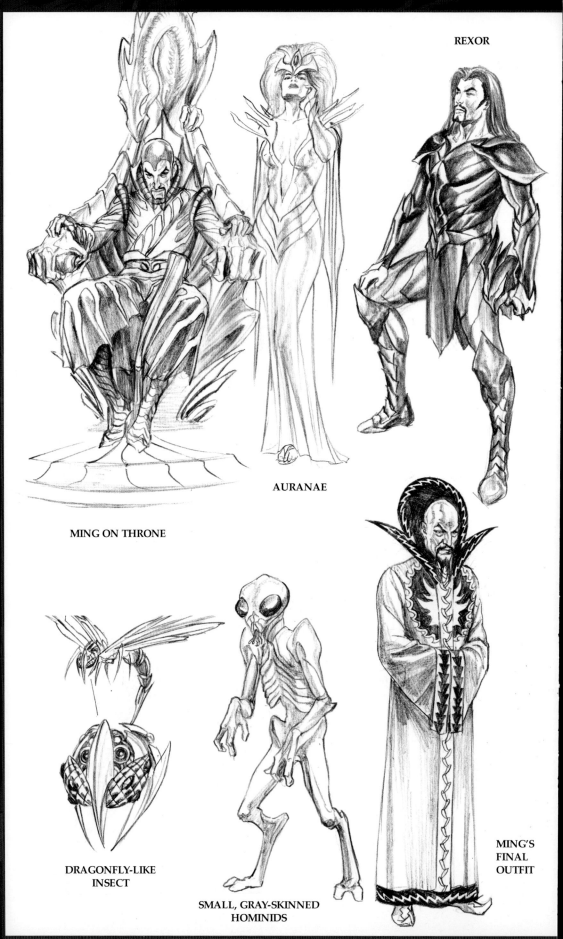

MING ON THRONE

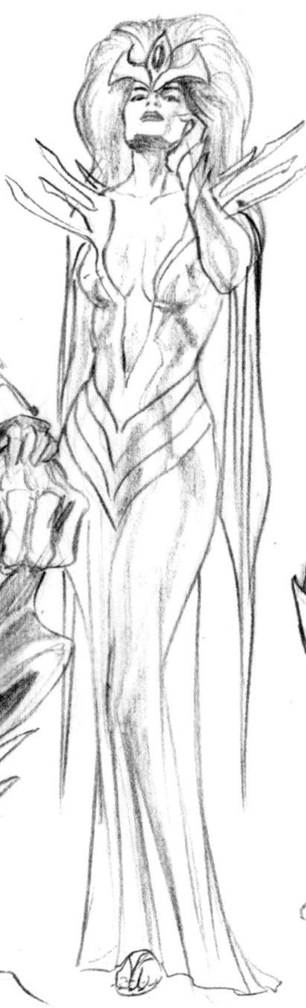

AURANAE

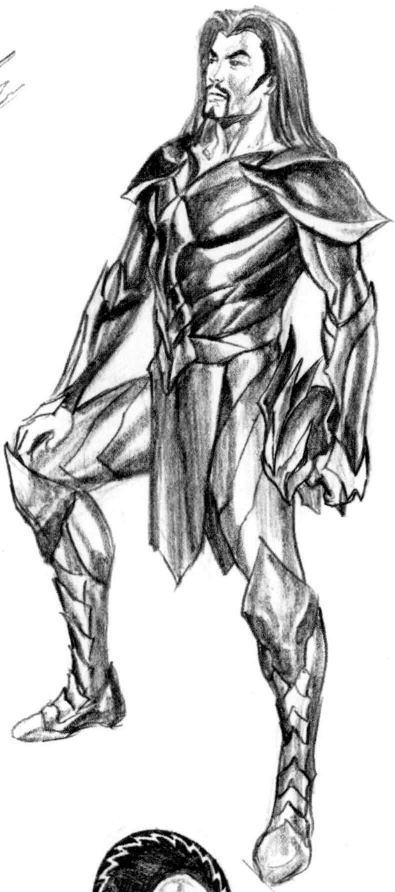

REXOR

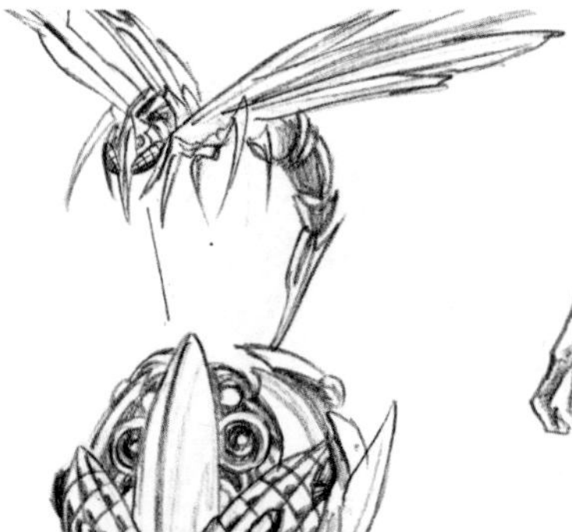

DRAGONFLY-LIKE INSECT

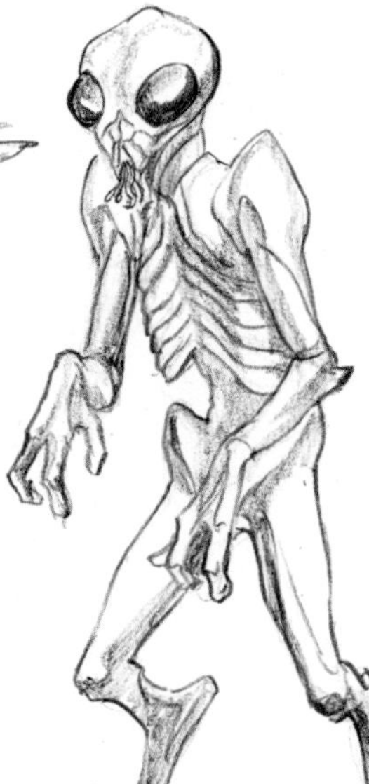

SMALL, GRAY-SKINNED HOMINIDS

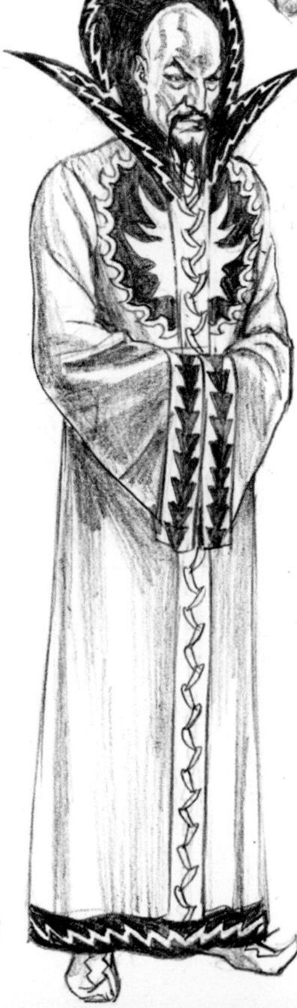

MING'S FINAL OUTFIT

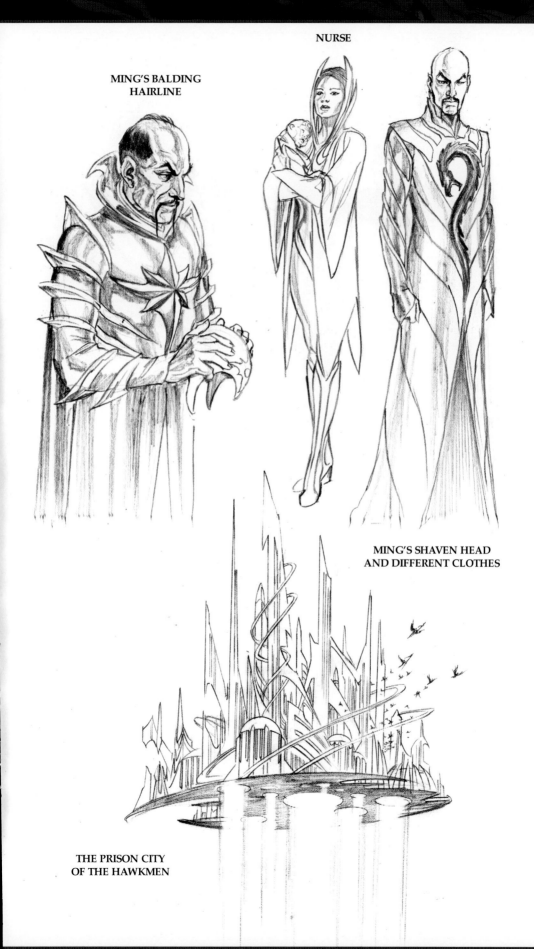

MING'S BALDING HAIRLINE

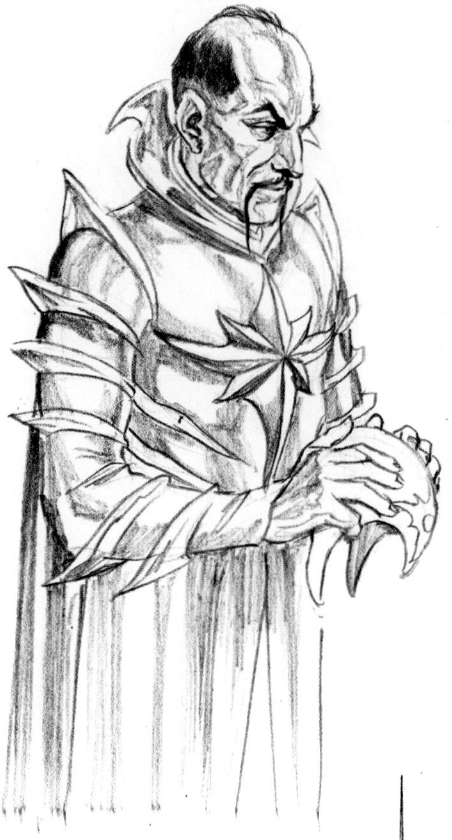

NURSE

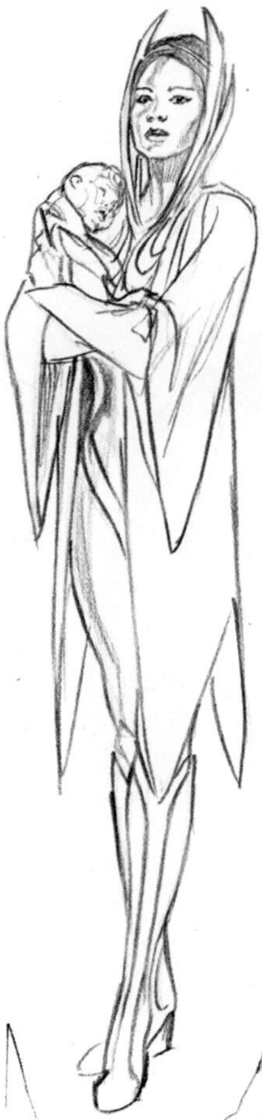

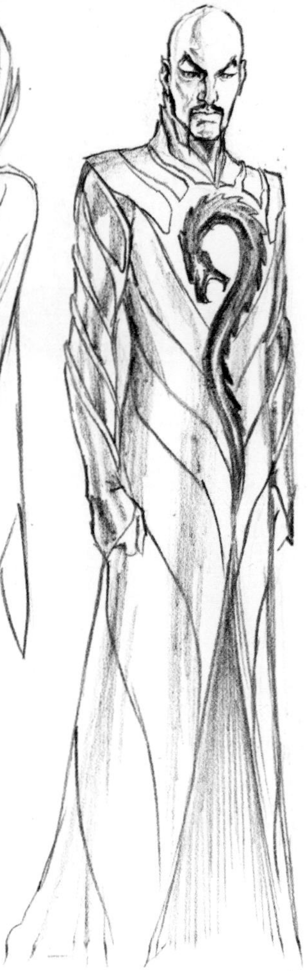

MING'S SHAVEN HEAD AND DIFFERENT CLOTHES

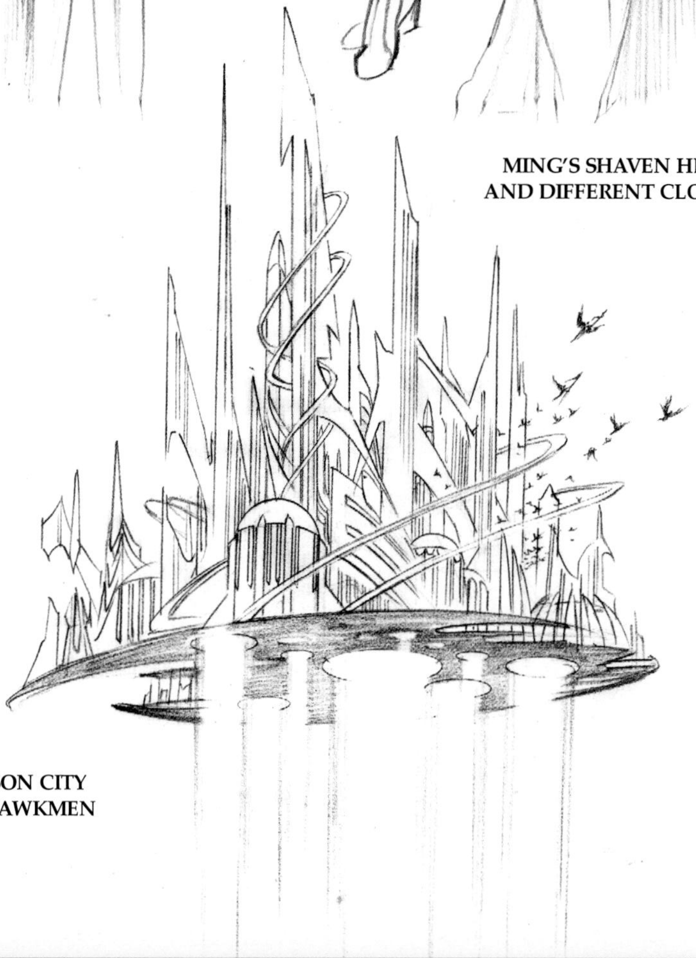

THE PRISON CITY OF THE HAWKMEN

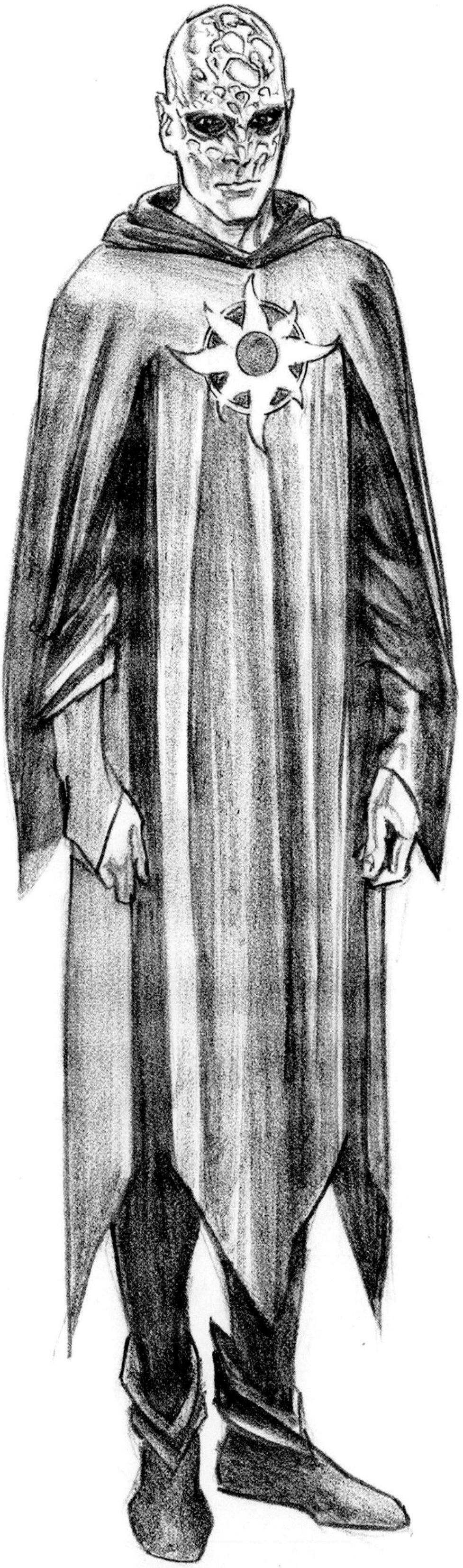

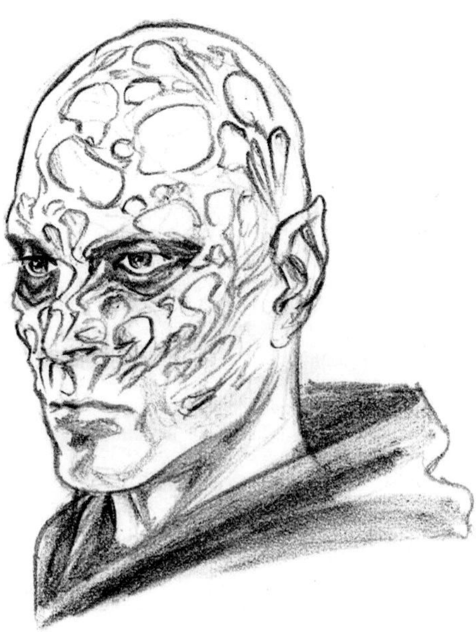

YOUNG KLYTUS WITH
SCARRED FEATURES
COVERED IN GOLD PAINT

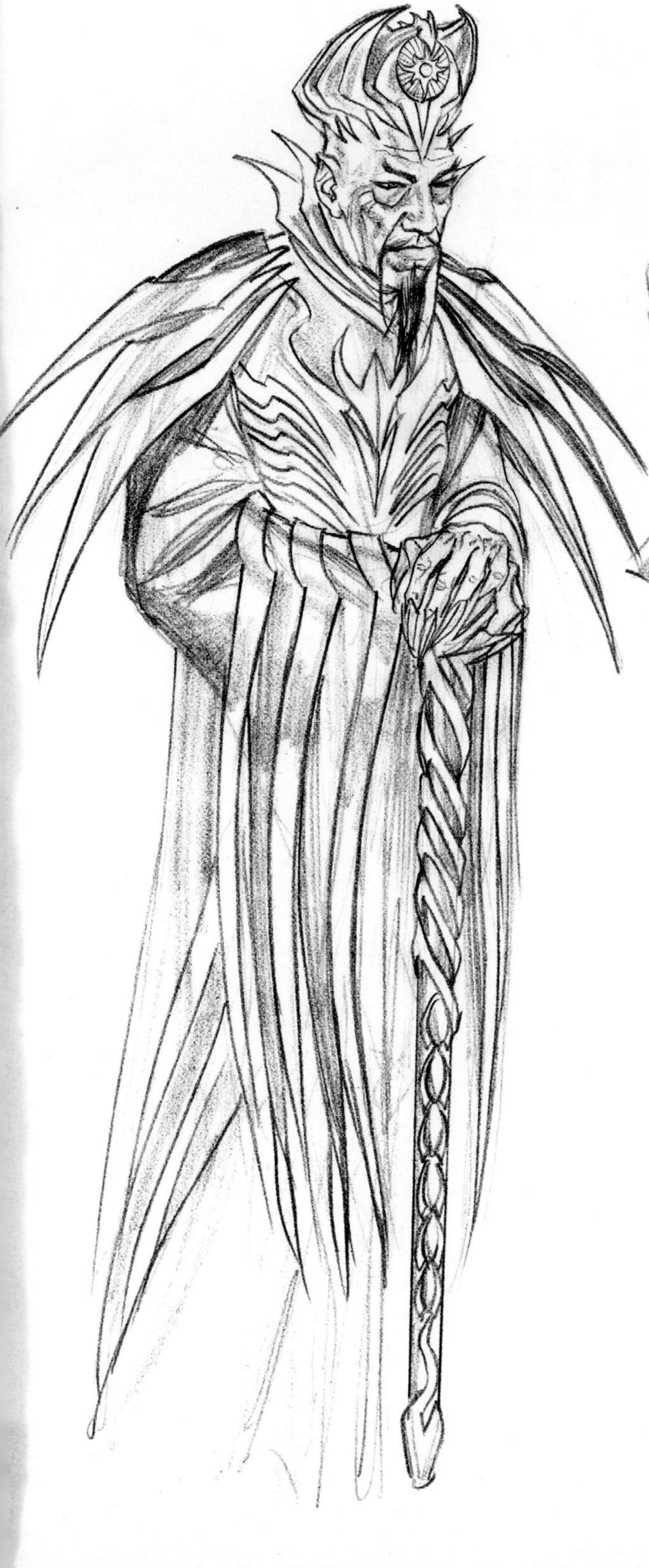

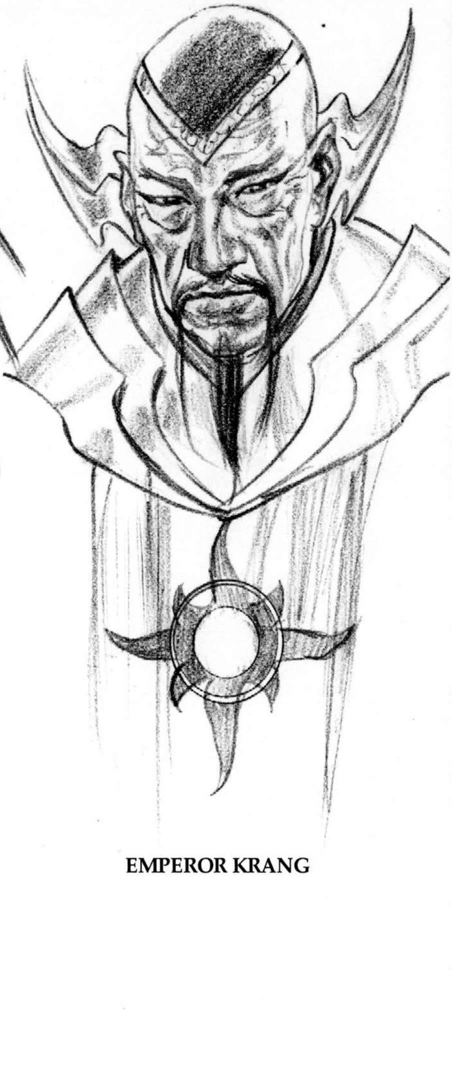

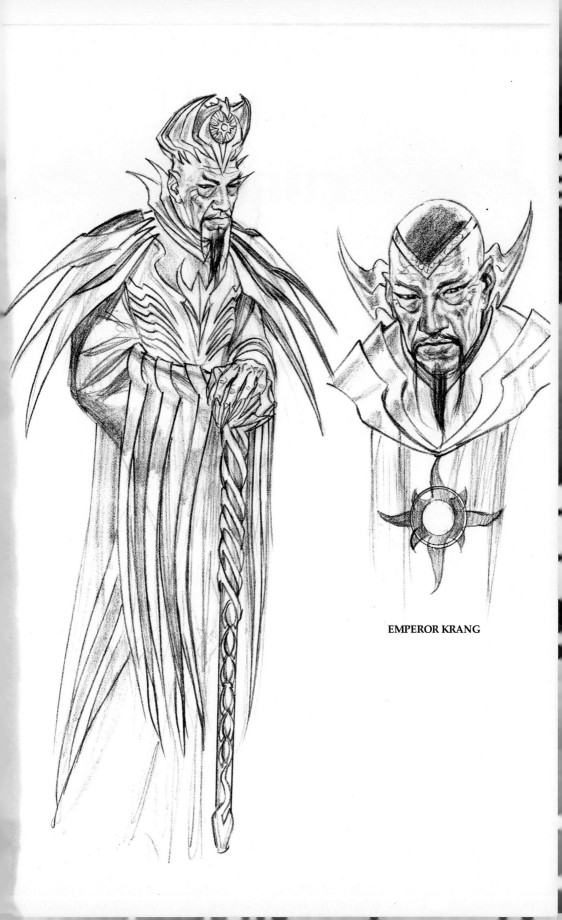

EMPEROR KRANG

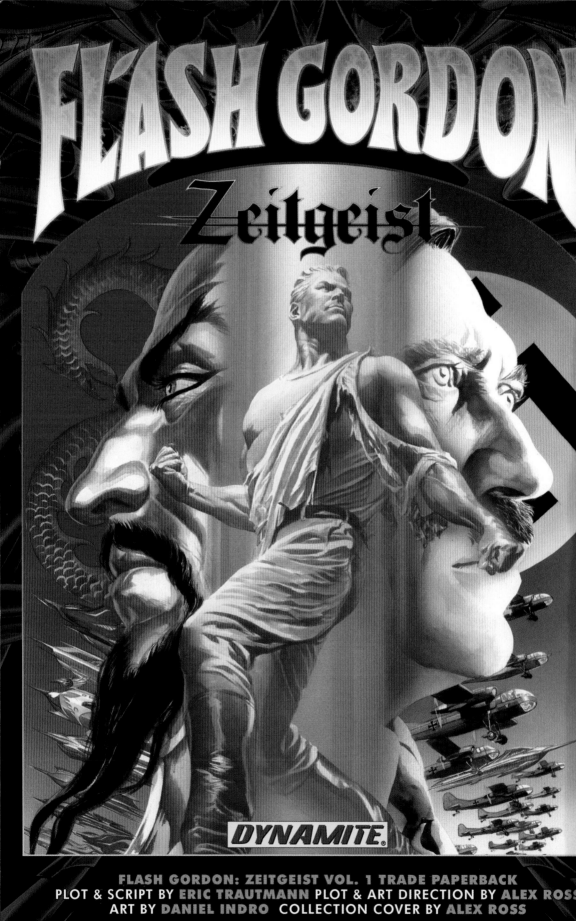

FLASH GORDON: ZEITGEIST VOL. 1 TRADE PAPERBACK
PLOT & SCRIPT BY ERIC TRAUTMANN PLOT & ART DIRECTION BY ALEX ROSS
ART BY DANIEL INDRO COLLECTION COVER BY ALEX ROSS